Realize Your
Horse's True Potential

Realize Your
Horse's
True
Potential

Lesley Skipper

Trafalgar Square Publishing

North Pomfret, Vermont

First published in the United States of America
in 2003 by Trafalgar Square Publishing,
North Pomfret, Vermont 05053

ISBN 1-57076-252-X

Library of Congress Control Number: 2003102743

2 4 6 8 10 9 7 5 3

Edited by Jane Lake
Design by Paul Saunders

Colour separation by Tenon & Polert Colour Scanning Limited, Hong Kong
Printed by Midas Printing International Limited, China

In Memory of

Balthasar

Pure-bred Arabian stallion
(Crown of Argosy x Coppermead Bel Echo)
1987–2001

Contents

Acknowledgements

WHEN WRITING A BOOK OF THIS NATURE, it has been necessary to draw on the knowledge of a number of experts, who have all been most generous with their advice. I must stress that any errors in the text are mine, and not theirs.

In the field of equitation I give particular thanks to the following: Paul Belasik, Erik F. Herbermann, Dr Thomas Ritter and Michael J. Stevens.

Fellow equestrian author and scholar Ann Hyland has, as always, been a mine of information, and I am deeply grateful to her for the hours we have spent in discussion.

For advice, guidance and thought-provoking discussion regarding equine biology, form, function and biomechanics, I thank Dr Hilary Clayton, BVMS, PhD, MRCVS, of the Department of Large Animal Clinical Sciences, Michigan State University; biophysicist Dr Averil Cox; McTimoney practitioner Dana Green; equine sports therapist Barbara Torney and veterinary surgeon Sara Wyche MRCVS.

The following have been most generous with their advice regarding scientific background research: Michael Bowling; Dr Gus Cothran of the Equine Blood Typing and Research Laboratory, University of Kentucky; and the late Stephen Jay Gould, Alexander Agassiz Professor of Zoology and Professor of Geology, Harvard University.

Many others have helped with information or advice on various subjects covered in this book; special mention should be made of Lisa Bradley, Jill Holding, Kelly Marks and Rose Tyrrell.

Mention must also be made of those who kindly provided me with, or assisted me to obtain, illustrations, particularly of unusual subjects. These include Lisa Bradley, John Cooke, Daylesford Stud, Elizabeth Furth, Gigi

Grasso, Erik F. Herbermann, Jill Holding, Holme Park Stud, Joanne Husband, Ann Hyland, Richard Lüst of Yeguada Iberica, Bob Langrish, Mrs Joanna MacInnes, Kelly Marks, Vanessa Payne, Marilyn and Peter Sweet, Dr Thomas Ritter, Mrs Shirley Watts of Halsdon Arabians and Diane Webber.

My dear friends Sue Coulthard, Lynn and Sara Debnam (whose much loved and greatly missed stallion Balthasar, to whom this book is dedicated, sadly died shortly before its completion), Lorraine Graham, Antoinette Harris, Joanne Husband and Alexander Mikaberidze have been extremely supportive, reading drafts, providing readers' comments, offering suggestions, and generally putting up with being ignored for weeks or even months on end while I toiled away at getting the book into shape.

The same goes for my husband, Brian, whose patience, understanding and general support have been typical of his kind and generous nature. The horses, too, have been most patient; their companionship and sometimes rather boisterous affection is a constant source of inspiration.

Last, but very far from least, my very special thanks must go to two remarkable people whose kindness and generosity has moved me more than I can say. Learning that I was trying to track down a copy of Dwyer's famous treatise, *On Seats and Saddles, Bits and Bitting,* Sylvia Loch and Elwyn Hartley Edwards both, unknown to each other, offered to lend me their own precious and irreplaceable copies of this book. Such willingness to help, and to share research material, is typical of them both. It is their example, more than any other, that has inspired my own equestrian researches and writings, and for that I am profoundly grateful to both of them.

Many of the photographs which appear in the book are of our own horses. They are:

Count Kruger	Arabian x Warmblood gelding
Guisburn Nivalis	Pure-bred Arabian stallion, son of Roxzella
Imzadi	Arabian x (Cleveland Bay x Thoroughbred) mare, daughter of Nivalis and Kiri
Kiri	Cleveland Bay x Thoroughbred mare
Mikenah (Tiff)	Pure-bred Arabian mare
Roxzella	Pure-bred Arabian mare
Toska	Belgian Warmblood x (Cleveland Bay x TB) gelding, son of Kiri
Zareeba	Pure-bred Arabian gelding, half-brother to Kruger

Author's Note

The text assumes at least a moderate level of competence, knowledge and experience among its readers: it is not intended for novice riders. Every care has been taken to alert readers to safety concerns but, ultimately, the responsibility for safety lies with the rider and/or handler. The author and publishers cannot accept any responsibility for any injury or damages which may arise as a result of following procedures mentioned in this book.

I must apologize to female horses for using the pronoun 'he' throughout the book, to represent horses of both sexes. This is not intended to slight or devalue mares; I used 'he' because the unisex pronoun 'they', perfectly acceptable when referring to humans, somehow did not seem quite right when talking about horses. To me, horses are 'he' or 'she', not an 'it' (the latter term treats the horse as if he were an object, instead of an individual), but it would have been too cumbersome to keep saying 'he or she' or 'him or her'. So I hope mare owners will forgive me!

Introduction

WHAT DO WE WANT FROM our horses? In an ideal world, we would all start off knowing exactly what we want, and would then set out to find a horse who matched our requirements. However, as we are only too aware, this is far from being an ideal world. Some of us have very clear goals in mind, and (if we are lucky) both the knowledge and the finances to go out and buy a horse who fits our criteria. Many – perhaps most – are not so fortunate. The average rider, who probably works full time, may have to juggle finances in order to keep a horse at all; a purpose-bred, ready-made horse is likely to be well beyond their financial reach. Most of us have to make do with what we can afford.

This does not mean we have to be stuck with a talentless plod capable of only the most limited activities. Some of the world's most renowned riders have made it to the top in spite of having less than ideal horses, simply because they have known how to make the best of the abilities their horses do have, while minimizing the latter's weaknesses.

One might be forgiven for thinking, 'Yes, but those are top class riders, who could probably get the best out of a three-legged donkey'. Fair enough, but most of them would tell you that whatever success they have had has been the result of grinding hard work, the ability to keep a clear goal in mind, and above all the knowledge and experience to 'read' the horses they ride and to know what approach will suit them best.

For this reason it is tempting, and in many cases perfectly sensible and legitimate, simply to hand a horse over to a professional, and rely on their expertise to produce the desired results. Certainly, the professional has many advantages over the amateur, everyday rider. They may have better facilities, such as an indoor school, or almost certainly an all-weather riding surface of some kind, whereas the everyday rider may have nothing more than a corner of a field in which to work. The professional will usually ride several horses every day, and will often have at least one assistant to help with real problems. They will have more time to devote to developing a horse's potential, and may be better placed to assess him neutrally, without any of the emotional involvement which can sometimes get in the way of judgement. Finally, the professional will have the advantage of a great deal of experience with a large number of horses of different types and temperaments. All of these observations may also apply to the more experienced amateur, who often differs from the professionals only in that they do not earn all or part of their living from their dealings with horses.

However, the everyday rider also has some very strong points in their favour. They may not have the wide experience with different horses that the professional has, but they will usually know their own horse far better than a professional might. Some riders (including professionals) with many years of experience may close their minds to new or unfamiliar ideas, simply because they feel there is nothing more for them to learn. Experience on its own does not guarantee either that the methods used, or the results obtained, are correct. Nor does competitive success, or, sadly, the possession of equestrian qualifications. I have come across riders with thirty or more years' experience of riding and training horses, who have some very peculiar ideas about what is correct, and whose methods leave a great deal to be desired. Yet, because they have always done things in the same way, they have never questioned whether it is, in fact, the best way (or even, in some cases, the only way!). The everyday rider, on the other hand, may be much more open minded and receptive. They will also be free of the pressure to produce results that besets many professionals.

Fortunately we are beginning to see, throughout the horse world, an increasing willingness to accept new ideas, to question entrenched beliefs, and above all to seek *understanding*. There is also a heartening tendency for riders and trainers from different disciplines to look at ways in which training principles from one discipline may be used to help horses specialising in another. Accompanying all this is an increased awareness – due in no small measure to people like Sylvia Loch, founder of the Classical Riding Club – of the principles of riding and training usually known as *classical*, about which I shall say more in Chapter 10 (for details of the Classical Riding Club, see Appendix II).

Way back in September 1995, the *Classical Riding Club Newsletter* printed a member's review of Sylvia Loch's video, *The Classical Seat*. Having shown the video to various people, the reviewer received from one of them the comment, 'That way of riding is okay for well-schooled horses but what about someone with an awful pony who has to get through a Pony Club test?' I remember thinking when I read this remark, how sad it is that so many people still fail to see the point of classical riding: that it is quite simply riding that is in harmony and balance, and that this kind of riding is relevant to everyone, no matter what their equestrian interest or discipline. There is also the implication that it cannot help those with 'awful ponies'. What is an 'awful pony'? Not many horses and ponies are truly awful (although there are *some* who make awfulness their life's work), but there are any number of ugly ducklings who would blossom into swans if given the chance.

This must surely give encouragement to those people who cannot afford a purpose-bred competition horse. If we approach training with the view that the real aim is not to win, thrilling though that may be, but to allow each horse to find his own potential by bringing out the best that he has to offer, then it really does not matter what kind of horse or pony you have.

However, from another point of view, the type of horse or pony you have may matter very much; it all depends on what you want to do. Before riders can decide whether a particular horse suits their needs, they need to be sure what they are aiming for. Do they want to take part in top level competition, or do they simply want to compete at Riding Club level? Do they, indeed, want to compete at all, or is their main satisfaction gained from just owning and riding their horse, and trying to get the best out of him? Whatever their goals, they need to understand how the way a horse is put together affects his athletic ability, and what his limitations are likely to be. They must also understand the enormous extent to which they, as riders and trainers, can affect a horse's capabilities and either enhance or decrease his potential.

This is the aim of this book. It will help riders to:

- Understand how the way a horse is put together affects his athletic ability.

- Recognize how conformation relates to the type of movement.

- Learn to look at the horse as an individual, rather than having preconceived ideas about temperament and personality.

- Realize the extent to which we can improve on nature, and learn to identify which aspects of a horse's conformation we can change, and what we must simply accept.

- Identify special problem areas, and know what remedial action to take.

- Understand how problems in their own riding may be affecting their horse's ability to use himself properly.

- Understand the role of training aids, and identify when these are appropriate and when their use should be avoided.

- Find expert help and support when they feel their own knowledge is inadequate.

Although I have placed emphasis on learning to recognize a horse's inborn limitations, I cannot stress enough that we must not hoodwink ourselves into accepting (or creating) artificial limitations for our horses. We should certainly not assume that such limitations as *do* exist mean that we can only expect mediocrity. On the contrary, accepting limitations in some areas can free us to explore excellence in others.

The emphasis throughout this book will be on the capabilities of *individuals*: just as every human being is a unique individual, so is every horse. Not every human can be a rocket scientist, a Pulitzer Prize winner, a Michelangelo or an Olympic gold medallist; in the same way, not every horse can be a Grand Prix dressage horse, an Olympic standard show-jumper, a Badminton star or a Derby winner. However, although we cannot decide what qualities we are born with, we are not stuck with what we have at birth, and neither are our horses. In the same way that every human has some abilities which can be developed and brought to excellence, every horse has some qualities which we can make the most of. We can identify strengths and weaknesses, and decide how we can make the most of the strengths while improving on, or at least minimizing, the weaknesses.

In other words, every horse has his personal best, and it is up to us to understand how we can help him to achieve it: in other words, to *realize*, in every sense of the word, his true potential. No horse is perfect, but almost every horse can be helped, through correct training and riding, to overcome such limitations as nature has imposed on him, and to become fitter, healthier, happier and more versatile as a result, thus enhancing the rider's enjoyment.

CHAPTER ONE

Improving on nature

'OF COURSE, WITH conformation/breeding like that, he'll never be able to jump/come on the bit/work in an outline…'

How often have riders heard those words, or something like them? Such a judgement appears to doom any horse who does not fit a theoretical ideal to a life of mediocrity. To the rider who may not be able to afford a 'better' horse, it may dash any hopes they might have had of reaching a respectable level of achievement.

In some cases the assessment may be justified. There are indeed many horses whose conformation severely limits their potential as riding horses. However, there are very many more who, while far from perfect, may still be capable of far more than a superficial judgement may suggest.

Look at the first picture of Arabian gelding Elmo. At first sight he is a pathetic little creature; undersized and suffering from malnutrition, he stands with lowered head, a picture of dejection. He appears to be croup-high, and as his neck is lacking in muscle and shape it looks too short, making his head seem disproportionally large and 'stuck on'. He also looks slightly 'camped out' behind (see page 54), although not enough to really worry about.

Lisa Bradley found Elmo standing in a field, in a very bad state. He had simply been turned out in a field, underfed and neglected, and wintered out for two seasons without rugs or any extra feed. Lisa felt so sorry for him that she offered to take him. It turned out that Elmo had been gelded late, and at the age of about seven was sent to a Thoroughbred racing yard to be broken in for general riding. What exactly happened to him at the racing yard is not known, but apparently they had difficulty in backing him, and whatever was done to him to make him more compliant left him traumatized and

Arabian gelding Elmo was in a pitiful state when Lisa Bradley found him
(Courtesy of Lisa Bradley)

fearful of being ridden, although in other respects he was willing and affectionate. He had been sent back to his owner as unrideable. His owner at the time Lisa Bradley saw him was a young girl, who was also unable to ride him. She had been paying someone to look after him, and believed he was being cared for properly. This was far from being the case. He had a heavy worm burden, was suffering from thrush, rain scald, mud fever, and had an open wound on his face from a badly fitting headcollar.

Now look at the photograph opposite. Is this the same horse? Indeed it is; this is Elmo after several months of Lisa Bradley's devoted care. After sorting out Elmo's numerous health problems, Lisa began, very carefully and under veterinary supervision, to build up his muscles on the lunge. This, combined with good feeding, brought Elmo to the point where he could be ridden. This proved extremely difficult at first, since his bad experiences at the racing yard had made him terrified of anyone wearing a riding hat. However, with the help of Monty Roberts's pupil Kelly Marks,[1] Elmo's phobia and his terror of being ridden were gradually overcome.[2]

1 For more information about Kelly's work, and that of Intelligent Horsemanship, see Appendix II
2 Elmo's plight, and his rehabilitation, appeared on BBC TV's problem-pet programme *Barking Mad* in July 2001.

Elmo transformed by Lisa
Bradley's devoted care
(*Courtesy of Lisa Bradley*)

Lisa now has a beautiful, willing riding horse with whom she can have the kind of fun she had originally dreamed of when she first took him on.

Naturally, we would not normally want to have to go to such lengths to obtain a good riding horse, but this is an example of just what can be done with care, dedication, knowledge, and timely advice from the right quarters. If we compare Elmo's posture in the first picture with the way he carries himself in the second, we can see that he is much more 'uphill' in his build than we had previously supposed. In the first picture he stands in a slumped posture, with his head low, because the undeveloped musculature of his neck can scarcely support its weight. This poor muscle tone, together with Elmo's general lack of wellbeing, has caused his torso to sink between his shoulder blades (see page 65), making it look as if he has undeveloped withers. The later picture shows that this is far from being the case. His croup area has muscled up and rounded out, as have his thighs and fore-arms. His neck has developed and stabilized, and he now looks like the kind of horse anyone would be proud to ride.

Many riders feel frustrated by the fact that in so many books on the training and riding of horses, the illustrations show magnificent, athleti-cally built horses performing flawlessly, with no indication being given of what the horse looked like before training commenced, or of what difficul-ties the rider/trainer had to overcome in the process of that training. It is tempting to believe that horses who go on to perform at advanced level must have started out as near perfect as possible, and certainly the horse which does so has an enormous advantage, and will usually prove much easier to train. However, it is quite remarkable what may be achieved sim-ply through correct training and riding.

Take a look at this horse (opposite), a 165 cm (16.1 hh) Thoroughbred x Percheron gelding called Atlantis, who started his training with Erik Herbermann at the age of ten. Before that he had been simply a family hack, who was occasionally taken out hunting. At first sight, Atlantis is not a particularly inspiring horse. Although he has plenty of bone and depth of girth, and his neck appears to rise nicely from his withers, his croup looks rather steep and short; this would restrict the forward reach of his hind legs, which are a little on the straight side. His shoulder is too upright, and the rather closed angle between the scapula and humerus indicates a lack of scope (see pages 60–62). The humerus itself is too short to compensate adequately for this shortcoming. For reasons which will become clear in the course of the next few chapters, we should not be too surprised to learn that his movement left a lot to be desired!

Erik Herbermann wrote of Atlantis, 'By nature he is a poor mover, his gaits are "klunky". Retraining this fellow to become active, supple and obe-dient was like schooling a heavy-weight wrestler to do ballet! He is a strong-minded, self-willed horse. It proved to be a challenging task.'[3]

Now look at the picture of Herbermann with Atlantis in collected canter: even in collection, there is the kind of impulsion (see page 168) that can only result when the horse flexes his joints and engages his hind legs

3 Erik F. Herbermann, *Dressage Formula,* 2nd ed., J.A.Allen, 1989, p.xvii

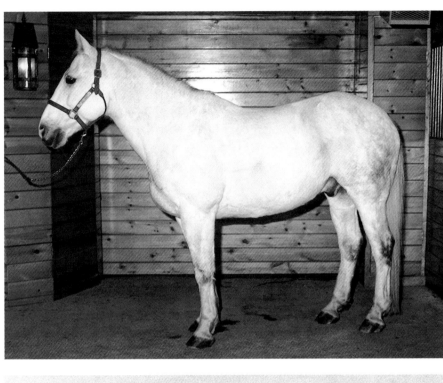

Training Atlantis was something of a challenge for Erik Herbermann *(Courtesy of Erik F. Herbermann)*

Atlantis in collected canter *(Courtesy of Erik F. Herbermann)*

correctly. All this has been achieved, not by the use of gadgets or exotic and arcane training methods, but simply through correct training and riding according to time-tested classical principles.

Certainly, Atlantis had the great advantage of being trained by an exceptionally good rider, who has studied with some very great horsemen. It would be unfair to raise false expectations by claiming that the everyday rider, who may be struggling even to find a decent riding school and to afford lessons, is necessarily going to be able to achieve the same degree of transformation of their own less-than-perfect horse. Nevertheless, with time, dedication and the pursuit of knowledge, all kinds of things are possible, and the above does at least serve to show just what can be achieved with some very unpromising material.

Even so, we must recognize that there *are* limits to what any horse can achieve, and learn both what those limits are, and how to work within them. So how can the horse owner decide, before beginning training, which aspects of their horse's conformation and movement can be improved upon, and which of them simply have to be worked around? We should be wary of accepting preconceived ideas. Instead we should look at every horse as an individual, using as many objective criteria as possible to measure his athletic potential. We must learn to assess which aspects of a horse's make and shape are fixed, and which can be altered by judicious feeding, training and gymnastic exercise.

You will need to create a profile of your horse, recording details of his conformation, movement and personality and, making a note of any potential problem areas, decide what, if any, remedial action you may need to take; such remedial action will be discussed in the chapters covering specific areas of the body, improving the gaits, etc. Only then can you start to draw up a training programme based on the horse's needs as an individual. It may be that extensive remedial action needs to be taken before the horse's training can even begin properly, or it may be that you can start to plan your work straight away, or at any rate without too much delay.

Whatever the case may be, remember that we must be realistic about what we can achieve. We must not start off with a fixed goal in mind, otherwise we will be concentrating so much on the goal that we may lose sight of the process. This could result in square pegs being hammered into round holes. A horse pushed beyond his capabilities (whether because of his natural limitations, or because he is not yet sufficiently trained or developed) can become very sour and even dangerous. He may allow himself to be coerced into performing, but his mind will always be seeking ways to escape. Some horses respond to this situation by reacting violently; a horse under intolerable pressure may try to run away (often the reason for rushing at fences), explode, or become savage. Others, depending on their individual temperaments, may respond by 'switching off', withdrawing into a zombie-like state, performing mechanically but with no zest or sparkle, and becoming dull and unresponsive to all but the crudest and heaviest of aids.

What we must do to avoid this is to take training step by step, continually reassessing our progress, and taking note of the horse's responses to decide whether the current work needs confirming, or whether it is time to move on to something new. Sometimes this means going back a step; sometimes we will progress much faster than we had thought possible. The important thing is that we do not get stuck with the idea that we *must* achieve this or that within a certain time frame, or in a fixed order. We need a system, but it must have an in-built flexibility. The more we learn about horses, and about training and riding them, the greater the number of options open to us, and the more flexible our system can become.

Skeletal structure we cannot change but, as we shall see, the horse's musculature is not set in stone. However, we also have to bear in mind that muscles will have developed according to what the horse has been doing and the way he has carried himself in the past.

Muscles cannot act on their own; they depend on impulses from the brain, which travel via neural pathways along the nervous system (see Fig.1.1). Every time the brain repeats an instruction for the muscles to act in

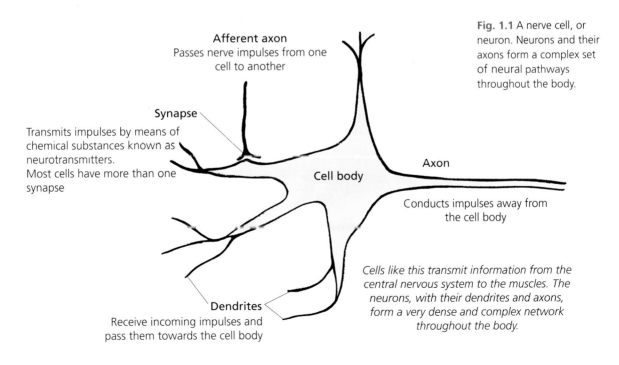

Afferent axon
Passes nerve impulses from one cell to another

Synapse
Transmits impulses by means of chemical substances known as neurotransmitters.
Most cells have more than one synapse

Cell body

Axon
Conducts impulses away from the cell body

Dendrites
Receive incoming impulses and pass them towards the cell body

Fig. 1.1 A nerve cell, or neuron. Neurons and their axons form a complex set of neural pathways throughout the body.

Cells like this transmit information from the central nervous system to the muscles. The neurons, with their dendrites and axons, form a very dense and complex network throughout the body.

a particular way, those instructions become more and more ingrained, so to speak. So if the horse has spent years moving in a particular way, his brain – as well as his muscles – will need to be re-educated before those movement patterns can be altered.

This process of education – or re-education – is precisely what dressage, especially at the lower levels, is (or should be) about; competition aside, dressage is nothing more than the basic education of the horse! Unfortunately many people seem to have forgotten this, and regard it instead as training the horse to perform movements in order to impress competition judges. For this reason, I shall henceforth refer not to 'dressage' (except in a competition context) but simply to 'training', although that is not really adequate to describe what is nothing more or less than the foundation for everything the horse will be asked to do under saddle.

Even the most perfectly conformed horse starts his career under saddle with a distinct disadvantage, as he carries so much of his weight – up to about 60 per cent – on his forehand. The ultimate aim of training is to build up his muscles and accustom him to a way of working which will take some of that weight off the forehand and transfer it to his hindquarters.

This applies no matter what we eventually wish to do with him and it is a great pity that so many people still regard the concept of lightening the forehand as solely the province of dressage, and competitive dressage at that. For no matter what he will eventually be called upon to do, the horse who can take more weight on his haunches, who is supple and light in hand, will stay sound longer, and be more pleasurable to ride, than one who is on his forehand, stiff, heavy in hand and difficult to manoeuvre. Some horses are so conformed that they will find it relatively easy to lighten the forehand; others will need a great deal of help before they can achieve the same result. It is up to us, their riders and trainers, to give them that help. It is not always easy – no knowledgeable person ever expects it to be – but if we arm ourselves with the necessary knowledge and understanding, we will make our task that much easier.

There are very few horses indeed whose overall conformation is so poor that they cannot be trained up to the equivalent of at least medium level dressage. In an ideal world, every riding horse would be trained to this level as a minimum requirement (and preferably to advanced medium level), before anyone considered going on to train him for more specialized work. You would not, for example, expect a human to undertake a university degree course in physics if they had no basic education in the sciences! There are always some extremely gifted exceptions, of course; however, we are not talking about exceptions but about generalities.

Unfortunately, in the English-speaking countries, very few riding schools or instructors will teach very much about actually training horses. There are simply not enough people with the theoretical knowledge, and the necessary practical experience, to train, or oversee the training of, the average riding horse, even to the standard cited above.

Nevertheless, it would greatly benefit the majority of horses if, instead of being plunged into training for a discipline for which they may have neither the inclination nor the aptitude, they were given a chance to gain a good basic education first. This would help to minimize their faults and nurture their abilities, while helping their trainers / riders to decide where a particular horse's talents lie.

In spite of the problems outlined above, the outlook is far from gloomy for riders who want to educate their horses for the latter's benefit. You do not have to be a dressage expert in order to give your horse this basic education, or to retrain him in such a way as to minimize any faults he may have. What you do need is patience (lots of it), a willingness to learn (from the horse as much as from anyone else), to be prepared to take as much time as it takes and a sound understanding of the basic principles of training. If the latter sounds daunting, it need not be, as I hope to show in the following chapters.

If we decide in advance that our horse is going to be capable of only very limited achievement, we will probably not put in sufficient effort to raise him above the mediocrity that we believe to be his lot. On the other hand, if we approach his training with a view to finding out just what he *can* achieve, who knows what hidden talents or unsuspected capabilities we may uncover?

All horses, no matter what their potential may appear to be, deserve to be treated as unique individuals, each of whom has some talent, some strength in performance, that can be identified, nurtured, and brought to fruition. As American trainer Vicki Hearne observes, 'Good trainers ride all horses as though they were potentially world-class; that's the only way you end up with world-class horses.' [4]

4 Vicki Hearne, *Adam's Task: Calling Animals by Name* Heinemann 1987, p.146

CHAPTER TWO

Getting the picture

I S THERE SUCH A THING as the 'absolute horse', who fits some abstract ideal of perfection? Of course there is not, any more than there is an 'ideal' human being. With the great diversity we find in both species, the best we can really say is that certain types will most probably be best fitted for this or that activity. I say 'most probably', because there are so many factors to be taken into account that it just is not possible to tell, merely from looking at the outside of a horse and how he is put together, what his true potential may be. (See Fig. 2.1.)

Those factors include such aspects as temperament, upbringing, general health and state of wellbeing, the manner in which the horse is kept and trained, and – extremely important – the kind of relationship the horse has with those who handle, train and ride him.

Nevertheless, we have to start somewhere. Since a horse's physical structure does have an enormous influence on potential, that is the logical starting place; it will at least tell us what his physical strengths and limitations are likely to be. We can then use this information as a base for our assessment of his potential.

The skeletal structure (see Fig. 2.2) cannot be changed, except by injury (for example when bone remodels itself following a fracture), or by surgery, which for both practical and ethical reasons is seldom practised on horses for that purpose. However, bones cannot move by themselves; that is the job of the muscles, with the length and weight of the bones providing the necessary leverage to move the limbs and joints. So, although we are mainly concerned with the skeleton, we must also look at muscular development.

Muscular tissue *can* change its shape: it can be developed and strengthened by exercise and correct nutrition, or it can waste and grow flabby.

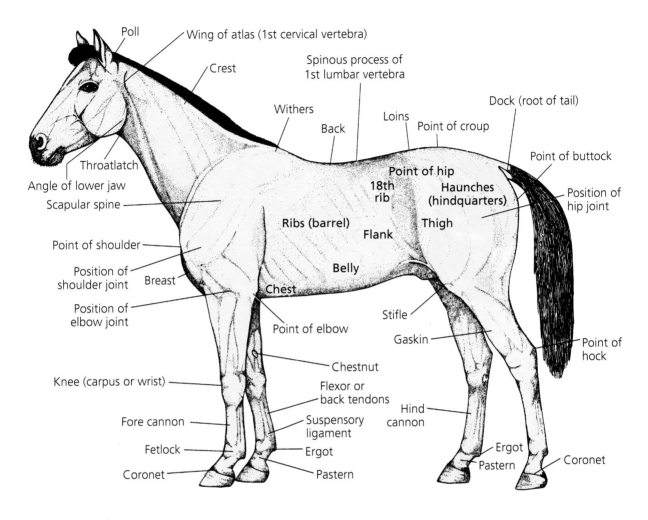

Fig. 2.1 Points of the horse

Sometimes, as in the case of Elmo, described in Chapter 1, what appears to be a fault of skeletal conformation may in fact be due to faulty posture, caused by insufficient or incorrect muscular development. Learning to recognize when this is the case is part of the art of assessing a horse.

The main thing is not to get stuck with the idea that only one type of conformation is 'correct'. With the exception of those conformation traits which predispose horses to injury or disease (which we shall look at in Chapters 3 to 7), no specific type of conformation is intrinsically 'better' than another. To decide whether or not a horse has 'good' conformation, we have to look at the type of work the horse will be expected to do, and understand how form relates to function.

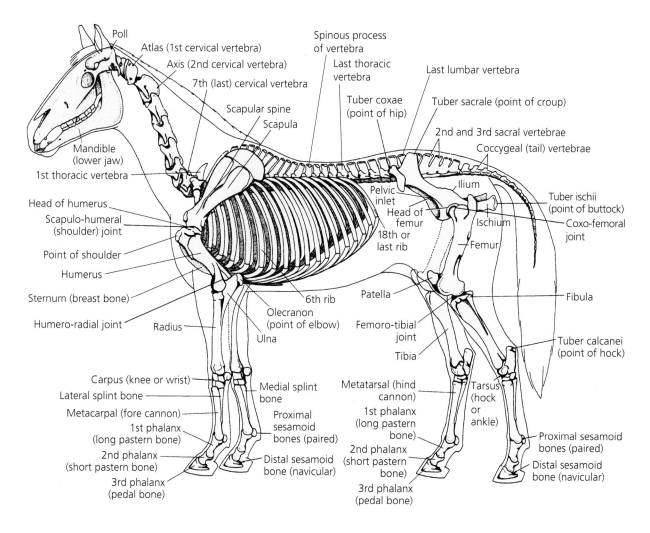

Fig. 2.2 The equine skeleton

Differing types

In the early twenty-first century, we have over two hundred recognized breeds and types of horse and pony, with widely differing standards regarding type and conformation. Most of these evolved to do a specific job, so their conformation reflects their suitability for that job. For example, we might consider a native pony's body too long and deep in proportion to his legs and height, when considered alongside a riding pony or a Thoroughbred. The native pony needs this body length to accommodate a larger than average gut, to enable him to cope with the extremely fibrous nature of the food available in his native habitat. This aspect of the native pony's conformation is therefore a breed characteristic, and is bound up with both function and habitat. Some people might not consider some of the mountain

Dales pony *(Bob Langrish)*

and moorland breeds, with their short, often bouncy strides, ideal riding types; but if you were crossing a moorland area you might well be glad of the sure-footedness of these breeds in an extremely unforgiving, often boggy terrain. The long yet strong back also helps these ponies with the traditional role of some native breeds as pack ponies – a role for which they are still in demand in some parts of the British Isles. Again, this conformational point is a breed characteristic which relates to function.

On the other hand the Cleveland Bay, also once a pack animal, was traditionally used to transport a different kind of load, and so a shorter back is more correct for the Cleveland. The hard 'blue' feet – another breed characteristic of the Cleveland – were necessary when traversing the steep, hard causeways of the Cleveland Hills – another example of type allied closely to function.

The Thoroughbred, bred exclusively for speed, can often be rather rangy, as can one of its probable relatives, the Akhal-Teke,[1] bred for war and for racing. Another of the Thoroughbred's ancestors, the Arabian, was

---

1 DNA analysis carried out so far has tended to confirm that some of the most illustrious ancestors of the Thoroughbred were almost certainly not Arabians, as is generally believed, but Turkoman horses closely related to the Akhal-Teke.

Cleveland Bay stallion
(L. Skipper)

originally bred exclusively as a war-horse, in whom agility and manoeuvrability were prized far more than mere speed for its own sake. As a result it tends to be rounder and more compact than either the Thoroughbred or the Akhal-Teke. Rounder still is the majestic outline of the Iberian horse, by which I mean the breeds of the Iberian Peninsula (Spain and Portugal), the Andalusian[2] and the Lusitano. These were bred for war, stock work and the mounted bullfight, where strength and agility are more important than speed. Combining power and speed is the Quarter Horse, whose bulky hindquarters form the powerful 'engine' which makes this horse the fastest of all over a quarter of a mile, yet strong and agile enough to make a very effective stock horse.

2 Since 1912 the Andalusian is more properly called the Pure-bred Spanish Horse *(Pura raza española)*. However, 'Andalusian' is still technically correct, and much less of a mouthful.

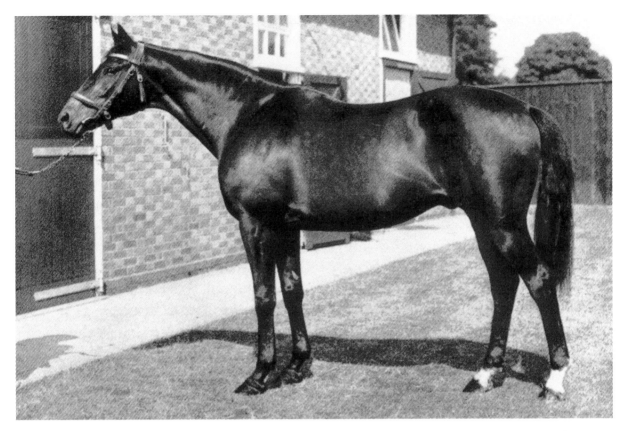

ABOVE A great racehorse: Thoroughbred stallion Nearco

A different type: Thoroughbred stallion Java Tiger. In 2000 he won the British Horse Foundation award for the leading TB and Leading British-Bred Sire of Dressage Horses *(courtesy of Joanna MacInnes)*

19

Akhal-Teke. The 'greyhound' type is exaggerated in this horse, shown here in racing condition (*Bob Langrish*)

Arabian stallion Carmargue: World Champion in 1985 (*Photo Sweet*)

ABOVE Iberian breeds: Andalusian stallion Ilustre IV (nearest camera) and Lusitano stallion Diabo (left) give a display (*L. Skipper*)

Quarter Horse Chunky's Sovereign (*Ann Hyland*)

Different again are the Warmbloods, originally bred in Central Europe as cavalry horses by crossing native light draught breeds with Spanish horses, Arabians and Thoroughbreds. Selective breeding, honed by the exclusion from breeding stock of horses which fail to pass a rigorous grading system, has resulted in the modern sport horses variously called after their place of origin, e.g. Brandenburg, Hanoverian, Holstein, Dutch, Belgian, Trakehner etc. These differ considerably in type, but all are characterized by a combination of strength and refinement, power and athleticism, and free elastic movement.

Most of the horses ridden by everyday riders in this and many other countries will not be pure-bred horses but cross-breds, which may have some of the characteristics of several of the breeds and/or types mentioned above. Yet in spite of all this diversity, when we come to consider desirability of form, there is still one factor which remains common to all breeds. This is the requirement that the overall appearance should be one of *balance*.

State Premium Brandenburg stallion Akzento *(with kind permission of Daylesford Stud, Gloucestershire)*

Showjumper Willi Melliger
and Calvaro (Holstein)
(Bob Langrish)

Trakehner stallion Holme
Park Krug *(Holme Park Stud)*

Hunter type *(L. Skipper)*

A horse or pony should have harmonious proportions, not only because this is pleasing to the eye, but also because a well-balanced horse is likely to find it much easier to carry a rider than one who is ill-proportioned *for his type* and, as a result, out of balance before a rider even comes near him.

Perhaps the most important thing to remember is that the horse is not just an inventory of parts. 'Conformation' consists of a huge number of variables, most of which can interact with each other in many complex ways. This being so, we must start by considering the horse as a whole.

So where *do* we start?

Objective judgement

Looking at horses objectively is something of an art. All of us carry around with us our own baggage of preconceived ideas; even people who know nothing to speak of about horses will still have a mental picture of what horses 'should' look like, whether from books, TV or films. Those of us who spend a great part of our lives with horses will have our individual preferences and prejudices, which may cloud our judgement when it comes to assessing our own horses.

Nevertheless, the ability to 'judge' horses is a skill that can be acquired with a little time and effort. You will not learn all you need to know overnight. In order to train your eyes to look at different types of horse (and, very often, to see past layers of fat to assess what the horse's skeletal structure is really like), it is best if you watch the breed classes at as many shows as possible. You do not have to be an expert on all the different breeds, but do some reading up on breed characteristics (the breed stands at some of the bigger shows are good sources of information, as are the excellent Dorling Kindersley books on horses: see the Recommended Reading section at the back of this book). Once you have read a few breed standards and looked at lots of photographs, you will be surprised at how quickly you will begin to recognize what is good conformation for a specific type. This, together with the information given in this book, will help you to understand how your own horse fits into the scheme of things.

Show judges usually have to look at a lot of horses in a short space of time, so they quickly develop the ability to assess a horse very rapidly. There must be many occasions on which such judges wish they had had more time to look at a particular horse, because if they had, they might have spotted a serious fault, or on the other hand marked a horse more favourably after a longer inspection. Thankfully, horse owners do not have this problem. You can take as much time as you like to give your horse a thorough top-to-toe scrutiny; the only factor that might limit this time is the horse's willingness to stand still!

Rather than test your horse's patience in this way, take photographs and work from those. You do not need a sophisticated camera; an ordinary 35 mm compact automatic model will do. Have prints made to a minimum size of seven inches by five inches, as it is much easier to work with larger print sizes.

Before you photograph the horse, you need to identify specific points on his body to use as guides in your assessment. These are various bony points of the skeleton, indicated in Figs. 2.1 and 2.2. First, though, there are a couple of points which need clarifying.

Kruger (Arabian x Belgian
Warmblood gelding)
(L. Skipper)

BELOW Kruger: front view
(L. Skipper)

BELOW RIGHT Kruger: rear
view *(L. Skipper)*

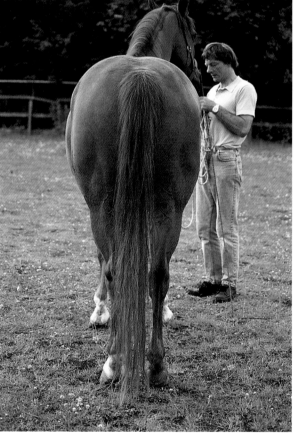

Angles of the upper limbs

Two of the measurements we want to make are of the angles formed by the scapula with the humerus, and of the pelvis with the femur. These measurements are usually taken as follows: withers/point of shoulder/ point of elbow, and point of hip/coxo-femoral joint/stifle. However, this gives a false measurement, because it is the angles made by the joints themselves that interest us. So we really need to measure a) along the scapular spine to the scapulo-humeral joint, then to the humero-radial joint, and b) from the point of hip to the coxo-femoral joint, and then to the femoro-tibial joint. Unfortunately these joints are not easy to find on many horses, particularly if they are well covered. So we will just have to make a best approximation (see the illustration on page 31 showing the appropriate points marked on one of my own horses, Kruger).[3]

'Uphill' or 'downhill' build

The other point concerns assessing whether the horse is built 'uphill' (good for a riding horse, as this will make it easier for him to come up off his forehand) or 'downhill', which will tend to put him more on his forehand. If the withers are higher (or lower) than the croup, this can give us some idea, but is not a very accurate method, as the croup can appear higher than it really is if the horse has a prominent point of croup.

There are two methods we can use. The lumbo-sacral junction – a very important structure – lies about 10-14 cm below the point on the horse's back that we call the loin coupling. The last cervical vertebra lies approximately under the widest part of the horse's neck. A line drawn between these two points will tell you whether or not your horse is built 'uphill' or 'downhill' (see the photograph on page 28 with these points marked).

Or will it? As we saw in Chapter 1, the torso can sink between the shoulder blades, giving a false impression. So we can use another method as a check. That great rider and trainer General Decarpentry tells us that the best way to measure this aspect of conformation is to see where the pivoting point of the shoulder (i.e. the bit that moves neither up nor down, forward or back, when the shoulder moves forward or back) lies in relation to the coxo-femoral, or hip, joint. This can be difficult to assess, so you need to watch the horse carefully in movement.

---

3 See Appendix I for an analysis of Kruger's conformation, based on the photographs which appear in this chapter.

Line from approximate pivoting point of shoulder to the coxo-femoral (hip) joint
Line from point where neck inserts into body, to lumbo-sacral junction

Identifying 'uphill' or 'downhill' build

Neither of these methods is entirely satisfactory on its own, but used together they can give us a reasonably accurate assessment.

Photographing the horse

Mark the points shown in the photographs opposite by sticking pieces of tacky paper, such as masking tape, over the precise points you want to indicate. Most horses, even thin-skinned ones, will not object to this as long as the paper does not stick so hard that pulling it off causes discomfort.

Unless your horse is a paragon who will stand still in the required position for as long as it takes for you to photograph him from all angles, you will need someone to hold him. Find the most level area you can, with (if it is at all feasible) as plain a background as possible (an open field is ideal, if it is level enough). Get the horse to stand square and, as far as possible, with his head and neck relaxed and carried naturally. This may take a bit of

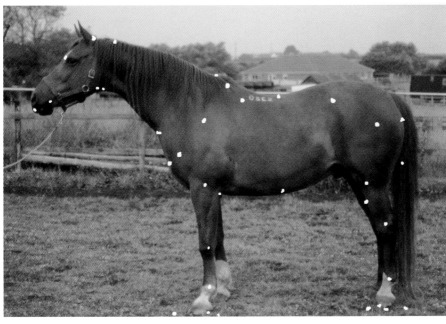

Kruger: side view with points marked

BELOW LEFT Front view with points marked

BELOW Rear view with points marked

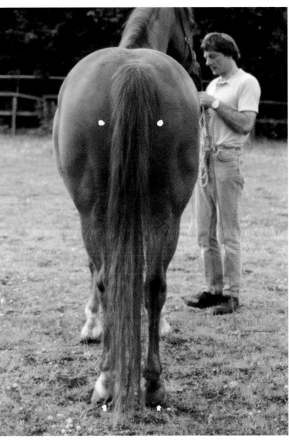

practice, and you might need to rearrange his legs a few times, but if you reward him whenever he gets it right, he will soon grasp what you want him to do.

The helper should stand well away from the horse if they can, to enable you to get clear shots free of distracting details. If it is a sunny day, try to have the sun behind you, or – unless you have one of the more sophisticated cameras – you may end up with nothing more than a silhouette against a bright background! Get as close as you can without distracting the horse; you want the image to be big and clear. If you are using a compact camera, remember that the viewfinder is not quite in the same plane as the lens (unlike that of a single-lens reflex, where what you see through the viewfinder is exactly what the camera lens sees), so if you get in too close you may end up cutting off part of the image. Most compact cameras have correction marks in the viewfinder to help prevent this, so use these to frame your shot.

Take plenty of shots from all angles, but pay particular attention to side, front and rear views, keeping the camera parallel to the squared-up horse.

Once you have your prints processed, select those that give the clearest side, front and rear views of your horse. If you do not want to mark the prints, have colour photocopies made (black-and-white copies will not give you enough detail to work from). Most towns of reasonable size have at least one quick-print shop offering a colour-photocopying service. If you use such a service, you can have the copies enlarged, which makes the images easier to work on.

Now, locate the points you marked with tape. Using a ruler and a pen of a type that will give a good, well-defined line (I find pens using gel-based inks the best for this kind of purpose; if you have a dark-coloured horse you can use one of the lighter metallic or pastel gel pens), draw connecting lines as in the photographs on pages 31 and 32. The reasons for doing this will become clear as you read Chapters 3 to 5.

Assessing the proportions

Next, we need to take some measurements. The idea is not to compare your horse with some hypothetical 'ideal' horse who never has and never will exist, but to assess his overall proportions by reference to some universal principles. As I said earlier, a well-made horse of whatever type should present a picture of harmony and balance, but what do we use as a yardstick? Oddly enough, the principles are the same as if we were assessing human proportions: we use the head as a reference point. I remember

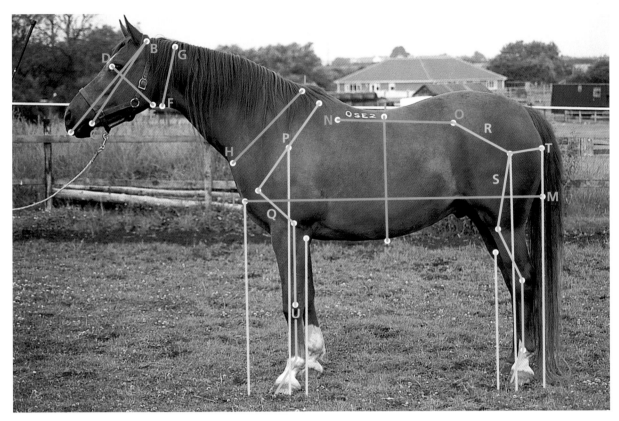

Kruger: side view with points joined up

············· Limb orientation
———— Joint angles and limb alignment
━━━━ Proportional measurements

Measure the respective lengths of the scapula (P) and humerus (Q) and the pelvic (O to T) and the femur (S)

Next, measure the angles of the scapula (P) and ilium (R) relative to the ground

Then measure the angle made by the scapula and humerus (P and Q) and the humerus with the radius (Q and U), and finally the angle of the ilium with the femur (R and S)

Now take the measurements from A to B, from B to C, from D to E, from F to G, from H to I, from J to K, and from L to M

On a well-proportioned horse, the measurements will be approximately as follows:

A to B = J to K and N to O
D to E = half of A to B
F to G = D to E
C to B = H to I and O to T
L to M = 2.5 to 2.66 x A to B

How do Kruger's measurements (and those of your own horse) compare with these proportions?

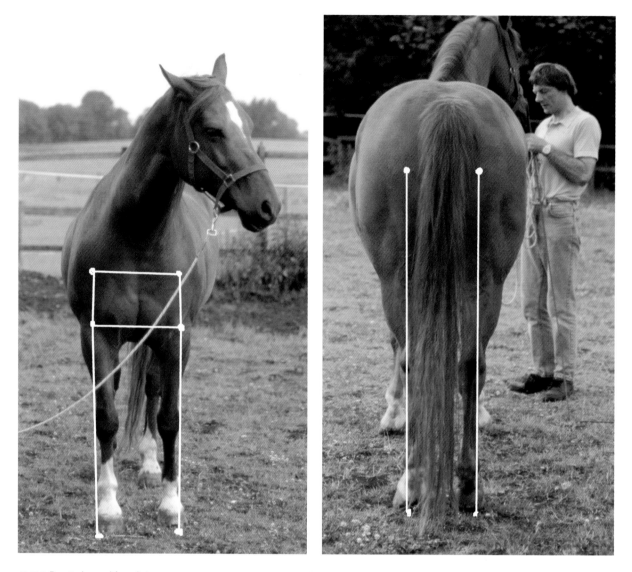

ABOVE Front view with points joined up

ABOVE RIGHT Rear view with points joined up

many years ago, in art classes, being taught to do this when drawing human figures. Although authorities who have studied equine conformation differ in their approach to the analysis of proportions, they all agree that the length of the head and the various proportions of the body are very closely related. The relevant measurements and proportions are shown in the side view photograph of Kruger on page 31.

You will see that, following the example of that great authority Captain Horace Hayes, I have not included the actual length of the limbs. This is because these can vary so much according to the type of horse (e.g. they will be shorter in draught types than they are in riding horses and, generally speaking, longer in racehorses than they are in ordinary riding horses, etc.). I have not included the length of neck either; not only can this vary according to type, but it also depends on the position of the head at any given time, as well as the line of the vertebrae themselves (which do not follow the top line of the neck).

I have also followed Hayes in measuring the length of the body from the point of shoulder to a point determined by a line dropped down from the point of buttock. This is more accurate than the usual method, which is to measure body length from the point of shoulder to the point of buttock.

Build a profile

Record all these measurements so that you can refer to them easily when building up your horse's profile. How you do this is entirely up to you; everyone has their own preferred working method. What is important is that you *do* have a method, otherwise you will find it very difficult to bring together all the information you have gathered. You may want to put it all in a file, with the photographs and marked-up copies for handy reference.

So, are you ready to start your assessment? Not quite, because all we have at this stage is a portrait of the horse *standing still*. While this is essential to our purpose, it really only gives us half the story. Horses are creatures of movement; that is one of their basic defining characteristics. *How* they move tells us a great deal, not only about their athletic potential, but also about their general health, soundness and state of wellbeing. So take some time to observe your horse moving about freely in the field; really watch him, looking carefully at everything he does, and recording the details of how he moves and any oddities of gait. Take more photographs of him moving about, in all gaits and, if you can, get some shots of him leaping and cavorting about (as all healthy horses, except the most elderly, tend to do when they are excited or full of energy). If you have (or can borrow) a camcorder, take video footage so that you can analyse your observations at leisure (even better, although not essential, would be a slow-motion playback facility). Make systematic notes, recording how he moves in all gaits:

■ when relaxed;

■ when he is startled or animated;

■ when he is tired;

■ how he moves on different types of surface (on a hard surface, for example, a horse may adopt a short, stiff stride in order to protect his limbs from the effects of concussion).

Then add all these notes and photographs to your profile file.

There is just one more thing to do before you can make a start on your assessment. This is, I am afraid, time consuming but essential, and it concerns the compilation of yet another profile of your horse: his temperament and personality.

Conformation problems, unless they are very severe, can usually be overcome, either by training or by working around them. Behavioural problems related to temperament (whether congenital or acquired) can be much more difficult to deal with, because it is not always easy to pinpoint the cause, or decide on appropriate action. So I think it is important that we get to know our horses as well as we possibly can.

Even if you have had your horse for some time, take some time to really observe him. Make notes about your observations, to help you draw up a psychological profile to add to your physical ones.

In the stable

- General demeanour: is he apathetic, or alert; dull and sleepy, or bright and interested in what is going on? Questions of health (which, of course, being a responsible horse owner, you will in any case have checked) apart, remember to take into account what he has been doing recently; if he has just been exercised, or has been running about energetically out in the field, he may be tired rather than apathetic.

- Does he have a good appetite, or is he a picky, finicky eater who leaves a good proportion of his hay? Is he a 'good doer', or is he difficult to keep weight on, even in summer? Again, remember to take circumstances into account. A horse who has recently had a change of home (or any other traumatic experience), or a recently gelded horse, may lose weight temporarily.

- How does he behave towards you in the stable? Is he friendly, or indifferent? How easy is he to handle generally? Does he like physical contact, or does he prefer to keep his distance?

- How does he react to anything new? Is he curious, or fearful? (He may be a mixture of both.)

In the field

- How does he get on with other horses? Is he a loner, or does he like to be close to the others?

- Is he energetic and playful, or does he just like to get his head down to graze?

- How does he respond to anything new or unusual out in the field? (This may be a very different response from that shown in the stable.)

- How easy is he to catch? Does he come up to you willingly, or does he try to avoid being caught at all costs? (Remember that this may be a learned response to previous bad experiences.)

Being tacked up

- How does he react to the sight of tack? Does he respond to it with interest, indifference, or does he try to avoid having the saddle and bridle put on (again, remember that this may be the result of previous bad experience, rather than lack of co-operation or desire to avoid work)?

Training and work

- How does he respond when you ask him to do something? Is he willing, or reluctant?

- Under saddle, is he forward-going or rather backward-thinking?

- Does he go forward calmly, or is he tense and spooky?

- If he is tense to begin with, how long do you have to ride him in before he starts to relax?

- How responsive is he to the aids? (This may depend on how well schooled he is to begin with. Always try the lightest, most subtle aids you can to begin with, increasing the strength of the aids as necessary to determine at what level he responds.)

- How easy is he to stop? Does fast work get him excited quickly?

- If you try him over jumps, how does he cope with them? Does he take them calmly and rhythmically, or does he rush? (Many horses who rush jumps do so because they are afraid, and want to get it over with as soon as possible.)

There are many other questions you can ask in order to build a psychological profile of your horse. The best way is to make notes recording his behaviour in as many different circumstances as possible, and then sort these into categories, similar to those above. How you do it is entirely up to you, but remember that any such profile will only be useful if it is based on observations over a period of time, preferably several months.

Does that mean you have to wait several months before you can start your training programme? Not necessarily; it all depends on the individual horse's character. Some are much easier to get to know than others. Do not be in too much of a rush, though; patience now can save you a great deal of trouble later on. Do take as much time as you possibly can to get to know your horse. You may feel as though you already know him well, especially if you have had him for some time, but you may be surprised by how much more you can learn by just observing him over a period of time!

What I would ask is that you make all your measurements and observations (other than those relating to temperament and personality) *before* you read through the chapters dealing with the various parts of the body. The reason I ask this is that for any observations to be truly accurate, we should really come to them cold, without any picture in our minds of what our horses 'should' look like. Even supposedly objective observations and measurements can be skewed by preconceived ideas. For example, if you think a certain feature should not be there, then you may literally not see it!

Once the profiles have been drawn up, we can then go on to see how a horse's make and shape affect his athletic ability. In the chapters that follow, I have tried wherever possible to confine myself to describing the effects that may follow from specific points of conformation. In this way I hope to have avoided, as far as possible, the 'ideal horse' syndrome. The thing to remember is that almost every horse has good points to balance any faults and weaknesses.

Having the right knowledge

Before we attempt anything by way of remedial action, there are a number of points to bear in mind. It is frighteningly easy, through lack of knowledge or understanding, or from an excess of ambition, to damage even the best conformed and soundest of horses. This means that, before we ever set out to remedy faults, or minimize deficiencies, we must first of all, a) understand exactly what we are trying to achieve, and b) ensure we have the knowledge and the technique to achieve it without harming what we are trying to improve.

If this makes it all sound rather daunting, it need not be so. If we are humble enough to recognize, first of all, what we do *not* know or fully understand, we can set about obtaining the necessary mental tools. As we gain more knowledge about ways in which the different parts of the horse work together in harmony, and our understanding of the principles of training grows, the range of options available to us when dealing with problems will widen, making such problems that much easier to solve.

When trying to solve problems, we must always look at the whole horse, considering a range of possible causes and solutions. It is all too easy to find a possible cause for a range of symptoms, and then to treat all those symptoms as having the same cause. The mind effectively closes itself to other possibilities. We must never fall into the trap of seeking a single explanation that will fit every case.

Much of the remedial action suggested in this book, should, in any case, form part of the basic training of every horse; it may simply be that in certain cases rather more emphasis needs to be given to specific aspects of that basic training. There is nothing arcane about any of it, and in most cases the work involved is well within the capabilities of a reasonably competent rider. You do, however, need to understand the principles behind what you are doing, so in many cases further reading may be necessary, as no one book can provide all the insight you need.

Please note that although remedial action is detailed in each chapter, you should read through the whole book before taking any such action. I stress this because you need to judge whether remedial action taken to improve one aspect might not be detrimental to another. The remedial action suggested should be regarded as a guideline only; as always, each horse should be considered individually. If you are at all unsure, then *do not proceed;* always, in cases of doubt, seek expert advice. This may be from your vet, from a farrier specialising in remedial work, a qualified equine physiotherapist, chiropractor or McTimoney practitioner, etc. Referrals to therapists, chiropractors etc. should always be with the approval of your vet; a list of organisations that will be able to provide details of suitably qualified people is given in Appendix II. Remember that it is illegal in the UK, and in many other countries, for unqualified persons to treat horses. Where remedial schooling is concerned, sadly, equestrian qualifications are not necessarily a guarantee of excellence. I would advise anyone seeking help to try to find a classically trained teacher. The Classical Riding Club maintains a list of such people; this is available from the CRC office for a small charge (see Appendix II). Where the problem is of a psychological or behavioural nature, the Intelligent Horsemanship Association may be able to help (Appendix II).

Such advice may not be cheap, but the extra cost is surely worthwhile if it helps you to overcome problems in ways that will not only enhance your horse's performance abilities in a humane, responsible manner, but almost certainly help to prolong his active life (with apologies to a certain well-known brand of dog food!).

Bearing all this in mind, let's start to look at individual parts of the horse's body.

CHAPTER THREE

No foot, no horse

THE OLD ADAGE, 'No foot, no horse' may be a cliché, but it is no less true for that, so we will start by looking at the feet.

The foot

Strictly speaking, what we refer to as the horse's foot is only part of the foot. The horse's elbow is the counterpart of the human elbow, so what we call the knee – the carpus – is actually the equivalent of the wrist joint. The cannon bone, or metacarpus, may be compared to the human hand, with its five rodlike bones (metacarpals), except that horses have only one of these bones. (See Fig. 3.1). So horses are in effect walking on their toes, or rather on one toe! Each limb, fore and hind, has only this one toe with which to support a weight of anything up to one tonne,[1] which helps to explain why good feet are a must for continued soundness.

The equine foot (see Fig. 3.2) is a complex structure comprising numerous small bones (ending with the coffin or pedal bone), tendon attachments, ligaments, cartilage, blood vessels, nerves, and the outer casing or hoof. The latter is attached to the pedal bone by thin leaves of tissue (laminae) and composed of tubules of keratin. Many people (including a great many farriers) believe that light-coloured hooves are weaker than dark

---

1 This applies to the bigger heavy horses; most riding horses range from about 400 to 600 kilograms in weight. At faster speeds, and in jumping, there may be times when only one foot is on the ground. The force involved is increased by the speed at which the horse is moving, so at a gallop each foot may at times be supporting a weight of up to 1,000 kilograms!

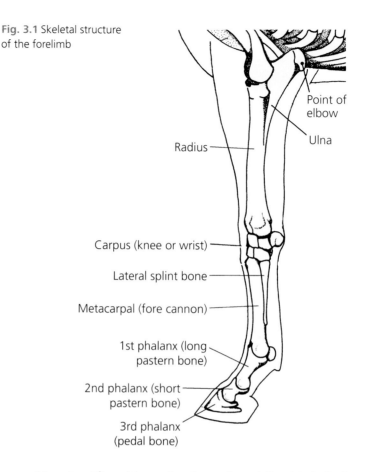

Fig. 3.1 Skeletal structure of the forelimb

Point of elbow

Ulna

Radius

Carpus (knee or wrist)

Lateral splint bone

Metacarpal (fore cannon)

1st phalanx (long pastern bone)

2nd phalanx (short pastern bone)

3rd phalanx (pedal bone)

ones. No scientific evidence has been found for this belief, and a comparative examination of light and dark hoof horn from our own horses has revealed no difference in strength or horn quality.[2]

As well as protecting the inner structures of the foot, hoof horn is a remarkably efficient shock absorber. Every time the hoof hits the ground, it absorbs and dissipates the energy created with each forward swing of the limb.

Because the foot plays such a vital role in support, and as a shock-absorber, imbalance in the hoof wall can affect every aspect of a horse's athletic performance, as well as soundness. If you had to walk in shoes with soles built up only on the outside, you would end up either putting more weight on the inside part of your foot, or by stepping more onto the outside, with more weight in the heel to compensate. Either way, your gait

2 Some breeds do tend to have harder hooves than most others, e.g. Arabians, some Iberians and Cleveland Bays; however, this hardness does not depend on colour but on genetics and, often, the climate in which the horse has been kept. Nutrition and general health can also affect the quality of hoof horn.

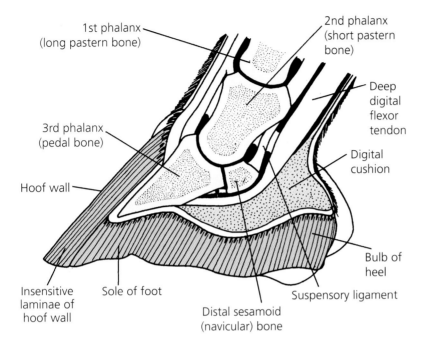

Fig. 3.2 The equine foot

1st phalanx (long pastern bone)

2nd phalanx (short pastern bone)

Deep digital flexor tendon

3rd phalanx (pedal bone)

Digital cushion

Hoof wall

Bulb of heel

Insensitive laminae of hoof wall

Sole of foot

Suspensory ligament

Distal sesamoid (navicular) bone

would be affected: you would probably end up straining muscles in your back as well as in your legs. In the same way, hoof asymmetry affects the horse's balance and use of his muscles (see Fig. 3.3).

Proper hoof alignment is therefore essential for good balance, soundness and correct muscle development.

The fore hooves should be more or less round (giving a greater weight-bearing surface), while the hind hooves are more oval in shape (see Fig. 3.4). If the toe of the forefoot in particular is too long, this will affect the horse's movement, as more force is needed to lift the heel. Excessively long

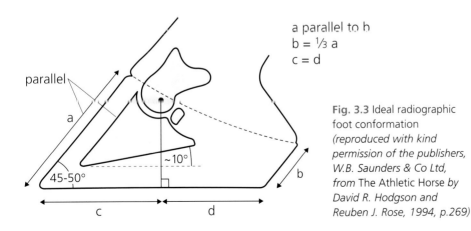

parallel

a parallel to b
b = ⅓ a
c = d

a

~10°

45-50°

b

c

d

Fig. 3.3 Ideal radiographic foot conformation (reproduced with kind permission of the publishers, W.B. Saunders & Co Ltd, from The Athletic Horse by David R. Hodgson and Reuben J. Rose, 1994, p.269)

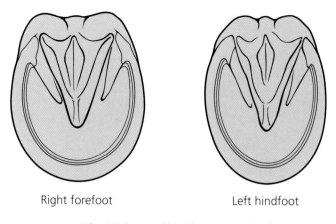

Right forefoot   Left hindfoot

Fig. 3.4 Fore and hind hooves: underside

toes cause gait problems, and may be a contributory factor to the onset of navicular disease.

Sometimes horses have odd feet, when one forefoot (or, more rarely one hind foot) is a different size and shape from the other. In some horses this asymmetry is congenital, in which case, as long as each foot is trimmed and balanced according to its individual conformation, mismatched feet are not necessarily a problem (Kruger, the horse used as a guinea pig in Chapter 2 and in Appendix I, has odd front feet). However, odd-sized feet are often a response to chronic pain. The horse attempts to relieve the pain by putting less weight on the affected foot; as a result, the foot contracts and becomes narrower and more upright. Because it bears more weight, the opposite foot may spread and become flatter. In such cases no attempt at remedial farriery should be made; instead, consult your vet about possible causes and treatments.

In some cases, the hoof and cannon bone are not properly aligned (or the cannon itself may be twisted), leading to the conformation known as toe-in (where the toes point in toward each other) or toe-out (the opposite). Sometimes this may be an optical illusion, caused by incorrect side-to-side foot balance; a simple exercise[3] can be carried out to test this (see photograph opposite). However, this is more usually the result of a conformation fault higher up in the limb, and so will be dealt with later in this chapter.

The feet must be in proportion to the rest of the horse. Feet that are too small and/or narrow for the size of the horse have a reduced area available for the dissipation of concussion. This lessens the foot's shock absorbing abilities and may result in the hoof wall becoming dry and brittle.

3 Suggested by Dr Gail Williams and Martin Deacon in their excellent book, *No Foot, No Horse*, Kenilworth Press 1999; thoroughly recommended.

Alignment of the forelimb: lift the horse's foreleg and, keeping it straight to the front, let it hang freely from the knee, as shown here. This will reveal whether the lower limb is straight, and the hoof and cannon properly aligned (L. Skipper)

Feet that are too large and wide, on the other hand, may not have sufficient strength in the hoof wall to support the horse's weight. Flat feet are common with this type of foot, often resulting in dropped soles prone to bruising.

Misshapen hooves or gait abnormalities may not always be a direct cause of lameness, but they can certainly be contributing factors. Many foot abnormalities may be the result of improper shoeing or trimming, but they can also result from poor conformation, so you need to discuss the subject fully with your vet in order to decide on proper corrective treatment. For this reason it is essential that the vet and farrier work closely together. Where gait abnormalities are the result of limb conformation such as toe-in or toe-out stances, corrective trimming and/or shoeing is aimed mainly at achieving better weight distribution and preventing interference. Where the feet themselves are poorly conformed, the emphasis is on restoring the correct balance and axis.

Shoes do interfere with the foot's natural shock absorbing qualities. There are many areas of the world where horses go barefoot over extremely rough and hard terrain, and yet do not suffer from lameness or foot problems. None of our own horses are currently shod, and all can happily work barefoot without detriment; in fact one horse's gaits improved dramatically once I stopped having him shod.

However, not all horses will benefit from being worked unshod. Horses bred in hot dry climates tend to have much harder, tougher feet than those bred in a moist, temperate climate such as that of the United Kingdom and western Europe. Working barefoot may not, therefore, be possible for all horses; much depends on an individual horse's type and breed, and the manner in which he is kept. If horses have previously been shod, they may have come to rely on their shoes for support. In addition, many foot problems can really only be treated effectively by remedial shoeing; this is why it is essential to discuss options thoroughly with your vet and farrier.

The forelimb

The pastern

HOOF/PASTERN AXIS

The angle of the hoof wall should make a continuous line with that of the pastern (see Fig. 3.5). The angle varies considerably with individual horses, but is usually within the range 45–54 degrees in the front feet, and 49–56 degrees in the hind feet. More important than the actual angle is the alignment with the pastern, since the foot/pastern axis can have a considerable effect on soundness (see Fig. 3.6). Keeping the foot/pastern axis aligned reduces stress on the joints of the lower limbs. The foot itself needs to be set squarely onto the cannon bone, and should be level and symmetrical from side to side.

Upright pasterns, especially if combined with an upright shoulder, will tend to make the gaits rough and the action choppy. They lack the springiness of more sloping pasterns, so their shock absorbing quality is greatly reduced. A horse with upright pasterns may be prone to lower leg injuries, as well as to arthritis of the fetlock joint, ringbone and navicular disease. **Long pasterns** may predispose the horse to sesamoiditis, as well as to ligament and tendon injuries. (See Fig. 3.7.)

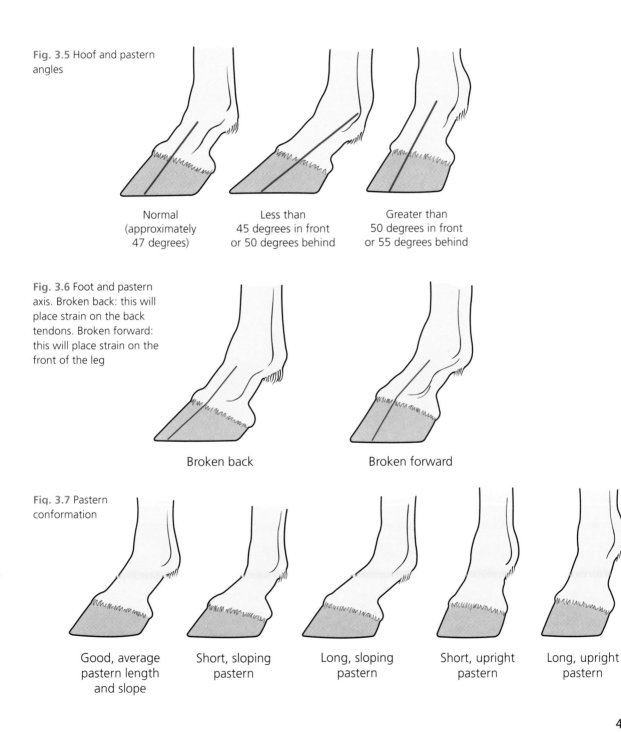

Fig. 3.5 Hoof and pastern angles

Normal (approximately 47 degrees)

Less than 45 degrees in front or 50 degrees behind

Greater than 50 degrees in front or 55 degrees behind

Fig. 3.6 Foot and pastern axis. Broken back: this will place strain on the back tendons. Broken forward: this will place strain on the front of the leg

Broken back

Broken forward

Fig. 3.7 Pastern conformation

Good, average pastern length and slope

Short, sloping pastern

Long, sloping pastern

Short, upright pastern

Long, upright pastern

The fetlock

These should be wide enough to allow for the attachment of the ligaments and tendons of the lower legs.

The cannon bone

If the radius and cannon bone are 'stacked' vertically on top of one another as they should be, this makes for a strong leg structure (see Figs. 3.8 and 3.9). If the cannon bone is not set directly under the radius (as seen from the front) the resulting conformation is known as **offset cannons or bench knees** (see Fig. 3.10). This may be congenital, or it may be caused by irregular growth of the bones. Uneven growth of the lower end of the radius may result in greater development at one side, or the unevenness may occur in the bones of the carpus – possibly a result of nutritional deficiencies.

Whatever the cause, the uneven stress this conformation causes to the knee may result in strains, and could in time create deformity of the carpus, and/or a tendency to form splints.

If the offset is only slight, this may not be so important, especially if the horse has big, well-shaped knees, which will be better able to absorb the strain caused by uneven stacking of the bones. In fact many horses have slightly offset cannons, and yet manage to perform well and remain sound

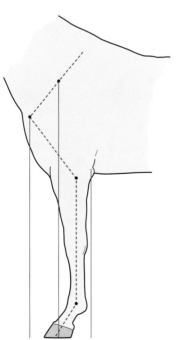

Fig. 3.8 Straight forelimb: side view. A vertical line dropped from the pivoting point of the shoulder passes approximately through the centre of the humerus and the centre of the hoof. In a well-balanced forelimb, this vertical line falls about half way between vertical lines dropped from the point of shoulder and from the point of elbow

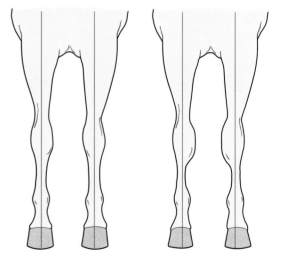

ABOVE LEFT **Fig. 3.9** Straight forelimbs: front view. A vertical line dropped from the point of shoulder bisects the knee, cannon, fetlock and foot

ABOVE RIGHT **Fig. 3.10** Offset cannon

in a variety of disciplines. One scientific study of Swedish Warmblood general riding and performance horses found that 60 per cent of the horses studied had offset cannons!

Sometimes the cannon bones line up, but the knee itself is offset, i.e. the radius and the cannon bone do not join the knee in the centre. If the knee is offset to the inside, as in Fig. 3.11, this may not be as much of a problem as it might seem. The forces generated by the hoof's impact with the ground do not travel up the centre of the forelimb; instead they are concentrated more to the inside of the limb. This is why the bone is denser there, and joints thicker. So a knee slightly offset to the inside may be well able to cope with those forces, provided it is large and well shaped. A knee offset to the outside, however, is a much weaker conformation; even so, as with a knee offset to the inside, a large well-shaped carpus may compensate for this weakness to some extent. As always, this aspect must not be viewed in isolation, but as part of the whole.

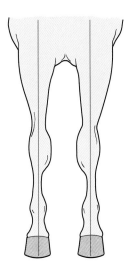

Fig. 3.11 Offset knee

The carpus

The carpus, or knee, is a compound joint, made up of several smaller bones. Its functions are:

- flexion of the forelimb
- absorption of concussion
- extension of the forelimb.

The carpus should be proportionally large, broad and shield-shaped, giving good shock absorbency. As seen in profile, it should appear flat, providing a smooth surface for the action of the tendons which straighten the knee, and the whole forelimb should appear to be almost straight. As the bones of the carpus provide attachment for the tendons and ligaments of the forelimb, any weakness here may cause damaging strain to these ligaments and tendons.

KNEE FAULTS

Calf-knees, or 'back at the knee' (see Fig. 3.12). This is a weak conformation in which the radius and cannon are not properly aligned from front to back. When the foot is flexed, the backward deviation of the cannon puts excess strain on the back tendons and check ligaments. Disciplines which impose a good deal of stress on the foreleg, such as racing, jumping or eventing, should be avoided.

Sometimes a foot with a long toe and low heel can make the forelimb look calf-kneed, because the heel is bearing too much of the weight. In such cases proper trimming may correct the forelimb stance.

Buck-knees, or 'over at the knee' (see Fig. 3.13). This may be a congenital conformation, or it may be the result of injury. It is a less serious fault than calf-knees; many successful racehorses and show-jumpers have been slightly over at the knee. If this is only moderate, a horse may suffer little or no strain; however, if it is pronounced, there is a danger of fetlock strain, injury to the suspensory ligament, or sesamoiditis.

As with calf-knees, an appearance of being buck-kneed may be the result of incorrect longitudinal foot balance; in this case it may occur because the toe is too short and the heel too high. Again, corrective trimming can restore the balance.

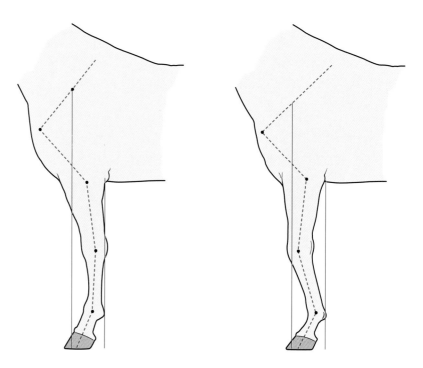

Fig. 3.12 Calf-knee ('back at the knee')   Fig. 3.13 Buck-knee ('over at the knee')

Knock-knees (see Fig. 3.14) are caused by deviation of the radius and of the cannon, so that the knees are angled in towards each other.

Bow legs (see Fig. 3.15) are also caused by deviation of the radius and cannon, but in the opposite direction.

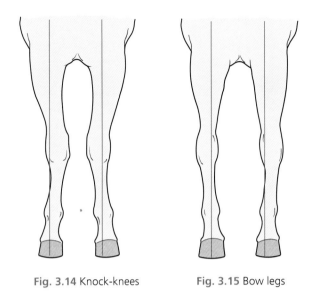

Fig. 3.14 Knock-knees   Fig. 3.15 Bow legs

Tied-in at the knee refers not to the knee but to the flexor tendon, which, instead of running parallel to the cannon bone, appears to slope inwards towards the back of the knee – hence the expression, 'tied-in at the knee'. Hard, cable-like tendons parallel to the cannon suggest strength and an ability to withstand hard work, whereas a tied-in tendon may be caused by the insufficient size of the bones forming the groove through which the tendons pass, and the tendon itself may be too small. Freedom of movement may also be affected.

The forearm

This consists of the radius and the ulna, the latter being fused to the radius for about half its length (occasionally the ulna is complete, as it would have been in distant ancestors of *Equus caballus* up to about 15 million years ago).[4] A good forearm is straight (i.e. in line with the carpus and cannon) when viewed from all sides. A forearm that is proportionally long and wide (seen from the side) provides plenty of room for the attachment of the muscles which propel the limb forward.

Camped under in front (see Fig. 3.16) refers to the pigeon breasted appearance of a horse whose forelegs angle under the body instead of continuing straight down from the elbow.

Camped out in front (see Fig. 3.17) refers to the opposite conformation, where the angle of the forelegs extends out away from the body.

4 A complete ulna is found in some (not all) Arabians.

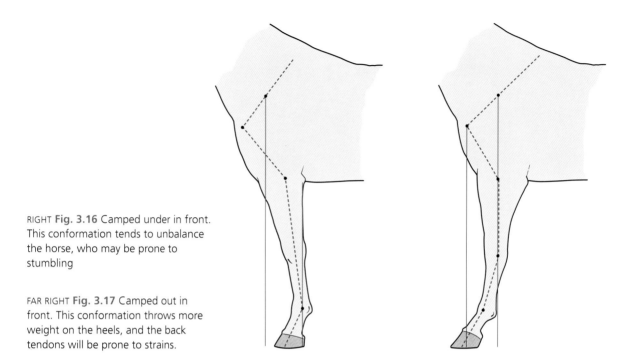

RIGHT **Fig. 3.16** Camped under in front. This conformation tends to unbalance the horse, who may be prone to stumbling

FAR RIGHT **Fig. 3.17** Camped out in front. This conformation throws more weight on the heels, and the back tendons will be prone to strains.

The elbow

The positioning of the elbow determines whether the horse will stand square, or whether he will be what is called base narrow or base wide.

Base narrow (see Fig. 3.18) is when there is a greater distance between the upper part of the forearms than between the feet. This places greater strain on the outside of the legs and feet.

Base wide (see Fig. 3.19) is the opposite of the above, i.e. there is more space between the feet than there is between the forearms. This places greater strain on the inside of the legs and feet.

These types of conformation are less than ideal because, as explained above, misalignment of the forelimbs, whether in the lateral or vertical plane, means that stresses cannot be evenly distributed throughout the limb, thus making it more prone to injury.

In a riding horse, the elbow joint should preferably be just in front of a line dropped down from the highest point of the withers. An elbow situated behind this point will tend to place more weight on the forehand. For the toes to point straight forward, the elbow must not be angled too far out away from the body, or the horse will probably stand with a toe-in stance. If it is angled in too close to the body, the horse may toe-out, and the range of movement of the forearm will be restricted, shortening the foreleg stride. (See Figs. 3.20 –3.23.)

A toe-in conformation can result in the gait abnormality known as 'dishing', where the horse swings his forelegs outwards and back in again, to avoid 'interfering', i.e. catching one foot (or leg) with the other. A toe-out conformation may result in the opposite gait peculiarity, often called 'paddling', where the forelegs swing inwards and back out again. (See Fig. 3.24.)

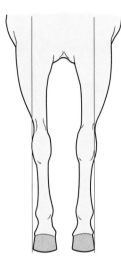

Fig. 3.18 Base narrow

Fig. 3.19 Base wide

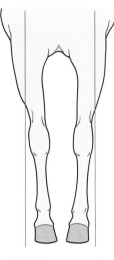

Fig. 3.20 Base narrow, toe-in

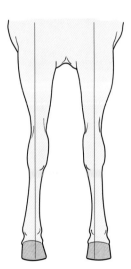

Fig. 3.21 Base narrow, toe-out   Fig. 3.22 Base wide, toe-in   Fig. 3.23 Base wide, toe-out

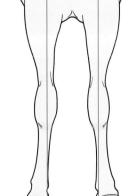

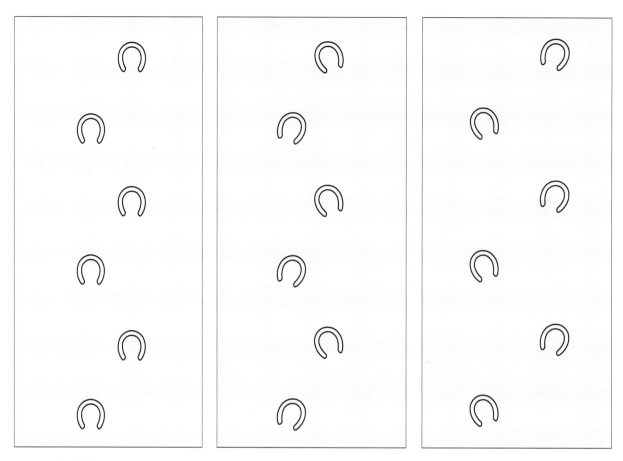

Straight movement	Toe-in	Toe-out
The hind feet follow in the tracks of the forefeet	The feet swing outwards and then back again. When exaggerated this is known as 'dishing', although some horses with straight limb conformation but having a broad breast may dish	The feet swing inwards and then back again. When exaggerated this is known as 'paddling', some horses with straight limb conformation but with a narrow breast may paddle

ABOVE **Fig. 3.24** How toe-in and toe-out conformation affects movement

The hind limb (See Fig. 3.25)

The hind cannon bone

The cannon bone of the hind leg is normally longer than that of the foreleg. There is some controversy regarding whether shorter cannons are more desirable than long ones. It should be borne in mind that longer bones need to be thicker in order to add strength to the added length. As with the forelegs, the back tendons should be clean and well defined.

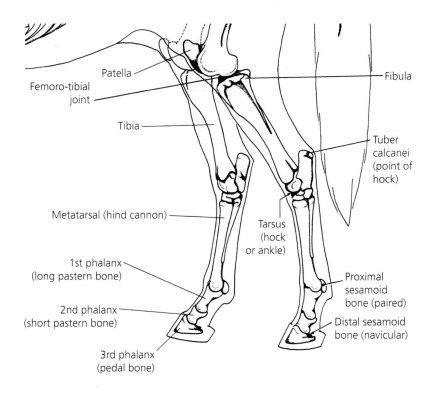

Patella

Femoro-tibial joint

Tibia

Fibula

Tuber calcanei (point of hock)

Metatarsal (hind cannon)

Tarsus (hock or ankle)

1st phalanx (long pastern bone)

Proximal sesamoid bone (paired)

2nd phalanx (short pastern bone)

Distal sesamoid bone (navicular)

3rd phalanx (pedal bone)

Fig. 3.25 Skeletal structure of the hind limb

The hock

Hocks need to be large, in order to sustain the horse's weight during flexion. Thin, weak hocks do not act efficiently as shock absorbers. Viewed from the side the hocks should be wide and strong, should appear clean, with the point clearly defined, and should appear neither too straight nor excessively angled (see Figs. 3.26, 3.27 and 3.28).

SICKLE HOCKS

Well-angled hocks favour flexion and collection, but too much angulation creates what are known as 'sickle hocks' (see Fig. 3.29). These place excessive strain on the rear of the hocks, and may be the cause of spavins, curbs and bog spavins.

STRAIGHT HOCKS

These are stronger than sickle hocks, and tend to give a longer swinging stride (see Fig. 3.30). This is fine for a racehorse, but in a riding horse a hock

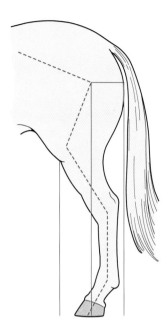

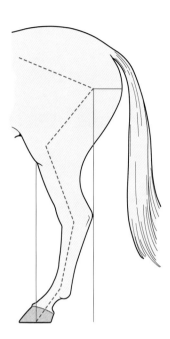

Fig. 3.26 Good average angles of the hind limb. A line dropped vertically from the hip joint passes approximately through the centre of the gaskin and the hoof. In a well-balanced hind limb, this vertical line passes about halfway between vertical lines dropped from the patella and from the point of buttock. The latter line also passes just behind, and parallel to, the rear of the lower hind limb

Fig. 3.27 Camped under hind limb. This is a rather unstable conformation

Fig. 3.28 Camped out behind. This conformation places strain on the lumbar portion of the back. A horse with this conformation may find it difficult to engage his hindquarters

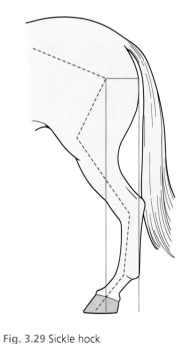

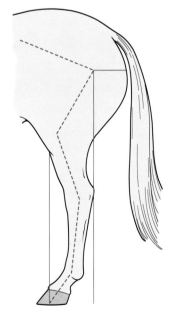

Fig. 3.29 Sickle hock

Fig. 3.30 Straight hock

that is too straight may be unable to flex sufficiently to allow the horse to collect himself efficiently.

COW HOCKS

When most people in the equestrian world talk about cow hocks, they are referring to hocks which turn inwards. In many cases these are not true cow hocks at all. We are usually told that, viewed from behind, the horse's hocks should be straight (see Fig. 3.31). However, this does not make anatomical sense. In order to prevent the front feet from getting in the way of the hind feet at the faster gaits, the horse has to place his hind feet further apart than in the slower gaits. This involves rotating the entire hind limb outwards from the hip joint, which for a brief moment brings the hocks out and makes the lower leg turn inwards, ensuring that the hind feet can land squarely. If the horse's hocks followed the textbook ideal, his toes would actually be pointing inwards at the gallop. This means that, in order to be biomechanically efficient, the horse's hocks have to start off by being turned inwards somewhat. Figs 3.32 and 3.33 illustrate the difference between normal hocks and true cow hocks.

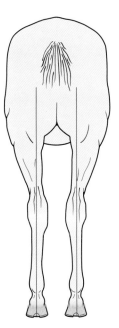

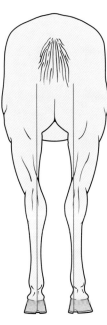

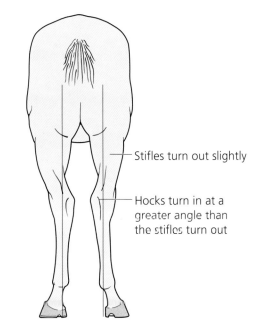

Stifles turn out slightly

Hocks turn in at a greater angle than the stifles turn out

Fig. 3.31 'Normal' hocks, as usually depicted in textbooks

Fig. 3.32 Correct 'normal' hocks

Fig. 3.33 True cow hocks: in 'normal' hocks the natural tendency of the structures is that the hock turns inward to the same degree as the stifle turns outward (which it should do, slightly, so that the upper hind limb can clear the ribcage). However, with true cow hocks the hock turns inward to a greater degree than the stifle turns outward

BOW HOCKS

The opposite of cow hocks is the conformation known as bow legs, bandy legs or bow hocks (see Fig. 3.34). In this case, the hocks are set further apart than the fetlocks, often resulting in the hind feet interfering with each other. This is much less common than cow hocks.

The gaskin

The gaskin or second thigh forms an important part of the horse's 'rear engine', and so the muscles need to be well developed. Racehorses need a long gaskin, as the longer muscles increase the swing of the hind leg and lengthen the stride. However, long gaskins, like long cannons, can be weak, and horses with this conformation tend to be cow-hocked or bow-legged. Riding horses do not need such a long gaskin, and it should therefore be at least 5–10 per cent shorter than the femur.

Gaskins that have the Achilles tendon attached well to the rear appear wide from the side; this gives the limb better leverage.

The femur

Unlike the forelegs, the hind legs are connected directly to the spinal column via the pelvis and the attached muscles. They effectively form the horse's 'engine', supplying most of the locomotive power. Because of this the bones of the upper hind limbs need to be bigger and stronger, and the muscles larger and more powerful, than those of the forelegs. A long femur gives greater power to the hindquarters, and is therefore desirable in a riding horse; a short femur will tend to make the horse take short, rapid strides.

Now that we have seen how various types of limb conformation affect the horse's soundness and athletic ability, what can we do to remedy, or at least minimize, any problems?

While we clearly cannot alter the skeleton, we can alleviate some of the stresses which may hamper athletic ability or create unsoundness. We have seen how vitally important foot balance is; before you make any judgements about your horse's limb conformation, make sure his feet are correctly balanced. Sometimes horses look camped out or camped under, appear as if they have calf-knees or are over at the knee, or their limbs look twisted, when in reality all that is wrong is that their feet are improperly balanced, causing them to stand awkwardly. So always check the feet first – in some cases corrective action here may be the only remedial action you

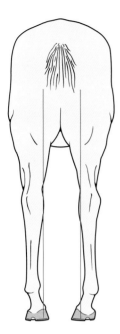

Fig. 3.34 Bow hocks

Table 1 Fore and hind limb remedial/corrective action

Limb part	Problem	Remedial action	Do	Do not	Further reference
Elbow	Loose	Lungeing, especially over poles and cavalletti	Work out a systematic programme of lungeing	Allow the horse to simply run around on the lunge. This will serve no useful purpose	Chapter 9; recommended reading: Reiner Klimke, *Cavalletti* (rev. ed.) J.A. Allen, 2000; Sylvia Stanier, *The Art of Long Reining* (rev. ed.) J. A. Allen 1993 and *The Art of Lungeing* (rev. ed.) J. A. Allen 1995
Elbow	Tight	Exercises to loosen and stretch the pectoral muscles. Manual massage	Proceed slowly and carefully	Carry out stretching exercises without first warming up the horse's muscles	Chapters 4 and 13
Feet	Hoof asymmetry	Corrective trimming	Discuss asymmetries fully with your farrier	Insist on corrective trimming without consulting your vet	Recommended reading: *No Foot, No Horse*, by Dr Gail Williams and Martin Deacon, Kenilworth Press 1999
Feet	Dry, brittle hoof walls	In dry weather, try to arrange for the horse to spend some time each day with his feet in water. Walking in a river or the sea is beneficial. Oil in the horse's diet can also help; see Chapter 13	Consult your farrier about any cracks which may appear in the hoof wall as a result of dryness	Use hoof oil; this is purely cosmetic and can actually prevent the hoof from absorbing moisture	Chapter 13 Recommended reading: *No Foot, No Horse*, by Dr Gail Williams and Martin Deacon, Kenilworth Press 1999
Feet	Toe-in, toe-out	Corrective trimming and/or shoeing, as uneven weight bearing will tend to cause one side of the hoof to wear down more in the unshod horse, or become compressed in the shod horse	Ask your vet and farrier to work together in deciding on the correct remedial treatment	Simply ask your farrier to carry out remedial treatment without prior consultation with your vet	Recommended reading: *No Foot, No Horse*, by Dr Gail Williams and Martin Deacon, Kenilworth Press 1999
Foreleg	Offset cannon (where the degree of offset is marked)	None	Undertake a programme of progressive training aimed at getting the horse to take more weight on the hind limbs	Ask your horse to attempt any kind of activities involving undue stress to the forelimbs	Chapters 9 and 12. Recommended reading: Sylvia Loch, *Dressage in Lightness*, J. A. Allen 2000
Foreleg	Over at the knee (to a marked degree)	None	As for offset cannons	As for offset cannons	As above
Foreleg	Back at the knee	Front heels should be kept fairly high for support	As for offset cannons	As for offset cannons	As above
Hindquarters	Short femur (short, rapid hind leg strides)	Encourage the horse to adopt a slow, regular rhythm in trot, while sending him actively forward	Establish and maintain forward movement at all times	Slow the horse down so much that you destroy the rhythm and forward momentum	Chapters 11 and 12
Hocks	Camped out, trailing hocks, giving a flattened movement in trot	Exercises to develop strength in the back and abdominal muscles, e.g. lungeing and riding over cavalletti	As for loose elbow	As for loose elbow	Chapters 9 and 12; recommended reading: Reiner Klimke, *Cavalletti* (rev. ed.) J. A. Allen, 2000; Sylvia Stanier, *The Art of Long Reining* (rev. ed.) J. A. Allen 1993 and *The Art of Lungeing* (rev. ed.) J. A. Allen 1995
Hocks	Weak hocks (sickle hocks, over-angulated hocks)	In order to stabilize the hocks, use lateral work to strengthen the abductor and adductor muscles in the thigh and gaskin (see Chapter 4 for more about these)	Make sure you understand how to perform lateral work correctly	Ask for too much at once, or try to introduce exercises for which the horse is unprepared	Chapter 12; Recommended reading: Sylvia Loch, *Dressage in Lightness*, J. A. Allen 2000
Pasterns	Long	The farrier may consider remedial shoeing, e.g. using an egg-bar shoe, to give more support to the heels and increase the weight-bearing area	Ask your vet and farrier to work together in deciding on the correct remedial treatment	Simply ask your farrier to carry out remedial treatment without prior consultation with your vet	Recommended reading: *No Foot, No Horse*, by Dr Gail Williams and Martin Deacon, Kenilworth Press 1999

need to take! This can work the other way, too; improving a horse's posture through correct work may in some cases help to alleviate or minimize foot defects.

If the problem lies in the skeletal structure rather than in foot balance, you may need to reassess what you plan to do with your horse. In some cases, limb defects may be severe enough to make a horse unsuitable for anything other than very light hacking. In most cases, though, it may simply be a case of assessing how bad any defects are, and avoiding any activities likely to place too much stress on the horse's limbs. Remember that no horse is perfect, and unless a horse's legs are really bad, things are not as black as they might seem. A careful choice of activities, allied to correct schooling and foot care, can ensure that even horses with defective limb conformation can lead useful lives and stay sound.

CHAPTER FOUR

The body beautiful

The shoulder and humerus

The shoulder

Viewed from the side, the bones and joints forming the shoulder and upper forelimbs make a series of angles, the shoulder (scapula) with the humerus, and the humerus with the radius and ulna (see Fig. 4.1). The length and angle of the scapula and humerus in relation to the body may vary considerably from breed to breed, and this affects the horse's type of movement. It also affects the amount of elevation and reach of the forelimb, and its shock absorbing capacity.

If the scapula is too upright, the forelimb will be limited in its scope, the forefeet will hit the ground more often, and the shock absorbing capacity of the limb will be reduced. A more sloping shoulder will not only provide a smoother ride, it will cause less strain on the forelimbs from concussion. (See Fig. 4.2.)

Scope and the ability to absorb concussion are also affected by the angle between the humerus and the radius and ulna. This should ideally be in the range 120–150 degrees; a more closed angle here can make for short, choppy strides and consequent decrease in shock absorbency.

Unlike that of humans and many other mammals, the horse's shoulder is not attached to the trunk, but supported entirely by muscles and tendons. This gives the whole joint great freedom of movement in the front-to-back plane, but this muscular support must be strong, so the muscles in the region of the shoulder joint need to be well developed. However, if they become overdeveloped, this may be a sign that the horse is working excessively on his forehand.

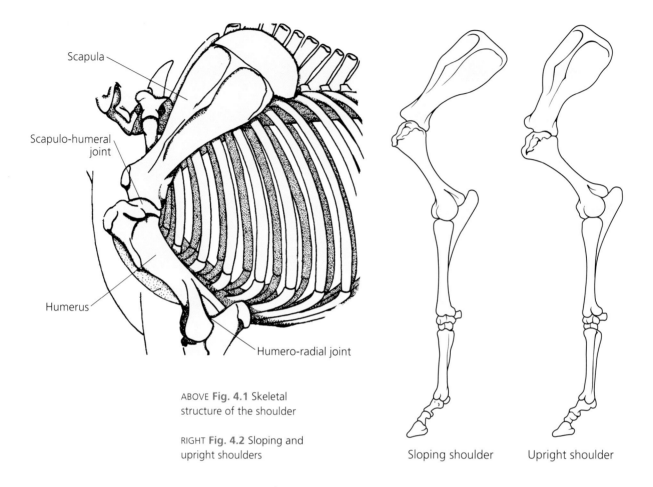

Scapula

Scapulo-humeral
joint

Humerus

Humero-radial joint

ABOVE **Fig. 4.1** Skeletal
structure of the shoulder

RIGHT **Fig. 4.2** Sloping and
upright shoulders

Sloping shoulder   Upright shoulder

The humerus

The structure of the horse's shoulder and forelimbs means that movement
is generally restricted to the back-and-forward plane. However, the ball and
socket joint between the scapula and humerus also allows a limited amount
of sideways movement. It is this joint which allows the horse to perform
lateral movements, moving the limb away from the body (abduction) or
towards the body (adduction). The range of these side-to-side movements
is nothing like as wide as it is in humans, of course, but it is there nevertheless.

The length and angle of the humerus largely determine the kind of
movement the horse will make with his forelegs. Perhaps the most important aspect of this is the effect it has on *scope,* i.e. the freedom of movement
of the elbow, either to the front or to the side.

ABOVE Arabian mare Roxzella scratches her belly on the ground: stretching the forelegs out like this shows good mobility of the shoulder and elbow (L. Skipper)

Adduction and abduction of fore and hind limbs: Arabian mare Tiff (L. Skipper)

61

A long humerus, i.e. one measuring 50 per cent or more of the length of the scapula, has to swing in a longer arc at the elbow, where it acts as a lever. This, assisted by the correspondingly long triceps muscle, gives the forelimb more scope.

Conversely, a short humerus will generally result in a shorter, choppier stride. The resulting lack of scope may restrict a horse's jumping ability, as well as making lateral work more difficult.

However, too long a humerus may make the action of the forelimbs slow and cumbersome, as the limb then has to swing through too large an arc.

The angle of the humerus also has a profound influence on scope. When the horse is in the normal standing position, if the angle formed by the humerus with the scapula is significantly less than 90 degrees, elbow movement will be restricted. If the shoulder slopes sufficiently to give a smooth, elastic ride, the humerus will need to be somewhat upright. An upright humerus will increase the horse's ability to raise his knees, whereas a more horizontal humerus will result in lower action.

Showjumping horses need plenty of scope to tackle large fences, and the most successful ones generally have a long, sloping shoulder and a long, upright to moderately upright humerus. For this reason, although we see plenty of cross-bred horses and ponies of the ride-and-drive type (who

Showjumping horses need plenty of scope to clear fences like this (L. Skipper)

often have rather upright shoulders) taking part successfully in showjumping at the lower levels, they are likely to struggle once the fences start to get bigger.

Having said this, I used to ride a pony whose rather upright shoulder gave him a short, very bouncy stride. He not only stayed sound and clean-limbed, he could jump almost anything a bigger horse could tackle, and in the hunting field and across country he was unbeatable. Another, bigger horse whom I later owned, had similar deficiencies of shoulder and gait, yet he too was a paragon across country and over jumps, and like his predecessor stayed sound and clean-legged. Even so, I always had the impression that he was being stretched to his limit, so as he grew older we hardly did any jumping with him, confining his activities instead to general riding and hacking out.

The latter point is important: many successful jumping horses are being, or have been, pushed to the limit of their ability. This leaves little or no margin for error, and the bigger the fences, the tougher the course or the more gruelling the distance, the greater will be the chance of your horse sustaining physical damage, and the higher the level of competence required in training and riding. So bear this in mind when assessing your horse's potential!

The effects of limb lengths and angles on movement will be more fully discussed in Chapter 11, but the above brief overview shows how important it is to recognize these effects when assessing a horse's athletic potential.

The body

The breast

The breast is often confused with the chest, which is actually the area of the thorax just behind the forelegs. The term breast refers to the muscular area below the neck and above the forelegs, which is defined by the left and right points of the shoulder and by the two points which lie in the same back to front plane as the elbows. A lack of squareness here indicates asymmetry in the horse's frame, which may make him liable to strains in the back and limbs. A narrow breast can place the forelegs too close together, and make the horse prone to interfering with his front feet. However, the breast can appear narrow in a horse who has tight elbows.

If the breast is too wide the horse may try to balance himself by turning his toes in, which helps to give him a more 'square' stance. This may result

The breast should be 'square'; lop-sidedness here indicates asymmetry in the horse's skeleton. Check the horse's stance: Kruger was slightly off-square when this photograph was taken
(*L. Skipper*)

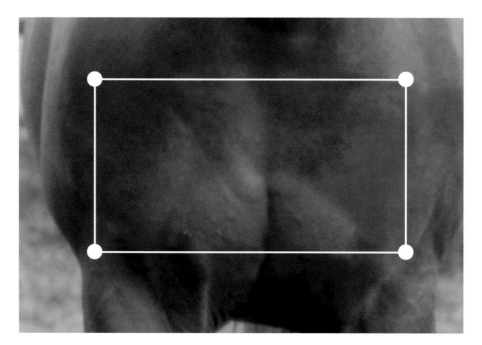

in the gait abnormality known as dishing, mentioned in Chapter 3. Two of our own horses have a slight tendency to dish, although both have straight forelimbs; it may be no coincidence that both have rather wide breasts.

Although well-developed pectoral muscles help to stabilize the forehand, a 'bosomy' appearance, with overdeveloped muscles in this area, may be a sign that the horse habitually moves on the forehand.

The withers

These need to be well defined to give a sufficient area for muscle attachment, and of medium height, sloping well back (although not too far back, or there will be insufficient room for the saddle). As such withers often go with a long sloping shoulder, they will contribute to greater length of stride and freedom of movement.

Very high withers, while they assist with the lever action of the neck, can make saddle fitting very difficult, which is why saddles with cut-back heads were originally devised (nowadays they seem to be regarded as essential for dressage, even though a cut-back head is not always necessary from the horse's point of view, and from the rider's can be a positive disadvantage, as it places the rider towards the back of the saddle). Very high withers may also indicate a shoulder which is too upright. Low, thick withers, on the other hand, often go with a 'loaded' or thick, heavy shoulder, which makes the forehand heavier and less agile.

As we saw in the case of Elmo in Chapter 1, the fact that the shoulder blades have a purely muscular attachment to the trunk means that the withers are not always a reliable guide to whether a horse is built 'uphill' or 'downhill'. The equestrian master Seunig describes how, after correct dressage training, the withers of some horses appear to increase in height.[1] This is because correct training builds up the muscles which support and elevate the neck; the withers, being part of the spine, are also elevated, and the horse appears much more 'uphill' than he did before training commenced.

Because of this, we should not use the height of the withers to measure whether a horse is 'uphill' or 'downhill'; instead we should use the method described in Chapter 2.

The barrel

The barrel needs to be wide and deep to provide good heart room, and to enable the lungs to expand properly. The ribs should have a good space between them, and be well arched (sprung), projecting backwards, rather than straight down; all this assists with expansion during respiration. Too wide a barrel, however, will cause the horse to roll in movement, as he has to swing his hind legs wide to clear the ribcage. A horse with flat sides (slab-sided) may have poor heart and lung capacity. A belly rising steeply to the flanks, like that of a greyhound, is a weak conformation, although this should not be confused with the 'tucked-up' appearance of a horse in racing condition. The latter is not suitable for a general riding horse, who needs good musculature in the belly to be able to function athletically. This is because the external oblique abdominal muscle arising from the ribs, and the long muscle running the whole length of the belly (*rectus abdominis*) play such an important part in lifting the horse's ribcage, as part of the process of raising and arching the back (see Chapter 5).[2]

The thigh

The thigh, situated between the hip and the stifle, needs to be long and well developed, on the inside (as viewed from the rear) as well as the outside (over the stifle). Weakness here – as with the rest of the hindquarters (see Fig. 4.3) – reduces the amount of power available for propulsion. Viewed from the rear, the stifles should form the widest part of the hindquarters.

---

1 Waldemar Seunig, *Horsemanship* (tr. Leonard Mins), Robert Hale & Co., 1958.

2 Dr Deb Bennett demonstrates this action in her video, *Secrets of Conformation;* see under Recommended Reading.

Kruger's belly clearly shows the line of the *rectus abdominis* muscle.
Note this should not be confused with the 'heave' line exhibited by some horses with breathing problems. There is nothing wrong with this horse's breathing! (*L. Skipper*)

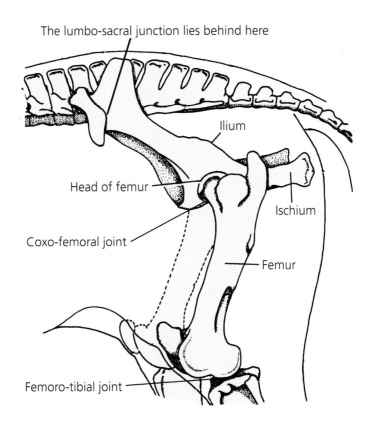

Fig. 4.3 Skeletal structure of the hindquarters

They need to be well forward in position; if they are too far back, this indicates a short thigh. A low stifle is a sign of a long femur. This helps to keep the hock low (for strength) without making the gaskin too long.

As with the forelegs, movement of the hind-legs in the side-to-side plane (abduction and adduction) is limited, but less so than many people realize. Some authorities maintain that horses cannot kick sideways effectively, but that has not been my experience (nor, I suspect, that of most farriers!). Two of our own horses can reach sideways more than one metre with a determined side-kick!

For a riding horse to be comfortable to ride at all gaits, he must be able to flex his hind limbs, so that they can function as shock absorbers as well as fulfilling their major role of propulsion. However, this flexion is hard work for the horse, because at the same time we want him to maintain impulsion (see Chapter 11), so we have to develop the muscles of the haunches by means of systematic gymnastic training of the kind described in Chapters 9, 11 and 12.

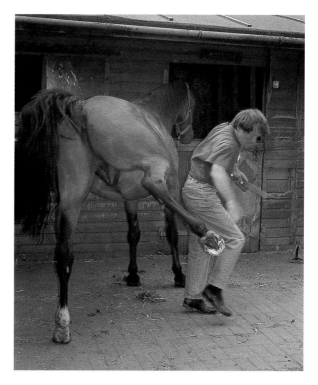

Warmblood gelding Toska proves that horses can kick sideways very effectively!
(*L. Skipper*)

Improving the body and upper limbs

We cannot change the shape of the horse's ribcage, or the angles of the upper limb joints. We can, however, tone up the musculature of his belly, and increase the flexibility of his joints, and so improve his ability to use what he *has* got.

When we say that a horse is supple, or alternatively that he is stiff or lacking in suppleness, what we are really talking about is the range of motion of which his joints are capable. In some joints this range cannot be increased because of the shape of the bones which make up the joint. For example, the long transverse processes of the lumbar spine (which we shall look at in the next chapter) mean that lateral movement in this area is rather limited. However, in many other joints, mobility is affected not by the shape of the bones but by the state of the muscles and the connective tissues (muscle fascia, ligaments and tendons).

Tension from many possible causes, and old injuries (including scar tissue), may affect joint mobility. Exercises for increasing the range of motion of equine joints stretch the muscles and connective tissues, lengthening the fibres and allowing them to return to a more elastic state.

The purely muscular nature of the equine shoulder's attachment to the torso means that we can use the properties of the muscles – i.e. their ability to stretch – to increase the range of movement of which the shoulder, humerus and elbow are capable. We can do the same, to a lesser extent, with the upper part of the hind limbs.

The suppling exercises take two forms: those carried out while the horse is standing still (considered here and in Chapter 5), and those carried out when he is in motion (which we shall look at in Chapters 9 and 12).

The first type of exercise is carried out in a slow, controlled manner. This is essential because the muscles have a built-in defence against sudden stretching, which might otherwise damage the tissues. When this defence kicks in, the muscle actually tenses to counteract the stretch.[3] This is not what we want, so the key words are: **slow** and **controlled**.

The idea is to move a joint to the limit of its range of motion, hold it there for a short period of time (20–30 seconds) and then release **slowly**. I will describe stretching exercises for the neck and topline in Chapter 5; in this chapter we will look at exercises for the shoulder and hind limbs.

Cold tissues are prone to injury, so you need to warm up the muscles first. This can be done by walking the horse around for 10–15 minutes, either in-hand or on the lunge.

Exercises for the shoulder and hind limb joints

Get someone to hold the horse if possible, and make sure he is standing as square as possible (the photographs illustrating this exercise show how difficult it is for one person to manage!).

1. Stand in front of the horse. Take hold of his foreleg at the fetlock joint, raise the limb carefully, and slowly move backwards so you are stretching the whole leg forward. Do not straighten the leg completely, but allow a little bend at the knee, or there will be excess tension in the suspensory ligament and flexor tendons. Hold this position for 20–30 seconds.

2. Still holding the foreleg in the same position, place your inside hand (i.e. the one closest to the horse's midline) just above his knee and, applying

3. Damage is still possible, of course, if the suddenness and force of the stretch are great enough.

gentle pressure, move the leg outwards as far as you can, and hold for 20–30 seconds. Then move the leg slowly back to its normal position, but still holding it up and forward.

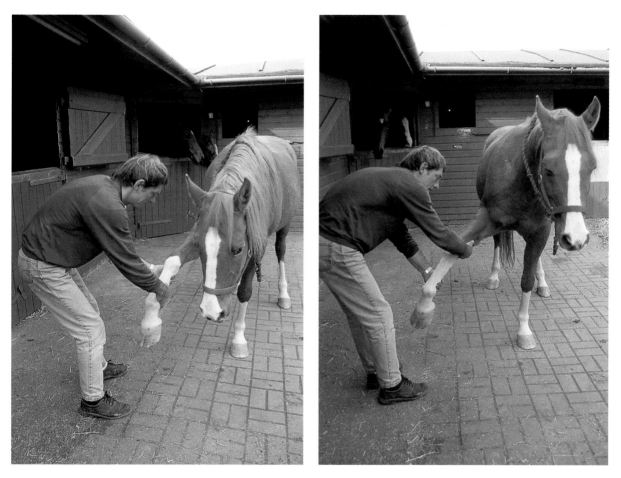

Foreleg stretch to front (*L. Skipper*)   Foreleg stretch to side (abduction) (*L. Skipper*)

3. Equally slowly and gently, move your own position forward and to the side, moving your inside hand to the front of the horse's leg just above the knee. Then move the limb back, with the knee still flexed, and hold for 20–30 seconds.

4. Move the limb forward again, and bring it slowly across the horse's front as far as you can in the direction of the opposite leg. Hold for 20–30 seconds.

5. Bring the leg back to its normal position and lower it slowly to the ground.

The same exercises should be repeated with the other foreleg and the hind limbs, using the same sequence of movements.

Carried out every day, these simple exercises can bring about a remarkable improvement in limb suppleness within the space of three to four months. Once they have become accustomed to them, most horses appear to enjoy them; as you can see from the photographs, Zareeba is very relaxed about the whole thing! Obviously, you need to be very careful if you have a horse who strikes out or kicks when his legs are handled, but this is a problem you will need to address in any case (for possible sources of help, see Appendix II).

In this way, we can help to lay the foundations for improvement of the horse's way of going under saddle.

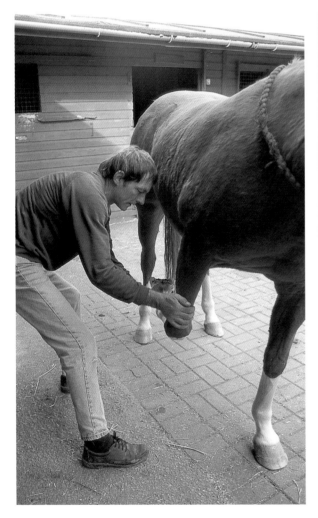

Foreleg stretch back (L. Skipper)

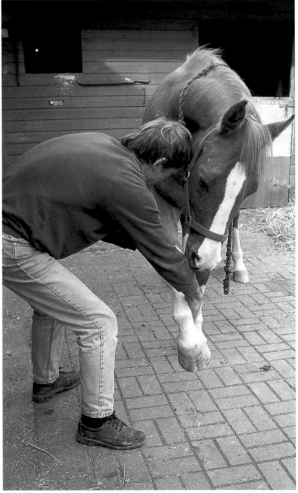

Foreleg stretch across front (adduction) (L. Skipper)

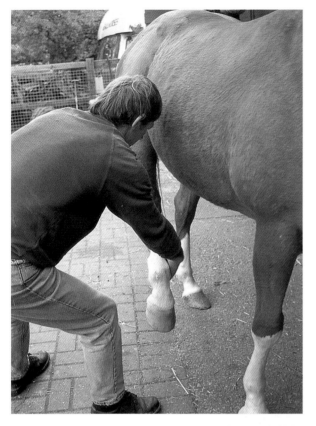

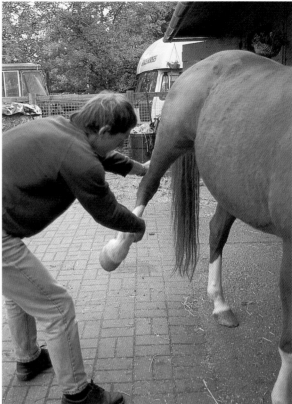

ABOVE Hind leg stretch forward
(L. Skipper)

ABOVE RIGHT Hind leg stretch to side
(abduction) (L. Skipper)

RIGHT Hind leg stretch back (L. Skipper)

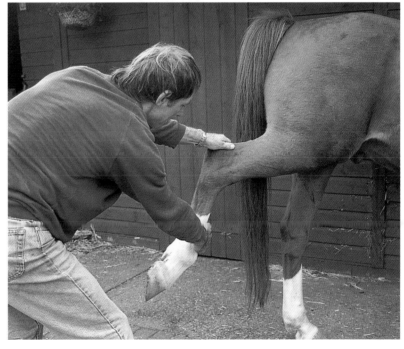

Table 2 Remedial work for the body and upper limbs

Body part	Problem	Remedial action	Do	Do not	Further reference
Belly muscles	Weak and/or undeveloped	Lungeing and riding with neck low and the hindquarters engaged, especially over raised poles or cavalletti; turns; transitions from one gait to another and within a gait; cantering and galloping; belly lifts	Ensure the horse is moving actively from behind	Allow him to rush, or trundle along on his forehand	Chapters 5, 9, 10 and 12. Recommended reading: Reiner Klimke, *Cavalletti* (rev. ed.) J. A. Allen, 2000; Sylvia Loch, *Dressage in Lightness*, J. A. Allen 2000; Sylvia Stanier, *The Art of Long Reining* (rev. ed.) J.A. Allen 1993 and *The Art of Lungeing* (rev. ed.) J. A. Allen 1995; Sara Wyche, *Understanding the Horse's Back* Crowood Press, 1998
Breast	Narrow	As for underdeveloped breast (see below). As training progresses, horses who are narrow in front will often broaden out	As above	As above	As above
Breast	Overdeveloped	Progressive training aimed at getting the hindquarters to take more weight	Ensure the horse is adequately prepared for any new exercises	Ask the horse to perform exercises for which he is not yet ready	As above
Breast	Underdeveloped	Work on the lunge and over raised poles or cavalletti, with neck low and the hindquarters engaged	Ensure the horse is moving actively from behind	Allow him to rush, or trundle along on his forehand	Chapters 5, 9, 10 and 12. As above
Hindquarters	Restricted movement	Stretching exercises as described in this chapter; lungeing and riding over poles on the ground; work over raised poles or cavalletti	Always make sure the horse's muscles are 'warmed up' before carrying out the exercises	Perform the exercises forcefully or too rapidly	Reiner Klimke, *Cavalletti* (rev. ed.) J. A. Allen, 2000; Sylvia Loch, *Dressage in Lightness*, J.A. Allen 2000; Sylvia Stanier, *The Art of Long Reining* (rev. ed.) J. A. Allen 1993 and *The Art of Lungeing* (rev. ed.) J. A. Allen 1995; Sara Wyche, *Understanding the Horse's Back* Crowood Press, 1998
Hindquarters	Underdeveloped	Lungeing and riding over raised poles or cavalletti, with the hindquarters engaged; transitions from one gait to another and within a gait; schooling over low jumps	Ensure the horse is moving actively from behind	Allow him to rush, or trundle along on his forehand	As above
Shoulder	Restricted movement	Stretching exercises as described in this chapter; progressive training aimed at getting the hindquarters to take more weight	Always make sure the horse's muscles are warmed up before carrying out the exercises. Ensure he is adequately prepared for any new exercises	Perform the stretching exercises forcefully or too rapidly, or ask the horse to carry out exercises for which he is not yet ready	As above

CHAPTER FIVE

The topline

The neck

The vertebrae of the neck form an 'S' shape (see Fig. 5.2). The curves of this 'S' are what largely determine the kind of neck the horse will have, and how easy or how difficult it will be to train and ride him (see Figs 5.3 and 5.4).

This is because any riding horse, no matter in what discipline he is to be ridden, must be able to make what palaeontologist Dr Deb Bennett calls the 'neck telescoping gesture': that is, his neck opens out like a telescope, arching up and forward from the withers. This is important in the riding horse because of the effect it has on the horse's ability to use his back and hind limbs.

The muscles of the hind limbs are connected to those of the front limbs by the abdominal and back muscles, which in turn are connected to certain muscles of the neck. In this way, these muscles form a continuous 'chain'. Running from the poll to the third thoracic vertebra is a powerful ligament, the nuchal ligament or *ligamentum nuchae,* which helps to support the weight of the head and, in addition, acts like a tension spring. It attaches to the cervical vertebrae by the *lamella,* a sheet of ligamentous fibres. On either side of this are the numerous muscles of the neck, which play various roles in the support, flexion, extension or rotation and lateral flexion of the neck. The nuchal ligament is continued beyond the third thoracic vertebra by the supraspinous ligament, and together they link the tips of all the spinous processes of the vertebrae (see Fig. 5.5).

When the horse's neck is stretched forward, the nuchal ligament is also stretched. At the withers, the long spinous processes of the thoracic

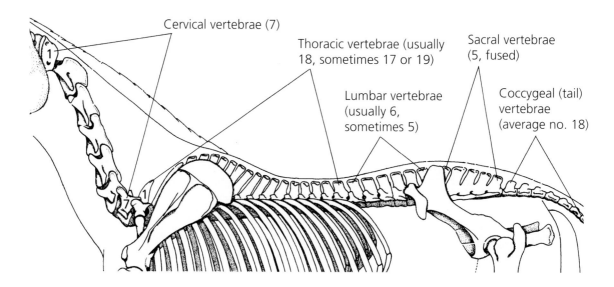

Cervical vertebrae (7)

Thoracic vertebrae (usually 18, sometimes 17 or 19)

Sacral vertebrae (5, fused)

Lumbar vertebrae (usually 6, sometimes 5)

Coccygeal (tail) vertebrae (average no. 18)

ABOVE **Fig. 5.1** Skeletal structure of the back

LEFT **Fig. 5.2** The neck vertebrae form an 's' shape: here the top and bottom curves are about equal. A horse with this neck structure will have little difficulty in making the 'neck-telescoping gesture'

BELOW LEFT **Fig. 5.3** High-set neck: here, the top curve is larger than the bottom one. A horse with this type of neck structure will find the neck-telescoping gesture easy

BELOW **Fig.5.4** Low-set neck: here, the bottom curve is larger than the top one. This type of neck structure is often referred to as a ewe-neck or 'upside-down' neck. Such a neck conformation makes the neck-telescoping gesture difficult for the horse

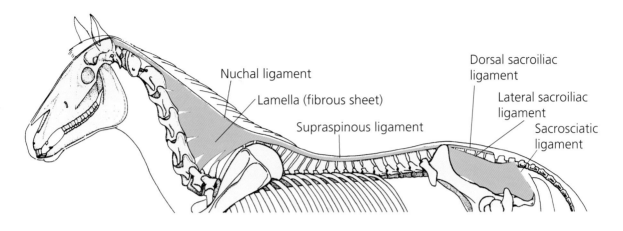

Fig. 5.5 Ligaments of the neck and back

vertebrae function like a lever; when the neck is lowered, the leverage exerted by the forward pull of the nuchal ligament is transmitted to the rest of the thoracolumbar spine by means of the supraspinous ligament and the *multifidus* and *spinalis* muscles (see Fig. 5.7). The resulting muscular and ligamentous tension supports and stabilizes the vertebral column, leaving the deeper back muscles to do their job of facilitating forward movement.

To begin with, the uneducated horse needs to be allowed to stretch forward and down, not only to balance himself, but also because his neck muscles will not yet be strong enough to lift the weight of his head in addition to helping to support the spine (which is still learning to cope with the weight of the rider). Eventually, the neck muscles will be strong enough to fulfil their role, and enable the horse to raise the base of his neck.

Most of the equestrian literature gives the impression that this neck-telescoping gesture starts with flexion at the poll, which misleads riders into thinking that if a horse has flexed at the poll, or has his nose at or near the vertical, this is sufficient. In fact, the neck-telescoping gesture begins at the base of the neck, with the contraction of the *scalenus* muscles which lie deep under the surface, close to the vertebrae (see Fig. 5.7). This straightens out the lower part of the neck, which in turn enhances the arch of the neck along the crest. When a horse makes the neck-telescoping gesture correctly, the *complexus* – a deep muscle which runs below the crest – (see Fig. 5.7) and the deeper-lying *multifidus* muscle, fill out to create the strong, arched, the neck seen in correctly trained dressage horses (see Chapter 8).

From this we can see that the neck-telescoping gesture will be much easier for the horse whose neck has its curves in the right proportions.

Arabian gelding Zareeba (left) and his friend, Arabian mare Anazar (owned by Sandra Nevin), both make the neck-telescoping gesture (*L. Skipper*)

Arabian filly P A Salomai: a beautifully set-on head and neck (*Photo Sweet*)

There are numerous variations on the types of neck shown in Figs. 5.2 to 5.4. Not all low-set necks, for example, are disadvantageous. A low-set neck which has its curves in the right proportions is a better conformation than a high-set neck with the widest curve at its base, as the latter will not make the neck-telescoping gesture easy for the horse. However, not all necks which have a bulging underside as in Fig. 5.4 are built 'upside down'. Overdevelopment of the muscles here may be a sign of incorrect training (usually the result of trying to impose a superficially pleasing head carriage with the reins – see Chapter 8), or it may be that the horse is still weak in the muscles at the base of the neck and has got into the habit of propping his neck up by using the muscles on its underside. Correct training or retraining will usually remedy this.

Many people are misled into thinking that if a horse has a high head carriage, his neck must be set on high. However, a high head carriage, especially if the horse is a 'star gazer', is frequently a sign of a ewe-neck. We have to look more closely at the neck's overall structure before making a judgement; a sharp dip in front of the withers is often a good indication of whether this is so.

We are often told that a long neck is desirable, but length of neck can only be judged in proportion to the rest of the horse. *In itself* mere length is no advantage. Long necks (especially if they are fine and poorly muscled) can be stiff, and are not necessarily more flexible than a shorter neck: much depends on the shape of the neck and its musculature. Horses did not evolve with long necks. Giraffes have evolved biomechanical strategies to cope with extra length; horses have not. Furthermore, giraffes' necks are not particularly flexible. Horses' necks have the same number of cervical vertebrae as giraffes; neck length increases by elongating the vertebrae, not by adding more vertebrae, so a long neck has exactly the same number of joints as a short one!

The horse uses his head and neck to help him balance, but too much length will *overbalance* him, while if the neck lacks muscle it will tire easily, since the muscles must not only support the weight of the head, but assist in raising the forehand. The long-necked horse can easily stiffen his neck into two lateral curves, forming an S-shape and starting with a bulge to the inside at the base of the neck. This makes it very difficult to turn such horses in a balanced manner.

So if you have a horse with a disproportionately long neck, you then have a lot of very hard work to do in order to develop sufficient muscle for the horse to function efficiently as a riding horse.

A neck that is proportionally too short, however, can restrict the foreleg stride, as the muscles which move the shoulder and forelegs forward are situated in the neck. A short, thick neck may be difficult to flex laterally or longitudinally.

If the horse can reach the ground to eat short grass without having to bend his knees or splay his front legs apart, and if his neck, from poll to withers, measures about the same as (or, at most, slightly more than) the length from withers to root of tail, then it is quite long enough. Anything else is superfluous!

If a horse whose legs are not disproportionally long can graze short grass without bending or splaying his forelegs, his neck is as long as it needs to be (*L. Skipper*)

The back

Fig. 5.6 A straight back

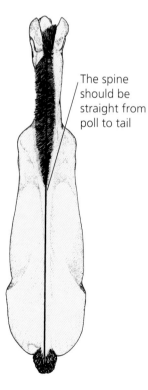

The spine should be straight from poll to tail

As well as acting like a bridge between the horse's hindquarters and fore-hand, transmitting the 'drive' from the hind legs to propel the forelegs and the body forward, the muscles and ligaments of the equine back create a kind of sling for the heavy organs contained in the thorax. It is a happy acci-dent of nature that the back also happens to be the right shape to carry a rider! The latter, however, adds considerably to the weight the spine and its muscles and ligaments have to support, so in a riding horse strength here is essential if the horse is not to be crippled in a very short time.

Seen from above, the back should appear symmetrical from left to right (see Fig. 5.6). No animal – human or non-human – is perfectly symmetrical. In most cases this asymmetry is slight and does not affect performance, but when two asymmetrical creatures such as a horse and rider try to work in harmony, the horse's asymmetry may be compounded by that of the rider. This is one reason why – as we shall see in Chapter 10 – the rider's posture in the saddle is of such vital importance.

When asymmetry is marked or severe, the horse will be unable to move straight. This may be the result of kinks in the vertebral column, or in the limbs. Horses with severe asymmetries are generally unsuitable for all but the mildest of pleasure hacking. Fortunately, in most cases the asymmetries are relatively slight.

A relatively short back is desirable for a riding horse, although too short a back may be stiff. Although the equine spine has limited flexibility in comparison with, say, humans, cats or dogs, the amount of bend possible is more than adequate for flexing the spine laterally and longitudinally. If horses' spines were as rigid as some authorities maintain, they would not be able to reach round and scratch their hindquarters with their teeth – as I have seen a great many horses do![1] Even the longest-necked horse would be unable to do this without some bend in his spine. And, in fact, if one is able to observe horses bending round to scratch themselves like this from above, one can see clearly that the spine *does* bend laterally. Experiments with equine cadavers have shown that most of the lateral bend takes place in the region of the 11th and 12th thoracic vertebrae, while almost all of the longitudinal bend occurs in the lumbar region.

A long back may be more flexible laterally than a short back, but a long-backed horse may find collection difficult. The back may also be weaker, especially if the loin coupling is also long. The loin is the weakest part of the back because, unlike the thoracic spine, which is supported by the ribcage and its attached muscles, the lumbar part of the spine has no support other than that of the muscles and ligaments.

As we saw in Chapter 1, a large part of a riding horse's training is aimed at relieving the forehand by getting the horse to take more weight on his hind limbs. In order to do this, he must flex the lumbo-sacral joint, as well as flexing the joints of the hind legs.

Some equestrian literature states that lumbo-sacral flexion is of little importance. However, we have only to watch slow-motion video footage of horses in all equestrian activities, to see how wrong this is. The cantering or galloping horse must be able to flex the lumbo-sacral joint in order to get his hind legs underneath him. This is why a horse who has only limited flexibility in this area is unlikely to be fast or to have a good, free canter. The jumping horse needs this flexion to make a 'bascule' over jumps.

Finally, the lumbo-sacral joint plays a major part in engaging the so-called 'ring of muscles' (see Fig. 5.7) which enables the horse to carry weight more easily, as well as to collect himself and come 'on the bit' (see Chapter 8 for a definition of the latter). When the horse flexes the lumbo-sacral joint, this exerts tension on the dorsal sacroiliac ligament, helping to raise and stabilize the back. The muscle which helps to create this lumbo-sacral flexion is the *rectus abdominis,* running the length of the horse's abdomen; when this is contracted, it brings the sternum and the pelvis

---

1 I often see our home-bred mare Imzadi (aged five at the time of writing) scratching the side of her face with a hind foot. Recently, she topped even this; out in the field one day, she lowered her head, brought her nearside hind foot forward, and casually scratched the top of her head!

ABOVE Nivalis reaches round to scratch his flank. This horse's back is certainly flexible enough! *(L. Skipper)*

Nivalis shows excellent lumbo-sacral flexion *(L. Skipper)*

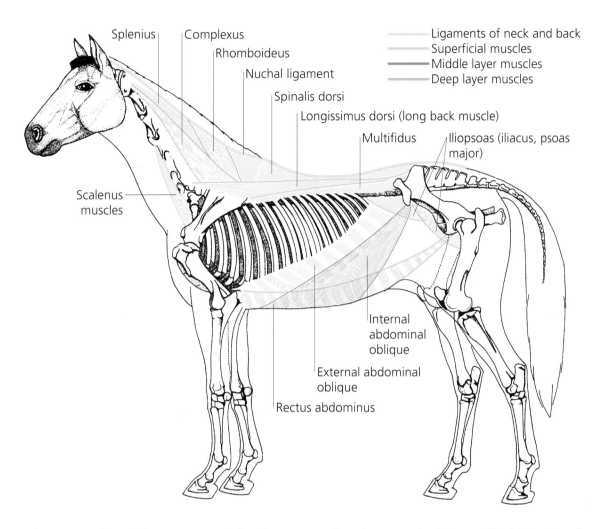

Splenius | Complexus
Rhomboideus
Nuchal ligament
Spinalis dorsi
Longissimus dorsi (long back muscle)
Multifidus | Iliopsoas (iliacus, psoas major)
Scalenus muscles
Internal abdominal oblique
External abdominal oblique
Rectus abdominus

Ligaments of neck and back
Superficial muscles
Middle layer muscles
Deep layer muscles

Fig. 5.7 The 'ring of muscles'

closer together.[2] This is assisted by the external and internal oblique abdominal muscles, as well as the *iliopsoas* and various muscles in the hindquarters, which help to bring the hind legs forward. This is the 'ring of muscles' referred to above.[3]

The loin area should be broad, and the coupling itself as smooth as possible, arching slightly upward to the point of croup. A short level coupling is very strong but can be stiff, whereas a slightly 'peaked' coupling may not be quite so strong, but is very often more supple. Ideally, there should be no more than about four inches between the last rib and the point of hip.

The most functional short back is one in which the ribcage is long, and the loin coupling short. Arabian horses are usually considered to have short

2 The action of this muscle can be seen quite clearly in the photograph of Atlantis cantering, in Chapter 1.

3 There are actually many more muscles involved in this process, but these are the principle ones.

backs because they have fewer vertebrae than horses of other breeds; in fact, studies have shown that approximately four out of seven Arabians have 17 thoracic vertebrae as opposed to 18. The number of vertebrae may vary in other breeds, too; some horses have 19, although 18 is the commonest number. However, as with the neck, back length is determined not by the number of vertebrae but by the length of each vertebra.

One factor which affects the state of a horse's back is its resting muscle tone. Highly reactive horses, i.e. those who are extremely sensitive to external stimuli, usually have fast reflexes to match; this enables their muscles to respond instantly to signals from the brain. Such horses generally have a high resting muscle tone, which may make their backs seem stiff in comparison with those of more naturally laid-back types. They may also have a tendency to hollow, especially if the rider is clumsy, ill-balanced or insensitive. This is the source of the nonsensical idea that Arabians – who as a breed tend to be highly reactive – are 'bred to go with their heads in the air'. The high head carriage so often seen in Arabians and their close crosses is most often the result of tension or excitement. *Any* horse, if tense or excited, will tend to put his head in the air. When correctly trained, and worked and ridden sympathetically, Arabian horses do not poke their noses or stick their heads in the air.[4]

This high resting tone, coupled with their reactivity, can make training such horses something of a challenge. However, although this, being a result of muscle property, is to some extent a conformational trait, it can be easily overcome with appropriate training and management – and most of all by good riding!

If you are bringing on a young horse, do not be deceived by claims that certain breeds or types are 'early maturing'. Some breeds may indeed mature later than others, but no horse is physically mature at four or even five years of age. We are often told not to work very young horses because the growth plates in their legs have not yet closed. However, there is another factor which may be even more important. Dr Deb Bennett, who has spent many years studying form and function in horses, states unequivocally that 'No horse, at any time, anywhere, has ever been physically mature before the age of five and a half.'[5] This is because the cartilaginous growth plates throughout the whole skeleton do not finish closing until the

4 One often sees photographs or films of Arabians being ridden in the desert, with their heads held very high. This reflects their response to the way in which they are being ridden, in particular if a harsh bit is used without the finesse such a bit demands. This is especially true in North Africa.

5 Dr Deb Bennett, Ph.D, Conquerors: *The Roots of New World Horsemanship,* Amigo Publications, USA, 1998, p.124

horse is at least five-and-a half. The last plates to close are those of the spine; this may not happen until the age of six, seven or even eight, especially in the case of bigger horses.

I know that in some European countries, stallions being graded for entry into their relevant stud books are put through gruelling performance testing when they are as young as three. To me this is unacceptable. Although these horses are usually big, and may appear strong, they are physically and mentally still babies. The wastage rate from such testing is very high (a fact not often publicized) and huge numbers of these promising young horses break down and are never seen again. This is the opposite of what we are trying to achieve, so if you are even considering working a young horse hard in order to bring him on quickly, my advice is: do not do it. The old masters of equitation knew what they were doing in this respect and in the seventeenth and eighteenth centuries they would not generally start serious work with a horse until he was at least six or seven.

No, it is far better to be patient than to ruin a horse by doing too much too early. In training horses, patience is indeed the greatest virtue of all!

The croup

The croup extends from the loin to the base of the tail (see Fig. 5.8). For maximum athletic ability, the croup should be long, the measurement being taken from the point of the hip to the point of the buttock This gives a larger area for the attachment of the powerful muscles of the loin and quarters, and provides greater leverage when the horse flexes the lumbo-sacral joint. When the horse is viewed from the side, the point of hip should ideally be almost underneath, or just in front of, the point of the croup (*tuber sacrale*).

As discussed in Chapter 2, the height of the croup is not a reliable guide to whether a horse is built 'uphill' or 'downhill'. However, the *angle* of the croup can affect the horse's ability to bring the hind legs underneath him. This angle is often measured from the point of the hip to the point of the buttock (*tuber ischii*) relative to the ground, but this is misleading. The pelvis (whose angle relative to the ground is what we are really measuring) does not form a straight line from the point of hip to the point of buttock. The *ilium* slopes down to the coxo-femoral joint, and then the *ischium* continues to the point of buttock, at a slight angle to the ilium. The ischium often slopes up again slightly. Two horses whose pelvises are set at exactly the same angle relative to the ground may have the point of buttock placed higher or lower, depending on the angle of the ischium. As it is the

Fig. 5.8 Skeletal structure of croup

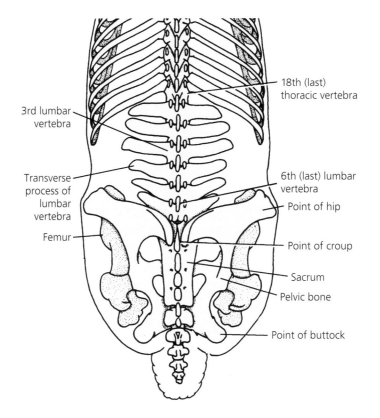

18th (last) thoracic vertebra

3rd lumbar vertebra

Transverse process of lumbar vertebra

6th (last) lumbar vertebra

Point of hip

Femur

Point of croup

Sacrum

Pelvic bone

Point of buttock

Arabian stallion Sorrento: the line of the ilium, ischium and femur can be clearly seen in this photograph *(Photo Sweet)* See also the photograph of Nearco in Chapter 2

placement of the coxo-femoral joint which matters, it is the angle of the ilium which should be measured.

Another factor which can be misleading is the set of the tail. The kind of tail carriage found in Arabians and horses with a lot of Arabian blood can make it appear as if they have a flat croup. However, this tail carriage is the result of the way the sacral vertebrae are set; contrary to that which some riders assert, it does not affect the horse's ability to flex his lumbo-sacral joint or to get his hind legs underneath him. A very muscular loin and quarter can also give the impression of a flat croup, so it is important to be able to recognize the angle of the pelvis itself; this can sometimes be difficult with horses who have very round quarters, such as some Spanish horses and Lusitanos. Horses who have developed a sway-back may also appear to have a flat croup, because the lack of support for the spine makes them tend to stand with their hind legs out behind them, tipping the pelvis upward. The same applies to horses who are not sway-backed as such, but who move hollow-backed for whatever reason. Those show exhibitors who admire a hollow-backed carriage, and the consequent flattening of the croup, are actually encouraging a pathogenic condition!

Flat croup

A flat croup resulting from a comparatively level ilium is preferred by some people. However, this conformation places the coxo-femoral joint too high and far back. This makes it difficult for the horse to engage his hind legs, as the pelvis must be rotated through a much greater angle than with a more sloping ilium. In addition, as Dr Deb Bennett has pointed out,[6] in horses with a level ilium the attachment of the rectus abdominis muscle is then placed at a disadvantage (remember the role this muscle plays in flexing the lumbo-sacral joint). Finally, a too-level ilium makes the pelvic structure shallow, with less room for the powerful muscles which play a major role in propulsion.

Steep croup

This is often referred to as a 'goose-rump', but a horse may have a fairly steep croup and not be truly goose-rumped. The latter kind of croup is usually short as well as steep, limiting the range of motion and, because there is less room for muscle attachment, also reducing the amount of power that can be generated. Some horses, particularly Andalusians and

6 In 'The functional flat croup', *Arabian Horse Express*, Vol. 6, No. 2 (February), 1983

Lusitanos, may have fairly steep croups that are also long, giving plenty of room for muscle attachment. This kind of croup does make it easier for the horse to bring his hind legs under his body, which can be a great advantage in disciplines which require rapid turning and stopping.

Hunter's bump

This is the name often given to the sharp 'peak' which some horses have at the point of the croup. The true hunter's bump is the result of injury to the ligaments at the sacro-iliac joint; this causes the displacement of the sacrum and the ilium. Long-backed horses with weak loins are particularly prone to this problem, as the back structure makes it more difficult for the horse to collect himself, particularly when jumping – hence the term, 'hunter's bump'. This condition should not be confused with a croup which merely has a very prominent point of croup. The true hunter's bump can usually be identified because one side of the croup, viewed from behind, appears higher than the other (although they may sometimes be the same height, so if in doubt, have your horse checked out). It is often accompanied by poor muscle development over the croup.

Improving/preserving the topline

As well as the various stretching exercises described in Chapter 4, there are several which will help to stretch the topline and mobilize the neck.

Longitudinal stretching

Stand the horse close to, and parallel with, a wall or fence so that he cannot simply swing round. Hold a titbit between his forelegs (make sure he knows where it is!) to encourage him to stretch his neck down. Do not ask him to stretch too far to begin with; start with what's comfortable for him, and gradually ask for a bit more with each session.

Lateral stretching

Hold the titbit to one side, as in the photograph, to encourage the horse to reach round for it. Again, ask for only a little at a time, increasing the amount of stretch very gradually.

Carry out these simple exercises every day, and you will be surprised to see how much difference they can make!

Basic neck and topline stretching exercise *(L. Skipper)*

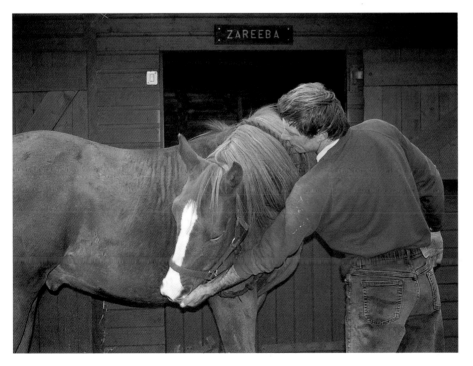

Sideways neck stretch to right *(L. Skipper)*

Sideways neck stretch to left
(*L. Skipper*)

Strengthening the 'ring of muscles'

Treat your horse's back with respect. In canter, even when schooling, ease your seat off the saddle as often as possible. Weak-backed horses may need to be ridden like this for some time, until their 'ring of muscles' has been strengthened. When trotting, go rising as much as possible. Even if your aim is dressage, sitting trot is by no means essential in the early and middle stages of training. If you take the trouble to learn the correct techniques of the rising trot, you can still school your horse very effectively indeed.[7]

Riding uphill at a walk or canter helps to strengthen the back and hindquarters. If you do not have any real hills nearby, even gentle slopes will help.

Perhaps the most effective technique for strengthening the horse's back and abdominal muscles involves working the horse with a lowered head and neck, which can be extremely beneficial and therapeutic. However, as with all such exercises, this work must be treated with caution, and must not be carried on for too long or too frequently. Start off with five minutes on each rein, working up to no more than ten minutes on each rein, several

---

7 The best explanation of the rising trot mechanism I have ever come across is given by Mary Wanless in *Ride With Your Mind Masterclass*, Methuen, 1991.

times a week. With horses built rather 'downhill', or who have a tendency to 'plough the ground' with their noses, head-lowering exercises should be kept brief and infrequent. This work can be carried out on the lunge (see Chapter 9) or under saddle (see Chapter 12).

The benefits and drawbacks of working with the horse's head and neck lowered are briefly listed below.

Benefits

- Lowering the head and neck exerts a strong traction on the nuchal ligament at the withers, which assists with raising the back and improving its weight-carrying capacity. The stretching of the vertebral column itself helps to make the back more supple, increasing its lateral and longitudinal mobility.

- It helps to develop the muscles at the base of the neck.

- It stretches the topline and, because the abdominal muscles have to work harder, strengthens the 'bottom' line.

Nivalis works low and round on the lunge. Note the engagement of the hindquarters that comes with flexion of the lumbo-sacral joint (L. Skipper)

- The muscles of the forehand must also work harder, developing the pectoral muscles; this in turn improves muscular support of the forehand.

- If, as well as lowering the head and neck, the horse also engages his hindquarters by flexing the lumbo-sacral joint, this helps to supple the latter, as well as developing and strengthening the muscles of the hindquarters, and improving the mobility of the hip joint. All of this in turn makes engagement easier.

Drawbacks

- If the hindquarters are not engaged, overloading of the forehand can increase stress on joints and tendons of the forelimbs.

- An excessive increase in tension can damage the supraspinous ligament and its attachments, as well as causing damage to the intervertebral discs and to the vertebrae themselves.

For the above reasons, such exercises must be carried out with great care. In spite of this, the benefits from judicious use of these exercises are potentially enormous, so in cases of doubt, seek expert advice (see also Chapters 9 and 12).

This kind of work is also very effective in cases where tension is the cause of stiffness and/or hollowness in the back and neck, as it can help to relax tight muscles along the thoraco-lumbar spine (see Chapter 12).

Finally, there is an exercise which benefits the muscles round the spine and pelvic area, by stimulating the muscles of the belly (belly lifts). We saw how the rectus abdominis muscle forms part of the 'ring of muscles'; if you use your fingers to groom the horse in this area, he will contract the abdominal muscles, including the rectus abdominis. As he does this, you should be able to see his back come up. If you place your hand on the long back muscles, you should certainly be able to feel this 'lift'. If it does not occur, it may be because the abdominal muscles are weak and need building up as described above.

Tapping the horse on the rump should make him respond by 'tucking' his pelvis; this will help to encourage lumbo-sacral flexion.

Correct training and saddle fitting, balanced riding and, above all, adequate preparation, can make all the difference between a horse whose back is hard, stiff, painful and as comfortable as a plank of wood, and one whose back is soft, supple, pain free and a joy to sit on.

Table 3 Remedial work for back and neck (Please note: if your horse has an underlying back problem, seek veterinary advice before starting any remedial work)

Body part	Problem	Remedial action	Do	Do not	Further reference
Back	Stiff	Suppling exercises on the lunge and under saddle	Encourage relaxation, especially if the stiffness is caused by high resting muscle tone	Ask the horse to do any serious work until his back is relaxed and he can start to move freely	Chapters 8, 9, 10 and 12 Recommended reading: Sylvia Loch, *Dressage in Lightness*, J.A. Allen 2000
Back	Weak	Ensure the back is strengthened before attempting serious ridden work	Progressively encourage the horse to stretch his neck forward and down in trot and canter; lunge over raised poles or cavalletti, progressing to similar exercises under saddle. Riding up hills will help to strengthen the back. Ensure that tack fits correctly, and that the rider's position and riding technique are not contributing to the problem	Trot over rough terrain, or use sitting trot, until the back muscles have been strengthened; even then use rising trot wherever possible. Avoid placing haynets and hayracks too high up, as this will force the horse to stand with his back hollowed; if possible, feed hay from the floor	Chapters 8, 9, 10 and 12. Recommended reading: Reiner Klimke, *Cavalletti* (rev. ed.) J.A.Allen, 2000; Sylvia Stanier, *The Art of Long Reining* (rev. ed.) J. A. Allen 1993 and *The Art of Lungeing* (rev. ed.) J. A. Allen 1995; Sara Wyche, *Understanding the Horse's Back* Crowood Press, 1998
Neck	Dip in front of withers	Work on the lunge and over raised poles or cavalletti, with neck low and the hindquarters engaged	Work systematically and ensure you know what you are trying to achieve	Ask the horse to work in any kind of outline until his neck muscles have strengthened sufficiently	Chapters 8, 9, 10 and 12 Recommended reading: as above
Neck	Ewe-neck	Lungeing with side reins attached low, working on transition: from one gait to another and within a gait. Until the scalenus muscles become strengthened, all lunge and ridden work should be carried out with the poll no higher than the withers	As above	As above	Chapters 8, 9, 10 and 12 Recommended reading: as above
Neck	Low-set	In lunge and ridden work, the outline should be long and low to begin with. The head and neck will be raised as the horse begins to take more weight behind	Always ensure the horse is working actively from behind	Allow him to slop about on his forehand	Chapters 8, 9, 10 and 12 Recommended reading: Sylvia Loch, *Dressage in Lightness*, J.A. Allen 2000
Neck	Short, thick	Stretching exercises as described in this chapter	Always make sure the horse's muscles are warmed up before carrying out the exercises	Perform the exercises forcefully or too rapidly	Chapters 8, 9, 10 and 12 Recommended reading: as above
Neck	Stiff	Stretching exercises as described in this chapter	As above	As above	Chapters 8, 9, 10 and 12. *Understanding the Horse's Back* by Sara Wyche
Neck	Undeveloped	Work on the lunge and over raised poles or cavalletti, with neck low and the hindquarters engaged; exercises which encourage the 'neck telescoping gesture'	Make sure the horse is properly a prepared (i.e. by warming up before schooling session)	Ask the horse to work in any kind of outline until his neck muscles have strengthened sufficiently	8, 9, 10 and 12. Recommended reading: Sylvia Loch, *Dressage in Lightness*, J.A. Allen 2000
Neck	Weak	As above	As above	As above	8, 9, 10 and 12. Recommended reading: as above

CHAPTER SIX

The head

The shape and size of the head

Good heads come in all shapes and sizes. Some people prefer heads of one type, others heads of a quite different type. So long as a head is well constructed and functional, one type is not better than another, just different.

It is a great pity that so many textbooks state that the head should have a straight profile. A convex profile, for example, is often regarded as evidence of 'common' blood, yet there is nothing at all coarse or common about the noble, hawked profile of the old-fashioned type of Andalusian or Lusitano. Such a head can be every bit as refined as a straight or dished profile. In the same way, a dished profile is often dismissed as somehow defective, but as long as the dish is not exaggerated, a dished head is as good as any other type of head.

Different types have different strategies for various functions. For instance, the Iberian breeds have a relatively long head, which gives plenty of room for the nasal passages. Arabians, with a generally shorter head, have instead wide nostrils. One writer on animal behaviour states that Arabian horses have nostrils which appear flared all the time. This is not so; in repose, an Arabian's nostrils are no more flared than those of any other horse, although they are generally wider. I should be seriously concerned about the health of *any* horse, Arabian or not, who had permanently flared nostrils!

Cleveland Bay X Thoroughbred mare Kiri: a good head with a straight profile
(*L. Skipper*)

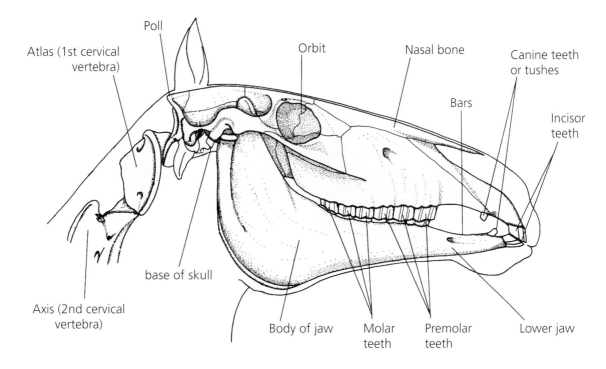

Poll

Atlas (1st cervical vertebra)

Orbit

Nasal bone

Canine teeth or tushes

Bars

Incisor teeth

base of skull

Axis (2nd cervical vertebra)

Body of jaw

Molar teeth

Premolar teeth

Lower jaw

ABOVE **Fig. 6.1** Equine skull

A dished head: Arabian stallion Rusleem. Unlike many modern Arabian show horses, multi-champion Rusleem does not have exaggerated features. This is a good, functional head *(Photo Sweet)*

A sub-convex head: Lusitano stallion Prazer *(L. Skipper)*

I like to see a straight profile on Thoroughbreds and hunter types, a dished (but not exaggeratedly so!)[1] profile on Arabians, and a noble, convex (or, as it is sometimes called, 'sub-convex') profile on an Andalusian or Lusitano – each type of profile being appropriate for the breed or type.

A good head should first of all be in proportion to the size of the body. A horse's head is heavy, weighing between 30 and 40 pounds, so a head that is proportionally too big will overweight the forehand. Large, clear nasal passages are essential, so the head should be long enough to accommodate these as well as the teeth. A broad forehead gives a good cranial space for the brain. The poll needs to be wide, and the throatlatch open. The latter is particularly important because a narrow throatlatch means less room for the upper cervical vertebrae to join the skull just below the ears. Consequently they must insert into the skull from below, making the horse's head look 'stuck-on' (hammer-headed), and reducing his ability to make the neck-telescoping gesture. This is particularly important if the horse has deep jowls.

Exaggerated features can sometimes be considered conformation faults just as much as bad legs etc. A very small muzzle not only reduces the space through which a horse breathes (horses can only breathe through the nose), it also reduces the space available for the upper and lower teeth. This can not only lead to breathing difficulties, but also to all kinds of dental problems, such as overshot jaws (parrot mouth [see Fig. 6.2]) and undershot jaws (monkey mouth [see Fig. 6.3]). In breeds with a dished profile, too pronounced a dish reduces the space available for air intake. The latter feature is one which modern breeders of Arabians all too often take to extremes in attempts to reproduce what they see winning in the show ring, but an exaggerated dish was never a feature of the desert horses bred by the *bedawin*.

Facial characteristics and personality

Perhaps understandably, given that we cannot help but notice it, we tend to place great emphasis on the shape of the head, even to the point of linking it with psychological characteristics. So we find certain psychologists

---

1 Many Arabians have an almost straight profile, and that, too, is perfectly acceptable.

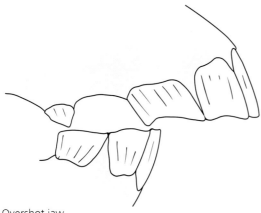

Fig. 6.2 Overshot jaw
(parrot mouth)

Fig. 6.3 Undershot jaw
(monkey mouth)

attempting to identify psychological traits in humans on the basis of their facial and other physical characteristics. In spite of much effort, no-one has managed to demonstrate convincingly that such ideas have any basis in fact. Even so, they have spilled over into equestrian culture, with certain people claiming to be able to 'read' a horse's temperament, personality and ability from his physical appearance, assigning personality traits to him which supposedly go with certain features.

Features such as small eyes or a too-small muzzle can certainly affect performance in so far as they affect vision, breathing, etc., and a horse handicapped in this way may develop personality quirks as a result of physical discomfort or psychological stress. Apart from that, I can find no objectively gathered evidence to suggest that the shape of a horse's facial bones affects its basic temperament or mental abilities.[2] We should instead concentrate on reading the whole horse – a subject to which I shall return in Chapter 14.

The eyes

Horses' eyes are the largest of any land mammal, yet the actual size of the equine eyeball varies comparatively little between individual horses, it is the size and prominence of the orbit (bony eye socket) which makes some horses appear to have eyes that are significantly larger or smaller than those

2 A larger brain may go with a wider forehead but, as with humans, there is no real evidence that this denotes greater intelligence as such. See my book, *Inside Your Horse's Mind*, Chapter 6. See also Chapter 14 of that book for more about the 'pseudo-science' of physiognomy.

of other horses. So when I refer to 'small' or 'large' eyes, I am actually talking about the orbit itself rather than the eyeball. Exaggeratedly large eyeballs, giving the appearance of 'bug eyes', can often be a sign of hormone imbalance, so if breeders select for the size of the eyeball itself, rather than size and prominence of the orbit, they could unwittingly be selecting for inherited hormone disorders.

Equine vision

As a grazing prey animal who needs to be aware of possible danger from any angle, the prominence and location of his eyes (at the sides of the head rather than facing forward) give the horse an enormous range of vision. The total field of vision is almost 350 degrees. However, there are blind zones (see Fig. 6.4). There is a blind zone immediately behind the horse, which is why horses suddenly approached from the rear tend to be startled. They may move away or, if they cannot move, they may kick out in defence.[3] There is another blind zone in front. This is why horses tend to back away from something – such as a human hand raised to touch the head – which suddenly appears in front of them; they need to step back in order to see it properly. It is a great sign of trust if a horse allows you to put your hand on his nose or forehead without making a gradual approach, as he cannot see what you intend to do!

Once an object approaches within three to four feet (with some horses, as much as six feet) of a horse, he must tilt his head so that the object can be kept in view with one eye. My Arabian gelding Zareeba learned, as a youngster, to take a Polo (gently!) from between my lips.[4] In order to see where I was he had to tilt his head sideways; he quickly found that people were enchanted by the comical look this gave him, and now it is his way of coaxing goodies from obliging humans.

Equine vision is not quite like ours, however. We have what is known as binocular vision. In order to see things three-dimensionally, the retinas of both eyes must simultaneously receive a focused image of the same object. This ability is found only in animals with forward-facing eyes, so can the horse have binocular vision, or does he see everything two-dimensionally?

---

3 In such a situation, a prey animal cannot afford to wait and assess the nature of whatever is approaching from behind. Sadly, too few people appreciate that while domestication has changed horses' appearance, it has not changed those aspects of their behaviour which are essential to survival.

4 Teaching him not to nip or snatch at people was part of his training as a youngster. See *Inside Your Horse's Mind*, Chapter 15.

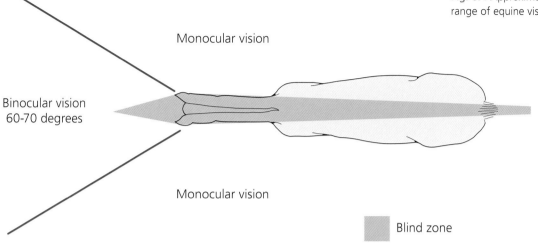

Monocular vision

Binocular vision
60-70 degrees

Monocular vision

Blind zone

Fig. 6.4 Approximate lateral range of equine vision

Horses do in fact have a limited amount of binocular vision. Although most of the horse's range of vision is what is called monocular, i.e. it is seen with one eye at a time, the wide field of vision resulting from the prominence of the equine eye means that there is an area in front of the horse where he does have binocular vision (see Fig. 6.4). This is because the visual field of each eye overlaps slightly with that of the other.

This area covers about 60–70 degrees in front of the horse, and it is this three-dimensional vision which enables horses to judge distances when jumping. So in disciplines needing good forward vision, such as jumping, horses with eyes placed rather closer together may do better than those with eyes set wide apart; the latter's reduced field of binocular vision may impair their ability to judge jumps accurately. This could explain why some Arabians, and other types of horse with wide-set eyes, are reluctant to tackle certain types of jump, especially if the rider interferes too much. Even so, horses with poor binocular vision can certainly learn to jump, if trained and ridden tactfully. Horses who are blind in one eye have been known to make successful jumpers; it seems that, with help and understanding from trainers and handlers, they can adapt quite well to lack of vision in one eye.

It is not quite clear just how good equine vision is in general. (See Fig. 6.5.) In most mammals, image focusing is achieved through the action of small muscles at each end of the lens, called *ciliary* muscles. These alter the shape of the lens to allow the image to reach the retina, a process known as 'accommodation'. If these muscles are inefficient, the image may focus too soon, i.e. in front of the retina; in this case the animal will be near-sighted (as I am). In other cases, the image may focus too late, when it is already

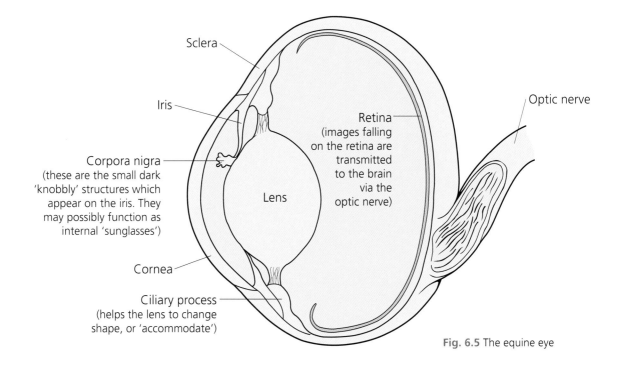

Sclera

Iris

Corpora nigra
(these are the small dark
'knobbly' structures which
appear on the iris. They
may possibly function as
internal 'sunglasses')

Cornea

Ciliary process
(helps the lens to change
shape, or 'accommodate')

Lens

Retina
(images falling
on the retina are
transmitted
to the brain
via the
optic nerve)

Optic nerve

Fig. 6.5 The equine eye

behind the retina; when this happens the animal will be long-sighted.[5] This is why humans with near or long sight will often squint or screw up their eyes; subconsciously they are trying to compensate for the ciliary muscles' inefficiency by increasing their action.

These ciliary muscles are not very well developed in horses, which suggests that they may have poor visual acuity; or, it may be that they do not need to rely so much on accommodation for focusing. This, together with the slightly asymmetrical shape of the equine eyeball, gave rise to the idea that horses had what was called a 'ramped' retina, which meant that they changed focus by raising or lowering their heads. Research has failed to find any conclusive evidence for this ramped retina, yet it is still cited in many books and articles. More recent work suggests that although the ciliary muscles are weak, they are adequate for accommodation; horses may simply be unable to adapt to changes of focus as fast as many other mammals can.

Peripheral vision in horses is much less acute than in humans. In the absence of any clear evidence for the ramped retina, it is not at all certain why images which fall on the centre area of the equine retina should be more detailed than those falling on the upper and lower areas; however,

5 Near-sightedness is quite common in dogs, and near- or long-sightedness may be more frequently found in horses than we generally realize.

this does appear to be the case. It means that in order to see things clearly within certain parts of their visual range, horses must either raise their heads, lower them, or tilt them sideways. If moving the head is not an option, or they simply do not feel like moving it, they may roll the eye instead, although this is not so effective.

This is one reason why some horses hollow when ridden. If they are tense or afraid, they will tend to put their heads up so that they can see around them more clearly. However, this reduces their ability to see what is in front of them, and so they may trip or stumble. I mentioned in Chapter 5 the common belief that Arabians are bred to go with their heads in the air. If this were true, such a horse would be a liability when ridden, as he would not only be difficult to control, he would not be able to see where he was going! The term 'blind panic' is no mere figure of speech; horses in a state of panic usually carry their heads high, and in this state they often crash into obstacles, because they have literally been unable to see them.

What equine vision *is* exceptionally good at is detecting movement, no matter where it may be in the visual field. This helps to explain why some horses shy for no apparent reason; they may have caught sight of some movement outside their range of acute vision and, again, survival behaviour kicks in, and they try to put some distance between themselves and a possible threat.

From all this we can see how different types of equine eye can affect performance. Small 'piggy' eyes restrict the horse's range of vision, especially if the spacing between them is narrow. A somewhat narrow spacing between the eyes can be perfectly functional, provided the eyes are of sufficient size and prominence to allow an adequate field of view. Large eyes spaced well apart give the widest range; it is this eye conformation which would benefit the horse most in his natural state, enabling him, while grazing, to see other members of his group, or the approach of potential danger. Wide spacing, however, may reduce a horse's range of binocular vision, and with it his ability to gauge jumps accurately.

There is still some controversy about colour vision in horses, with many books and articles still stating categorically that horses cannot see in colour. However, this is certainly incorrect, as closer examination of the equine eye structure, together with experiments involving colour recognition, have shown. The question remains, what colours *can* they see? Some studies suggest that they do not see red, others that they see light reds better than darker reds, and still others that they do not see blue too well. At the moment, findings are inconclusive, but it seems very possible that the way in which horses perceive colours may not, after all, be so very different from the way we do; it just might be that some of the shades (for example, dark reds as opposed to light reds) are not recognized quite as well. No doubt it will be some time before this controversy is resolved, if at all.

Horses may appear not to connect something they have seen, say, on their left, with the same object when they pass it again on their right. This seems to have given rise to the idea that the two halves of the equine brain are imperfectly connected. We are sometimes told that, because of this, the two sides of a horse's brain do not communicate effectively and so we have to teach the horse everything twice, once for each side (for example, teaching him to perform a school movement on one rein and then the other). In fact, experiments carried out by Dr Evelyn Hanggi in the USA have revealed that the two halves of the equine brain communicate perfectly well. The reason why horses appear to have this disconnection between their left and right may have more to do with the way they see things than with anything else. Because their range of binocular vision is limited in comparison with ours, it may well be that they do not immediately make the connection between an object seen from one side, and later from the other (try looking at a reversed image of a familiar scene, and you too may experience an initial lack of recognition).

It must also be remembered that, like humans, horses can be right- or left- 'handed': that is, they are one-sided, i.e. more supple on one side than the other. So, it is one-sidedness, not an imperfectly joined brain, that prevents them from performing equally well on both reins!

UNDERSTANDING EQUINE VISION

Understanding equine vision can help us to work through certain problems which arise in training and riding. If your horse frequently hits poles when jumping, consider whether his binocular vision might not be good enough for him to see the jumps properly. Because they cannot see the jump at the time they are actually taking off, horses have to rely on their memory of how it looked. If they are distracted, or prevented from looking at the jump (either by being held tightly so they are unable to turn their heads to look at the jump should they need to do so, or by looking at it too soon), this memory might not be good enough and so they misjudge the distance. This does not mean your horse is useless for jumping; he might be an exceptionally good jumper who just needs a bit of help and understanding from his rider!

Or, take the example of a horse who shies a lot. This may be because he gets insufficient work and therefore tends to be a bit fresh and silly when first ridden. On the other hand, it might be that he is a naturally reactive type, who needs to be allowed to look at things properly (a prey animal that did *not* react quickly to anything suspicious-looking or unfamiliar would not live too long). If such horses are always ridden on a tight rein and not allowed to turn their heads to look at anything close by, they may step sideways in order to see it properly; sometimes this side-step may be a leap sideways. I have found that such types need to be reassured that the chief look-out (the rider) is not worried. It takes a bit of nerve to drop the reins when you are sitting on a horse who seems about to explode, and remain calm and steady. It does work, though![6]

Outward appearance of the eye

Finally, what about the outward appearance of the eye? A so-called 'human' eye (i.e. where the sclera is white rather than brown) is not a fault, or a sign of viciousness; when a horse 'shows the white of its eyes' through bad temper or fear this is invariably accompanied by other signs, e.g. ears laid flat

6 Do be careful, though. I am not advocating riding around with loose, flapping reins; there must still be communication through the bit (see the next chapter). A sloppy riding style could be dangerous in such a situation, so if you are riding a horse of this type, please, do learn to hold yourself in the saddle in a manner which will enable you to control the horse without having to hang on to the reins. See Chapter 10 for more about this.

Arabian mare Nileisha (owned by Melanie Gaddas-Brown) is showing the white of her eye, but she is neither angry nor upset; she is simply glancing to her left, although her main attention is forward. In fact this mare is extremely good-tempered *(L. Skipper)*

back, or tension in the muscles of the lips and muzzle. A blue, or 'glass', eye is not necessarily weaker than a dark eye, but this is still a matter of controversy. D. Phillip Sponenberg, for example, maintains that most horses with light-coloured eyes see perfectly well and are at no disadvantage compared to dark-eyed horses.[7] However there is some evidence that blue-eyed horses are more sensitive to the sun, and that they actively seek shade in summer.[8]

When assessing your horse's abilities and deciding on riding and training strategies, take the nature of equine vision into account. Try to see things as your horse sees them, and you will understand much more clearly how this affects his performance, and how you can help to minimize any problems which may arise because of the peculiarities of equine vision.

7 D. Phillip Sponenberg, *Equine Color Genetics,* Iowa State University Press 1996, p.32

8 Ann T Bowling, *Horse Genetics,* CAB Publishing, 1996, p.28

Table 4 Problems and possible causes related to respiration and vision

Problem	Possible cause	Remedy
Intolerance of exercise (i.e. easily out of breath)	Heart or lung defects, lack of fitness, overweight. Insufficient space in nasal passages for oxygen intake	Consult veterinary surgeon to establish cause. If the cause is simply lack of fitness, build up fitness gradually (see Chapter 14). If the nasal passages are too narrow, you may need to avoid activities requiring fast work or prolonged exertion, such as cross-country or long-distance work
Horse frequently hits jumps; reluctance to jump	The horse may be simply lacking in confidence, or the set of his eyes may make it difficult for him to see jumps properly	For green or novice horses, or older horses who have lost their confidence, proceed gradually as outlined in Chapter 14. If the horse appears bold enough (consult the psychological profile you constructed!), encourage him to look at the jumps, if necessary allowing him to tilt his head. This may affect his accuracy, so take things carefully to begin with, starting off with small hops and building up very gradually to higher jumps. If he really seems not to see the jumps, consult your vet regarding possible vision defects
Horse is very spooky	Tension; freshness and lack of exercise; overfeeding. May be related to vision	Where tension is the cause, work on relaxation (see Chapter 14). Allow the horse to look around him. If shying is very frequent and severe, consult your vet regarding possible vision defects

CHAPTER SEVEN

From the horse's mouth

The equine mouth

As one of the main channels of communication with the horse, the mouth is of immense importance. Responsible horse owners understand the necessity for having their horses' teeth rasped regularly; yet how many of us actually take the trouble to find out how our horses' mouths are constructed? (See Fig. 7.1.) The shape of a horse's mouth affects his response to the bit, so if we want to get the best out of our horses, we owe it to them to make sure the bit is the correct type for that particular horse.

Some books and magazine articles suggest that you should attempt to examine your horse's mouth yourself. However, the usual method employed, that of grasping the horse's tongue and pulling it out to the side in order to avoid being bitten (since few horses will voluntarily bite their own tongue) does not always work: for one thing, it is easy to hurt the horse in an attempt to hold his tongue, and some horses understandably resist the whole process! It is far better to leave the actual examination to a veterinary surgeon or (even better) an equine dentist; even they can sometimes get bitten, but the likelihood is reduced by the use of proper dental gags, which should only be used by trained persons.

Things you need to know about your horse's mouth:

■ The width of his mouth as measured from corner to corner of the lips. This can most easily be measured by passing a piece of string through the horse's mouth. Mark it on either side of the lips using a non-toxic waterproof marker pen and measure the distance between the two marks.

- The depth of the mouth at the bars (this includes the height of the palate).

- The width and thickness of the tongue.

- The width of the tongue groove (i.e. the distance between branches of the lower jaw.

These measurements are important, as they will determine the best type of bit for your horse's mouth conformation.

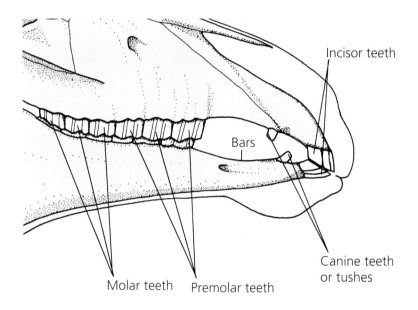

Fig. 7.1 The horse's mouth

Bitting

Bitting is a complex topic, so here I am really only talking about relatively simple, direct-action bits such as the snaffle in its many varieties, since, to all horses but those working at higher levels of dressage, highly trained Western horses etc., these are the bits most likely to be of use in training. By 'direct action' I mean that the communication – whether from the rider's hand to the bit, or from the bit to the rider's hand – is direct, i.e. unlike the action of a curb, it does not involve any leverage.[1] This does not

1 We are often told that the snaffle acts to raise the horse's head. Well, it can do so, but as it may also be used to encourage the horse to lower his head, such a statement on its own is meaningless.

imply that such bits are 'mild' in themselves; that depends on their construction, fit, and the manner in which they are used!

Head carriage

First of all, let us look at how the horse's head carriage affects the action of a simple snaffle with a smooth, jointed mouthpiece (see Fig. 7.2).

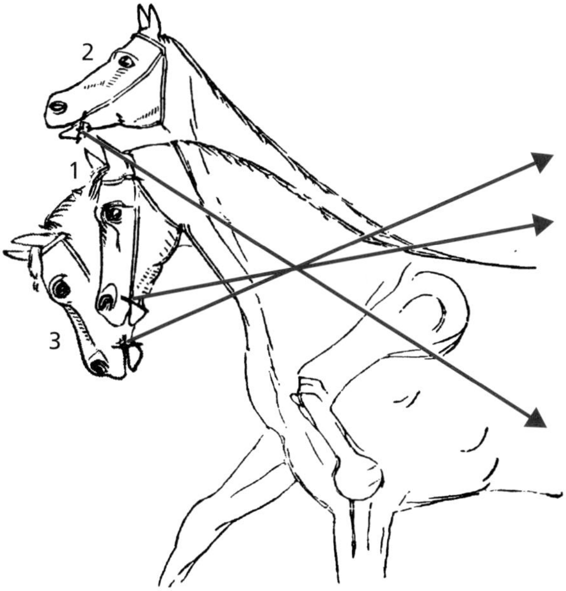

Fig. 7.2 How the horse's head carriage affects the action of the bit (adapted from Dwyer, *On Seats and Saddles, Bits and Bitting,* London 1869)

Head Carriage	Action
1. Horse lowers his head and flexes at the poll, with his nose at or just in front of the vertical.	The mouthpiece exerts pressure on the bars and tongue, but less on the corners of the mouth.
2. Horse pokes his nose and comes above the bit.	Most of the pressure is brought to bear on the tongue and corners of the lips, with very little contact with the bars.
3. Horse overbends and comes behind the bit.	The bit exerts little pressure on the tongue or bars; most of the contact is with the corners of the lips.

The space inside a horse's mouth is actually rather small. I think you have to see an X-ray of a horse's mouth with a bit in place (see Fig. 7.3) to realize just how uncomfortable even the mildest snaffle can be if it is not fitted correctly, with the individual mouth conformation taken into account.

Fig. 7.3 This drawing was taken from an X-ray of a horse's mouth with a single-jointed snaffle in place

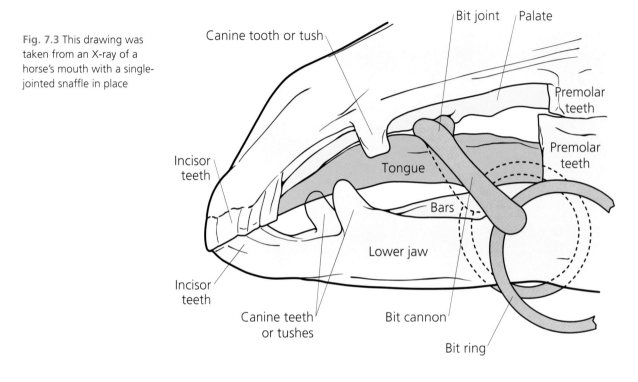

The upper jaw

The height of the palate and its width vary considerably between horses. This can limit the amount of space available for the tongue.

In some male horses, the canine teeth or tushes may be closer than usual to the molars (cheek teeth), which leaves less space for the bit.

The distance between the bars in the lower jaw, and the space between the incisors (and/or tushes) in the upper jaw, may be shallow (see the photographs showing the skull of an Arabian horse compared to that of a less 'refined' type). This again will affect the space available for a bit.

The lower jaw

The mouth may be short as measured from the end of the muzzle to the corners of the lips. This does not mean that the bars themselves are necessarily short. Arabian horses often have short mouths, yet the actual bars

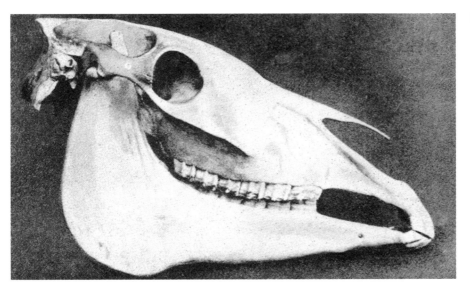

Skull of Arabian horse

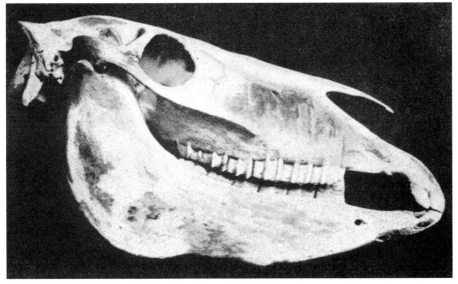

Skull of non-Arabian horse

may be longer than those of many other breeds with proportionally longer mouths (see the photographs of skulls for comparison). Some cobs may also have short mouths, although they are likely to be wider than those of Arabians. Such horses will need to have the bit fitted lower than usual, which can make bit fitting quite tricky, as horses with short mouths may also have the tushes closer to the molars. This is true of our own Arabian stallion, Nivalis.

If the lower jaw is also narrow, and the tongue fleshy, the latter may not fit into the space available in the lower jaw, and may overlap the bars, leading to resentment of the bit. Quite often horses who persist in getting their tongue over the bit, or in sticking it out to the side, have this conformation. On the other hand, if the tongue is too thin, the bit may have greater contact with the bars.

If the bars themselves are quite narrow and sharp, with insufficient fleshy covering (such as may be found in many Thoroughbreds and horses of Thoroughbred type), they may be easily damaged by the bit pressing down on them.

The tongue

The tongue is far more sensitive than is generally realized, much more so than either the bars or the lips. It also takes up a lot of room in the mouth. If the palate is arched and the tongue comparatively thin, then bitting may be relatively simple, even in horses with short mouths or narrow muzzles, but if the tongue is fleshy and the palate low (a very common combination), there is then very little room for a bit. In a short-mouthed horse who needs to carry the bit low, a thick tongue combined with a low palate (or even in combination with an arched palate) will make correct bitting even more crucial than it is for most horses, since the tongue is highest in the mouth at precisely the point where most horses with this conformation will have to carry the bit. Raising the bit is not the answer, as this will tend to stretch the lips too much in a short-mouthed horse, leading to rubbing and soreness.

This is where bit width is of such vital importance. If the bit is too wide – or if the horse has the type of mouth conformation referred to above – the joint of the bit may come into contact with the sensitive palate (see Fig. 7.3). This is especially the case if the rider takes up a strong contact. To relieve the pressure, the horse may either tuck his nose in and come behind the bit (which many people then mistake for a good outline – see Chapter 8), or he may stick his nose out and pull. Either way, the result is the same: he relieves the pain of the bit joint pressing against the palate.

Bitting for comfort

So how do we ensure that the bit fits correctly and is suitable for the horse's individual mouth conformation?

Having measured the width of the horse's mouth and examined (with the aid of a veterinary surgeon or equine dentist) its interior conformation, we need to decide what width the bit should be. It should fit closely without pinching in the corners of the lips; the mouthpiece should not protrude on either side of the mouth. Bits that are too wide are far more common than those that are too narrow. The saddlery trade seems to think that modern riding horses are all equine giants; many excellent bits are available through retail outlets only in sizes from 12.7 cm (5 in) upwards, yet many of the horses that would benefit most from some of the recent advances in bit design have mouths smaller than this.

In the mid nineteenth century, Lieutenant-General Oeynhausen of the Austrian army, an acknowledged equestrian authority, measured the mouths of a very large number and variety of horses. He found that the majority of horses of 155 cm (15.1 hh) to 160 cm (15.3 hh) had mouths averaging approx. 10.75 cm (4¼ in) in width. Major Francis Dwyer,[2] also of the Austrian Imperial Army, confirmed von Oeynhausen's findings with reference to his own experience, together with the observations of others. The average size of riding horses has increased since Oeynhausen and Dwyer were writing, but it would be wrong to assume that bigger horses necessarily have larger mouths. Many Warmbloods, for example, have relatively small mouths; our 168 cm (16.2 hh) Warmblood gelding takes the same size in a snaffle as my 150 cm (14.3 hh) Arabian gelding. I think it highly probable that large numbers of horses are going around in snaffle bits that are too wide, increasing the nutcracker action, and in many cases pressing on the sensitive palate. No wonder so many horses resist the bit.

As I mentioned above, a bit that is too low may also come into contact with the palate. However, most riders have the bit fitted too high rather than too low. We are usually told that there should be one or two wrinkles in the corners of the horse's mouth, but fitting the bit this high can lead to chafing and soreness. In addition, the horse can obtain no relief from the bit. Dwyer, writing in the 1860s, considered that in 99 cases out of 100, the mouthpiece lay higher than it should. It should not be so high that it wrinkles the mouth, but should not be low enough to come into contact with the canine teeth (if present). It should certainly not be low enough to bang against the incisors! Let the horse tell you, from his response, where the bit should be. You may need to experiment a little, but it is far better to spend a little time getting it right than to make your horse uncomfortable just for the sake of accepted practice.

The mouthpiece

What type of mouthpiece should you use? Many people believe that a mullen-mouth bit is milder than a jointed snaffle, but an unjointed mouthpiece tends to act most strongly on the tongue, and so may be unsuitable

---

2 Author of the justly celebrated *On Seats and Saddles, Bits and Bitting* (1869).

for horses with sensitive tongues. However, a greater degree of curve to the mouthpiece (especially if the latter is also soft) helps to take some of the pressure off the tongue and transfer it to the bars. Such a mouthpiece may be very useful for starting off young horses (we use a soft Nathe bit, which tapers in the middle). Many people maintain that, as a mullen mouth is a solid mouthpiece, acting on the whole mouth, it is more difficult to indicate changes of direction, or to ask the horse to flex to one side, than with a jointed mouthpiece. I have to say that I have not found this to be the case, although a jointed mouthpiece does, in theory, give more precise communication. It all depends on how sensitive your horse is, as well as on how effective your seat is (and consequently your ability to ask for a change of direction without relying too much on signals through the bit). After all, as we shall see, many horses trained in the old Spanish way reach quite an advanced stage of training without ever having a bit in their mouths.

The mildest jointed snaffle is a simple, smooth eggbutt design. I like eggbutts, because our horses all have sensitive lips that tend to be chafed by loose ring designs. I know you can use bit guards, but they add to the bulk and, to me at least, tend to deaden the signal down the reins, which should in any case always be the minimum necessary to communicate with the horse.

When choosing a jointed mouthpiece, go for one with a solid feel and with cannons that are not too wide in diameter (about the same as an

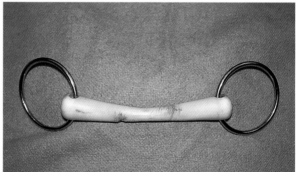

ABOVE Soft rubber mullen-mouth bit *(L. Skipper)*

ABOVE RIGHT Nathe bit.
The disadvantage of these otherwise excellent bits is that sometimes horses manage to chew on them, creating rough edges (as one horse has done with this bit!) *(L. Skipper)*

RIGHT Simple eggbutt snaffle *(L. Skipper)*

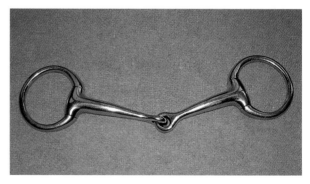

average-sized woman's forefinger) at their widest point; measure them about 2.5 cm (1 in) in from the butt. If they are too thin, they will be severe in their action; if too thick, they may be too much of a mouthful, as well as being insufficiently precise in their action. The cannons should be curved in order to accommodate the tongue; this will lessen the nutcracker action and help to prevent palate contact.

Mouthpieces with two joints are also very good in this respect, but the extra joint does tend to put more pressure on the tongue (see Fig. 7.4), so if you choose a two-jointed mouthpiece, take care in your choice, and be extra polite in your contact. The centre plate of the popular Dr Bristol is angled so that the edge presses on the horse's tongue. The idea is that when

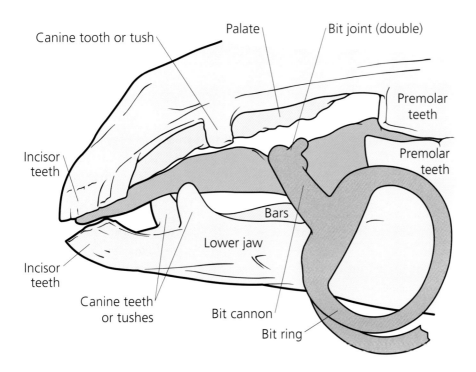

Canine tooth or tush — Palate — Bit joint (double)

Premolar teeth

Incisor teeth

Premolar teeth

Bars

Lower jaw

Incisor teeth

Canine teeth or tushes

Bit cannon

Bit ring

ABOVE **Fig. 7.4** This drawing was taken from an X-ray of a horse's mouth with a double-jointed snaffle in place

LEFT Dr Bristol two-jointed snaffle. Because the centre plate is angled, this is more severe in its action than the French link snaffle
(L. Skipper)

(if!) the horse flexes at the poll, the centre plate lies flat, relieving some of the tongue pressure. However, since poll flexion depends on many additional factors which have nothing to do with the bit, a French link snaffle with a centre piece that is flat at all times, which is much milder, may be preferable. In fact many horses (including my Arabian gelding, who has a short mouth and a fleshy tongue) go well with one of these.

French link hanging cheek snaffle *(L. Skipper)*

There are far too many variations on the snaffle to describe here and as more research is being carried out into the principles of bitting, new designs are constantly being thought up. At the time of writing I have been unable to test one of the Myler range of bits which has been highly successful in the USA, but I have heard very good reports of them. They incorporate all kinds of features such as independent side movement within the mouthpiece, curved mouthpieces for tongue relief, and many others designed to help the horse to accept the bit without discomfort and to allow the rider greater precision of communication.

The despised pelham

Although I am mainly considering direct action bits here, there is one enduringly popular bit which has some of the properties of both a direct action bit and a leverage bit. This is the pelham, whose use is decried (often loudly) in some quarters.

The reason for this disapproval seems to lie mainly in the fact that some riders use a pelham to impose a superficially pleasing head carriage on their horses. Yet the same can be said of many riders who use a double bridle, even at high levels of dressage! In such cases it is not the bit itself that is incorrect, but the rider's use of it. Some of the classical masters of equitation, while not specifically recommending the pelham, have not despised it either. The great eighteenth-century master François Robichon de la Guérinière thought the pelham was ingenious; while he did not precisely recommend it, he did not condemn it either. Conversely, like many of the great masters, la Guérinière was disparaging about the snaffle; he considered the widespread use of the snaffle to be part of the reason for the many problems which beset English horses during the eighteenth century. The snaffle was at that time regarded as the bit to be used by grooms, who did not have the finesse required to use a 'proper' bit (by which I mean a curb).

In theory the pelham is not as effective as either a snaffle or a curb bit, having a less precise action than either. In practice, many horses go very well in a pelham. They seem to like the mild poll action of the bit; massaging a horse's poll just behind the ears is an excellent way to relax him. (I do this a lot with our Arabian stallion Nivalis if he becomes tense or upset.) This beneficial action relies upon the pelham being used with two reins, not roundings, with the equivalent of the bradoon rein predominant, and on the rider being capable of using two reins effectively and politely. This is because the use of roundings renders the bit's action imprecise and ineffective.

My Arabian gelding Zareeba likes either a soft rubber pelham, or one with a ported mouthpiece, to accommodate his rather fleshy tongue. As he will already flex to one side with a slight outward rotation of the hand, the lack of a joint in the mouthpiece is not a handicap.

Another use for the pelham is as an intermediate bit between the snaffle and a full curb. As it has some of the characteristics of both types of bit, it can be very helpful here. It can also help those horses whose mouths simply cannot take a full double bridle, as there is not enough room in their mouths. Used correctly, the pelham is not a means of compelling the horse

BELOW LEFT Soft rubber pelham: many horses go very well in one of these (*L. Skipper*)

BELOW RIGHT The Kimblewick is a member of the pelham family. This has more in common with the curb bit than with a snaffle, and so the rider using this bit needs the sensitive hands that can only come with a secure, independent seat (*L. Skipper*)

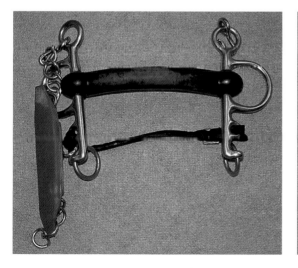

to come into a false outline, although it can certainly be misused in that way. However, if we use that argument, then we must also condemn the snaffle, because of its potential for misuse (I am well aware that this argument could be extended to 'gadgets' such as draw-reins, but there is a difference. See my comments on draw-reins and other training aids in Chapter 8).

Keep an open mind with regard to the pelham. Some exceptional horsemen and women find that this bit suits their horses far better than a conventional snaffle. If the horse goes correctly in a pelham, and seems happier with one than with a snaffle, then that is the bit to use. Let your horse be the judge.

Position of the hands

When choosing and fitting a bit, be aware that the position of the rider's hands also affects the action of the bit; you will need to take this into account when assessing how your horse responds.

Hand position	Action
1. Rider's hands held high.	Contact with the bars is reduced; more contact with the tongue and lips.
2. Rider's hands held low.	Contact with the bars is increased; less contact with the corners of the mouth.

The old advice to riders, to carry the hands no further apart than the width of the horse's mouth, was given for good reasons. In this position, the rider can use the bit to give precise – and subtle – signals down the reins. However, nowadays many riders are taught to hold the hands wide apart, sometimes by as much as the width of the rider's waist (an extremely variable distance!), or even more. If the hands are held wide (except temporarily, to encourage the horse to lower his head – see Chapter 12), almost all precision is lost, and all too often the rider resorts to pulling and fiddling, or a strong contact, to make up for the loss of communication through the reins.

As the late, great Dr Reiner Klimke used to say, 'Hands together! Hands together unites the horse!'

Choosing a bit

Please bear in mind that the solutions offered here are only *suggestions*. Every horse is an individual, and there are many possible variations in mouth conformation. You may need to experiment in order to find the bit which suits your horse best. Your horse will soon let you know, by his ready acceptance of the bit, when you have found the right solution. Understand how the bit and the horse's mouth interact and use that knowledge as a guide.

Table 5 Bitting solutions

Mouth conformation	Possible bitting solution
Canine teeth closer to molars than normal	Choose a bit with a narrow mouthpiece, but be aware that this is potentially more severe. A jointed snaffle may hang too low in the mouth. I have found a soft Nathe bit, slightly curved and with a tapering centre, to be very useful in such cases
Narrow distance between upper and lower jaws	As above, or try a mouthpiece with two joints (French link, or rounded centre link, for mildness)
Mouth short from front to back	As above.
Narrow lower jaw, fleshy tongue	A Nathe bit will be softer on the bars; a two-jointed mouthpiece will transfer some pressure to the tongue
Tongue too thin	Nathe bit
Sensitive tongue	A snaffle with hanging cheeks will help to prevent undue pressure on the tongue
Bars narrow and sharp	A soft Nathe bit may help, or try a bit with thicker cannons (one made in a soft material would be best). A two-jointed mouthpiece would transfer some pressure to the tongue
Tongue fleshy, palate low	A two-jointed bit may help, but as this puts more pressure on the tongue, the joint should be a French link or one with a rounded centre link. A mullen mouth-piece with a pronounced curve might help, as would a Nathe bit tapering towards the centre

As the above table shows, I have found the soft Nathe bits to be excellent; I also like French link snaffles, particularly combined with hanging cheeks – or perhaps I should say, my *horses* like them! If you choose an unjointed bit, remember that this is a trade-off: you lose something in precision, but if your horse is more comfortable, you have gained rather than lost. As always, treat the horse as an individual.

Going bitless

What happens if you have a horse whose mouth conformation simply defies every attempt to find a suitable bit for him? Such horses are far more numerous than you might think from reading equestrian literature. If you have this problem, do not think of your horse as defective; if his mouth is still functional from the point of view of eating efficiently, then the fault does not lie with him but with us, for imagining that horses were made just for us to ride and expecting them to conform to some impossible ideal.

What can you do? Consider whether you need a bit at all. There are a number of different types of bitless bridle available and, contrary to popular belief, these do not give the rider any less degree of control than a mouthful of metal would do. Some horses can even be ridden without a bridle, if the communication between horse and rider is good enough (a concept explored by Pat Parelli and his students). Ann Hyland, founder of the Endurance Horse and Pony Society, used to give bridleless demonstrations with her champion endurance horse, Arabian stallion Nizzolan, who died in 2001 at the grand old age of 34. (If you are interested in exploring the possibilities, you could try contacting a teacher of Parelli's methods, but be aware that this is not a gimmick; it is a serious exploration of human/horse communication and co-operation.)

Correctly trained and ridden, any number of horses can be managed using nothing more than a halter. We started our Arabian stallion Nivalis in a simple headcollar. He was lunged in a headcollar, backed in a headcollar and, for the first six months of his ridden career, ridden in a headcollar. At no time did his rider have any less control than would have been the case with an ordinary bit. What *was* lacking was the same degree of precision that could have been achieved with a bit or a proper nose bridle (see below), but at this stage we were mainly interested in getting the horse to go forward freely and calmly under saddle. Nivalis now goes happily in a bit (although fitting was tricky because of his short mouth and high canine teeth; after some experimentation, we eventually settled on a Nathe bit), but he can still be safely ridden in a headcollar.

We decided to start Nivalis in a headcollar partly because of his extreme sensitivity. We felt that bitting him at this stage, when he was already having to cope with so many new sensations, would simply lead to sensory overload. Another factor, which is often overlooked, was the eruption of teeth; young horses, especially stallions and geldings, may suffer great discomfort and/or pain if bitted while their permanent teeth are still coming through. For this reason the old Spanish horsemen used to start off young horses in a nose bridle, the true hackamore or *jaquima,* and would not use a

Arabian stallion Nizzolan could be ridden in the most intricate manoeuvres without a bridle *(Peter Connolly)*

bit until a stallion's canine teeth had come through, in his sixth year. Similarly, seventeenth- and eighteenth-century horsemen would start the horse off in a cavesson, or *caveçon,* and only progress to a bit when the horse was ready for it, usually at seven or eight years of age.

The Spanish nose bridle mentioned above has survived in the form of the Western hackamore, often known as a *bosal,* although strictly speaking

117

this refers only to the noseband (see Fig. 7.5). This sophisticated hackamore is still used by many of those Western riders who follow the Spanish tradition, bequeathed to the American West by the Spaniards who first colonized California. It is a very precise instrument of communication with the horse, and to use it properly requires a great deal of finesse. If you are interested in learning more about this type of bridle, seek guidance from a Western rider who understands the old Spanish bitting principles[3] (see also Elwyn Hartley Edwards's excellent book *The Complete Book of Bits and Bitting,* David & Charles, 2000, pp. 105–109). The other, more common, bitless bridles (whose use is also described by Hartley Edwards) also require sensitive riding and the good hands that come only with a secure, well-balanced seat, but they can be used very effectively indeed. If you use one of these bridles you will not be able to take part in affiliated dressage competitions, but there are other disciplines (such as showjumping and endurance riding) where the use of a bitless bridle is no handicap and may even be an advantage. Bitless bridles are also permitted in the Classical Riding Club Training Tests, as are pelhams (see Appendix II).

3 Western riders in the USA are in general far more sophisticated about bitting than most European riders. However, while there are many brilliant Western riders and trainers, there are also many bad ones, and too many of them employ force in their training methods. Try to watch trainers at work, and make your own judgements.

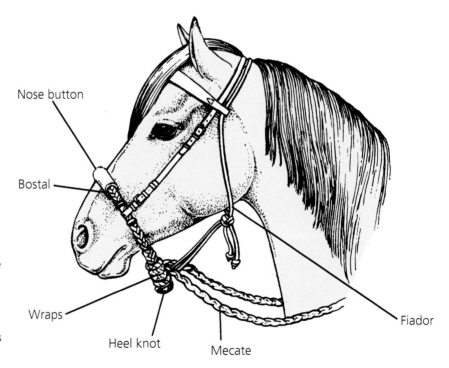

Fig. 7.5 The Western nose bridle or true hackamore (from the Spanish *jaquima*). The heel knot of the bosal, or noseband, together with the *mecate* (reins, attached to the heel knot by a series of wraps) acts as a counterbalance to the nose button. The *fiador* or throatlatch attachment can also help to balance the bridle, supporting the weight of the heel knot as well as keeping the bosal in place. Many riders who use this bridle prefer to dispense with the browband and in some cases even leave off the fiador.

Nose button

Bostal

Wraps

Heel knot

Mecate

Fiador

Weight in the hands

Whatever type of bit you choose for your horse, remember the truth of yet another cliché which, again, is no less true for being a cliché: any bit is only as good as the hands at the other end of the reins, and a rider's hands are only as good as the rider's seat! If you lack a balanced, independent seat, you will find yourself relying on the reins for support (see Chapter 10 for more about the rider's seat).

Unfortunately, there is a pernicious idea that in order to influence the horse's head carriage the rider needs to have 'X' number of pounds'[4] weight in either hand. It has been suggested that riders normally take at least two pounds of weight in each hand and, in the case of a large man on a strong horse, the weight of the contact could be seven pounds or more. Now try holding a one kilo (2.2 pound) bag of sugar in each hand. If you were a horse, would you like to feel that much pressure on your mouth, let

This horse is understandably opening his mouth in reaction to a harsh contact. Strapping his mouth shut would be inhumane, as it would do nothing to alleviate his discomfort
(L. Skipper)

4 The amount varies, depending on who is putting forward the idea.

alone seven pounds? Of course, horses' jaws are immensely strong, but that does not mean they are equipped to handle this kind of pressure. Such pressure will inevitably lead to tension in the jaw, and this tension will pass up through the poll and back down along the neck and spine, eventually affecting the hindquarters and the feet. It certainly cannot contribute to the soft, yielding jaw that should be the aim of all those who seek to train horses.

Those riders and teachers who have taken the trouble to study the horse/rider interaction in depth point out the falseness of this idea of weight in the hands. Mary Wanless, for example, writes about the rider's need to learn how to hold their body in place in the saddle in such a way that they can release their hold on the rein and ride the horse 'from back to front'. 'Any teacher who tells you that there should be a significant weight in each rein has not yet learned to do this; so seek out someone who has.'[5]

Any weight felt in the rider's hands should be the amount of pressure the *horse* is putting on the bit, not the rider. To begin with, the untrained horse, one who is weak in his neck muscles, or one who is conformationally built somewhat 'downhill', will tend to put rather more pressure on the bit than one who, by virtue of greater development of his muscles, is able to 'carry' himself without using the rider's hands as a prop. As his muscles strengthen and he begins to carry himself properly, with less weight on his forehand, he will gradually start to lighten this contact. This assumes that the rider has not let him get into the habit of leaning on the bit: encouragement to move forward will generally prevent this. A horse who put seven pounds of pressure in each of his rider's hands would be leaning on the bit very heavily indeed, and this is certainly not something we want to encourage him to do.

There will inevitably be times during the course of training when the horse will put more pressure on the bit than he normally does: it may be because he is tired, or because a new exercise is proving difficult for him (in which case it may be a warning that he is not yet ready for it). In every case the rider must 'read' the signals coming from the bit, which together with the sensations coming from under the saddle, will help them to recognize what needs to be done to help the horse at that particular moment.

The unbalancing effect of pressure

There is another, extremely important, point which, to my knowledge, has not generally been recognized: this concerns the effect of tongue pressure

5 Mary Wanless, 'On the bit?', *Horse & Rider*, April 1996

on the horse's sense of balance.[6] The root of the horse's tongue is based on the hyoid bones, which in turn root on the structures which house the semicircular canals, the looped, fluid-filled membranous tubes which control the sense of equilibrium and orientation. There is direct evidence from the results of surgery to the hyoids that immobility of the latter affects the horse's sense of balance. Given the tongue's origin on the hyoid bones, this is strong evidence that pressure on the tongue can also affect the sense of balance. So taking up too strong a contact may not only lead to tension, it may also destroy your horse's ability to go straight!

The sin of pulling

One of the most basic equestrian commandments is: 'Thou shalt not pull'. However, for many riders this is easier said than done. How about a new commandment: 'Thou shalt not pull, but if thou findest thyself pulling in spite of all thy best efforts, read the books of Sylvia Loch, Sally Swift and Mary Wanless;[7] these will help thee to avoid the sin of pulling. Thy horse will thank thee for the rest of his days'.

Nosebands

Almost every complete bridle seen for sale nowadays seems to come with a flash noseband; these are now so popular that the saddlery trade seems to expect all of us to use one. They are fine if not fastened too tightly, but if anyone is thinking of using one because their horse persists in opening his mouth when ridden, I would ask them to find out first *why* he opens his mouth. If it is because of pain from the bit, or a reluctance to accept the bit, then fastening his mouth shut may cure the symptom, but it does nothing to address the cause. If, on the other hand, it is simply a habit caused by the *memory* of pain from the bit, then provided he has overcome his fears about the bit, the flash may help, but do investigate first.

As for those abominations, the so-called crank nosebands, their use betrays either ignorance on the part of their users, or a complete disregard for the horse's wellbeing. A horse with his mouth clamped tightly shut (and the crank serves no other purpose), will not only be tense in his jaw, but

---

6 I am grateful to the Equine Studies Institute, California (www.equinestudies.org), for information regarding this topic.

7 See Chapter 10, and the section entitled 'Recommended Reading'.

unable to move the bit in his mouth (necessary for a moist, responsive mouth), and he may be prevented from swallowing properly. Moreover, his mouth can only be closed to the extent that his incisor teeth meet,[8] so any attempt to close it further is utterly futile. Such practices have no place in true horsemanship.

Communication before control

Those who think of the bit as primarily a means of control are missing the point. The bit can certainly *assist* in controlling the horse, but in the kind of riding which seeks to help the horse to perform with ease and fluency, as opposed to merely getting him to obey our commands, its main function is as a means of communication. Some of the curb bits used in past centuries look horrifically severe but, in the hands of a rider capable of guiding the horse effectively with their body, and possessing the ability to *feel* the mouth at the other end of the rein, such bits provided fingertip communication through a loose rein.

8 A fact seldom recognized, but pointed out by Dr Deb Bennett (see the Equine Studies Institute website).

Late eighteenth- to early nineteenth-century curb bit *(Byron Brett)*

Even today, when few riders possess such finesse, the bit should still be seen as a way of talking to the horse, not simply giving him orders. Through a light, elastic feel on the reins, which is steady enough to provide a continuous contact without becoming dead or unfeeling, the rider can not only give guidance to the horse, but they can also receive feedback *from* the horse. The quality of the contact, i.e. the amount of pressure the horse is putting on the bit, and the steadiness and evenness (or lack of these) of the contact, can help the rider to evaluate what is necessary to help the horse to achieve the self-carriage which is (or should be) the aim for every riding horse, no matter what activity or discipline will ultimately be the goal. Communication is a two-way process!

CHAPTER EIGHT

The elusive outline

LOOK AT THE PHOTOGRAPH opposite of Arabian stallion Endel trotting at liberty. His haunches are lowered, his back is rounded and lifted, his forehand is raised, and his whole posture speaks of strength and pride, power and agility. Whether he is showing off to mares, or impressing a potential rival, he is ready for anything. He is so poised, and so well balanced, that he can stop and turn on a sixpence, raise his body to launch an attack on an enemy, prance in a perfect circle around the mare he is courting, or hurl himself into an instant gallop. He is like a ballet dancer, full of elastic tension. He is in 'collection', and if he were to maintain this posture and this elastic tension under saddle, we would say he is working in an 'outline' and 'on the bit'.

I dislike both these latter terms because they are bandied about so freely, and frequently with so little regard to what is actually happening, that one must question how many of the people who use them really know what they mean. Too often, people assume that if a horse has his head tucked in and his nose vertical (or even behind the vertical), then that means he is working in a correct outline or on the bit. In fact, he may be doing nothing of the kind!

I think we need to be clear about these terms, because success in so many equestrian activities depends on the horse's ability to 'round up' and collect himself. The dressage horse is expected to work in collection at the more advanced levels (although many, even at the highest levels, are not truly collected); the showjumping horse must be able to 'round up' in order to produce a proper bascule over a fence; the eventer, even though he may take cross-country fences somewhat 'flatter' than a showjumper, still needs to collect himself before a jump. In Western riding, the working stock

LEFT Arabian stallion Endel, owned by Shirley Watts of Halsdon Arabians
(Gigi Grasso)

BELOW The dressage horse must work in collection: Kirsty Mepham and Dikkiloo
(Elizabeth Furth)

Trakehner stallion Holme Grove Prokofiev: in order to jump efficiently, a show-jumping horse needs to make a 'bascule' over the jump *(Holme Park Stud)*

horse and the competition horse taking part in activities such as roping, cutting or reining have little hope of succeeding if they cannot round up and get their hind legs underneath them. The same applies to all working stock horses. Even the endurance horse needs to be able to raise his back and engage his hindquarters in order to negotiate obstacles and take steep slopes. The horse who can work in a good outline, no matter in what discipline, will be able to use himself easily and athletically, and with reduced risk of fatigue or injury.

Collection and outline

The first thing to realize is that collection and working in an outline, are not just things the horse has to learn in order to impress dressage judges, or to fulfil some aesthetic ideal: they are essential if the horse is to work correctly and athletically in specific situations.

The second thing we must understand is that when the horse comes on the bit or works in an outline, this is something the horse does for himself, not something the rider does for the horse! All the rider should be doing is making it *possible* for the horse to perform the actions which bring him on the bit or into an outline.

OPPOSITE PAGE Andalusian stallion in the Spanish *doma vaquera* (training for the stock horse) equivalent of the Western 'sliding stop' *(Yeguada Iberica)*

Finally, we have to remember that no part of the horse's musculature

An advanced outline:
M. Philippe Karl of the Cadre
Noir at Saumur with Lusitano
stallion Odin *(A. Laurioux;
reproduced from* Long
Reining *by Philippe Karl, with
kind permission of M. Karl)*

acts in isolation. Pain or discomfort in one part affects the activity and efficiency of all the others.

So what do we mean when we say that a horse is on the bit? This term is actually rather misleading, because it suggests that something active to do with the bit is involved. It would be much better to use the term 'on the aids' or something similar, since that is much closer to what is actually happening. The FEI (Federation Equestre Internationale) defines 'on the bit' as follows:

A horse is said to be *on the bit* when the hocks are correctly placed, the neck is more or less raised and arched according to the stage of training and the extension or collection of the pace, and he accepts the bridle with a light and soft contact and submissiveness throughout. The head should remain in a steady position, as a rule slightly in front of the vertical, with a supple poll as the highest part of the neck and no resistance should be offered to the rider.[1]

1 FEI Dressage Rule Book, Object & General Principles, Clause 107

The outline that a horse makes when he is on the bit or on the aids depends partly on his conformation but largely on his level of training, because that will determine, to a great extent, his ability to flex his haunches, round his back and elevate the base of his neck. The outline of a novice horse will naturally be much longer and lower than that of a more advanced horse because the former will not have the latter's muscular development and therefore the ability to maintain his posture.

One of the most basic principles of riding and training is that we work the horse from back to front. The horse comes to the bit, not the other way round. However, if we concentrate on either the front or the back ends alone, the horse is disconnected in the middle. Sylvia Loch, in her excellent book *Dressage in Lightness,* uses a comparison which I like very much. She suggests that we think of the horse's back as being like an arched bridge, supported at both ends, and asks the rider to feel as if they are sitting just above the keystone. It is this bridge-like quality which is the key to the desired outline.

First of all, the ring of muscles described in Chapter 5 comes into play. Then, as the hindquarters engage, the joints of the hind limbs flex, enabling them to carry more weight and relieving the forehand. Finally, the horse makes the neck telescoping gesture. Then, and only then, will the rider feel that wonderful sensation that comes with the lightening of the forehand, and the feeling that the horse has lifted his back, making it easier to sit on, and raised himself up in front of the saddle. It should be clear by now that none of the above can be achieved by drawing the horse's head in, or indeed by restricting his use of his head and neck in any way. If we do so, and try to impose an outline by means of pressure on the bit, then instead of letting the horse round up and stretch his topline, we are compressing the latter; muscle contraction causes the bridge to become disconnected, and the horse cannot raise his back or flex his lumbo-sacral joint properly.

Unfortunately, there are many misunderstandings regarding the concepts of collection and on the bit. For example, many riders believe that raising the horse's head and neck brings his centre of gravity further back, and that this somehow has something to do with collection. Well, the centre of gravity will indeed come further back (though only slightly), if only because the resulting shortening of the neck brings the heavy head further back, closer to the body. Simply raising the head and neck, without a corresponding flexing of the hind limbs and lowering of the haunches, will hollow the horse's back (see Fig. 8.1). As a result, the muscles of the topline, and those of the abdomen, will be brought into opposition, and this in turn may result in peculiarities of gait and make it difficult for the horse to move forward freely.

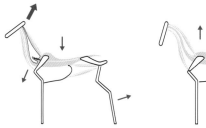 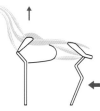 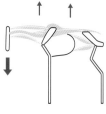

Raising of head and neck   Engagement of hind legs   Stretching of neck

Fig. 8.1 The effects of raising the head and neck *(adapted from* Long Reining, *by Philippe Karl, with kind permission of M. Karl)*

A hollow outline

Perhaps because there are so many different factors involved, it is easy for people to home in on one or more of those factors, while ignoring (or downplaying) the role of the rest. Huge numbers of people, including many of those competing at the highest levels in dressage, pay lip-service to the idea of working the horse from back to front and to the maxim that the horse's outline must never be imposed by the rider. But when they talk about methods, it is all too obvious that, in spite of what they say, they are in fact working the horse from front to back. Because we rely so heavily on the use of our hands in so many of our human activities, we tend to overemphasize the importance of the hands in riding. This tendency is made worse by the fact that it is relatively easy for us to manipulate the horse's head and neck, and to see the effects this produces. In this way, many riders (and, regrettably, their trainers) end up focusing almost exclusively on the positioning of the horse's head and neck.

In most disciplines the horse will not be penalized for a faulty head carriage, or for working in a hollow outline; in showjumping, for example, the outcome is what matters, not the form in which the horse achieves that outcome. Very often horses who work in a hollow outline, or overbent, will succeed in their disciplines, in spite of the fact that this almost inevitably puts them at greater risk of injury or unsoundness. In dressage or showing, the form in which a horse presents himself matters very much – in theory. However, showing is about external appearances, not correctness of training (although ideally the two go together). As for dressage, such is the obsession with 'outline' in certain circles that incorrect training is often rewarded (see Fig. 8.2).

Fig. 8.2 This horse is performing one of the most advanced dressage movements, but he is not in collection. He is 'strung out' behind, and his back is hollow. This was drawn from a photograph of a horse and rider competing at the highest level

The result of this is that there are countless horses appearing in ridden show classes and dressage competitions, who may appear to be working on the bit and in a nicely rounded outline, when in fact they are on the forehand – sometimes very much so.

Training aids

This obsession with outline has led to the widespread use of certain training aids. Although the manufacturers of some of these devices claim that they will not only help to work the horse in the proper outline, but also help the rider to sit more correctly and have softer hands, one must take these claims with a large shovel of salt. A horse who moves with choppy gaits and a tense, hollow back, will certainly make it very difficult for his rider to sit correctly. However, the answer lies in the elimination of possible causes, together with schooling from the ground, to help build up the right muscles and improve the gaits *before* any serious ridden work is attempted. This takes time and patience, but it is far better than attempting to mask the problem without ever trying to understand – and deal with – its cause. When a horse resists to the point where many riders reach for the draw reins or other such training aids, he is usually telling the rider that he simply cannot work in the way they want him to.

I am sure the majority of riders who use draw reins and similar devices would be appalled if they realized their potential for harm. The irreparable damage[2] that can be caused by their use, even in some supposedly expert hands, is something seen all too often by physiotherapists, osteopaths and chiropractors.

However, it would not be true to say that auxiliary reins and/or equipment are *always* detrimental. The use of auxiliary schooling aids when lungeing, for example, can be very beneficial. Correctly fitted side-reins, or tactful use of an aid such as the Chambon or the de Gogue (see Chapter 9), can be of great value in encouraging the horse to stretch forward and down, and to strengthen the muscles of the back and abdomen. A note of warning is due: the lunger must still understand the principles of what they are doing. Even so, I think that this work, which is often overlooked, is where the real value of schooling aids lies. It is in the ridden work that we find the greatest potential for damage – and a corresponding degree of misuse.

For me, one of the greatest objections to draw reins, balancing reins etc., apart from their potential for damage, is that they encourage riders to abandon part of their responsibility to the horse. Instead of riders trying to understand how they and the horse interact, they effectively stand back, and turn all the burden of understanding over to the horse. It then becomes *his* responsibility to learn how to come on the bit or work in an outline. The result is that the rider stops listening to the horse, and the feedback process is blocked before it can even begin.

Looking at the whole picture

Horses may, as we have already seen, come above the bit for a variety of reasons. Before deciding which of these apply, we must look long and soberly at the whole picture, and our role in it. Factors we need to consider are:

- Is the horse tense? Tension from fear, anxiety, excitement or hypersensitivity can all cause horses to become hollow-backed.

- Does the saddle fit correctly? Pain from an ill-fitting saddle is a major cause of tension in the back.

---

2 Often this consists of damage to the nuchal ligament as a result of excessive flexion of the cervical vertebrae, and the consequent overstretching of the ligament. This damage can be permanent. Horses worked in draw reins may also suffer from extremely painful muscle spasms in the back.

- Are the horse's feet properly balanced, and has he been shod correctly? Pain or discomfort in the feet, or imbalances in the feet can also lead to tension in the back and neck, as the horse attempts to compensate or ease the discomfort.

- Does the bit fit correctly? Is the horse in pain from teeth needing attention? Pain in the mouth causes tension in the jaw, which in turn can pass all the way down the neck, through the back and down to the hind legs. Remember the chain of muscles!

- Following on from the last point: are the rider's hands hard and unyielding, or soft and allowing? If the former, then tension in the mouth and jaw will be the inevitable result.

- As we saw in Chapter 7, the rider's hands are only as good as their seat. Is the latter independent, balanced and secure, or are the reins being used as a crutch for a wobbly, insecure seat? Does the rider sit slumped heavily in the saddle, lurching around with every movement the horse makes and grinding the seatbones into the saddle, or do they sit lightly, taking responsibility for their own weight? The way the rider sits makes an enormous difference to the way a horse carries himself. See Chapter 10 for more about the seat.

It may be that a particular horse's conformation is affecting his head carriage and the state of his back. Rather than make any prior assumptions about this, we must first of all look at all the factors mentioned above, and eliminate them one by one. Riders must be especially ruthless in evaluating their own abilities – even (or perhaps especially) experienced riders; we all fall into bad habits, or may be blissfully unaware that what we have been doing for years is incorrect. Having (hopefully) eliminated all these, we can then use the conformation and personality profiles we have drawn up and see what conformational or personality factors might be affecting the horse. This will help us a) to understand the problem(s) and b) to understand (perhaps with a little help) how we can work around them.

CHAPTER NINE

Working from the ground

MANY TRAINERS FEEL THAT, once the horse has been backed and ridden away, work from the ground has little further place in his schooling. I disagree. While it is true that ridden work is the best of all methods for producing a riding horse, working from the ground has many advantages. The horse can be worked without having to cope with the weight of a rider and the trainer can see far more clearly how the horse is responding. For example, the trainer can see whether the horse is truly light in front, or whether the rider is receiving a false sensation of lightness because the horse has got behind the bit; whether the horse is truly tracking up, whether he is swishing his tail in annoyance, or whether he is really straight, etc. The trainer can also get close to the horse, both mentally and physically, before actually riding him. All of this helps to make the ridden work much easier and more pleasant, as well as laying sure foundations for it. I would certainly always do as much work from the ground as possible to prepare a young or green horse for ridden work, as it helps to build up the horse's musculature in the right places.

Lungeing

This is the obvious place to start, as most people who ride horses will have tried it at some stage or another. Most horses will also have been lunged at some point, although some trainers prefer long-reining (we use both, often in combination, as I shall describe later in this chapter).

Many people think of lungeing simply as a means of settling down a fresh horse, but in fact there are better methods of doing so, the most obvious being to allow the horse enough freedom and exercise so that he is not too fresh in the first place!

The kind of lungeing we are concerned with here is aimed at strengthening the horse's back and abdominal muscles (as described in Chapter 5), as well as helping to relax tight muscles along the thoraco-lumbar spine. Some trainers dislike lungeing because of the potential strain continual movement on a circle can impose. However, there is nothing to say that you cannot vary this by periodically taking the horse on straight lines during a lunge session! (See Fig. 9.1.) We frequently do so, but this variation is most effective when working with two lunge lines. With the latter, it is easier to control the amount of bend in the horse's body, and the outside line passed round the hindquarters can work wonders in encouraging a horse to go forward. Working with two lines takes more skill than with just one, and there are a number of different techniques you can use. As it is basically a combination of lungeing and long-reining, I highly recommend Sylvia Stanier's two classic books, *The Art of Lungeing* and *The Art of Long-Reining* (both published by J. A. Allen).

Nivalis moves actively forward on the lunge
(L. Skipper)

Fig. 9.1 Some schooling patterns you can try on the lunge, instead of simply working in circles *(adapted from* Long Reining *by Philippe Karl, with kind permission of M.Karl)*

One rein around the horse's hindquarters can help to encourage him forward. Nivalis does not mind this, but some horses dislike the sensation, especially if the line gets trapped under the tail, so take care when using two reins *(L. Skipper)*

Before undertaking any of this work on the lunge, check your own lungeing abilities (I am assuming here that readers are familiar with the basic principles of lungeing). If you are unsure of the principles involved, or have any doubts about your own capabilities, then *do not attempt to work the horse with his head lowered.* Instead, seek advice from someone, prefer-ably an instructor committed to classical principles, who does have the necessary expertise in lungeing. Watch videos of experts carrying out lunge work; I can think of no better example than Arthur Kottas (see Recommended Reading). If you are confident of your ability to lunge effectively and safely without compromising the horse's wellbeing, you can go on to try exercises over raised poles or cavalletti, which we shall come to shortly.

Before starting work on the lunge, walk the horse round for five to ten minutes to loosen up his joints and muscles and to help him to relax. If he is stiff and tense, he will derive no benefit from the lunge work.

Whether you fit your horse with boots or bandages or not is up to you. Although these have traditionally been used to provide support and/or protection from injury, some trainers are now beginning to question whether they are really necessary. I have to say that we do not normally use them with any of our horses because none of them brushes, overreaches or otherwise interferes. However, if you have a horse who, whether because of conformation or injury, does any of those things, then boots or bandages may be a good idea. If you do use them, make sure they are fitted correctly; ill-fitting boots or bandages can be worse than nothing at all and may actually cause, rather than prevent, injury. The choice is yours! Horses with a tendency to overreach should wear overreach boots.

Loose work

This should not be confused with loose jumping, which is also often referred to as loose schooling, although the two can be combined. The kind of loose work we practise is more akin to the liberty work found in circuses, although its aim is not to provide a display as such, but to have the horse working freely with the trainer, giving his full attention and concentrating on his work. Once the horse is able to do this, he can exercise his muscles without feeling in any way restrained or restricted. Most horses appear to enjoy it, too!

We like to get the horse thoroughly accustomed to working on the lunge before starting loose work. Horses for whom responding to the trainer's voice and body language has become second nature, will tend to accept the idea of loose work more readily. Indeed, they can become so absorbed in their work that they appear to forget that they are not actually being controlled by the lunge line.

When working the horse loose, do not simply let him rush around the training area in an uncontrolled manner. If he is at all fresh, lunge him first to get him relaxed and concentrating, remembering to ask for increasingly precise responses. Horses who have learned that lungeing means work, and is not just an excuse for letting off steam, will soon settle to their work and will be more ready to progress to loose work in a calm and consistent manner.

Trotting poles and cavalletti

These can be used in much the same way as for ridden work (see Chapters 11 and 12), although the kind of variations you can use depends on your ability to place the horse accurately on the lunge. Once your horse is accustomed to going over poles or cavalletti under saddle or on the lunge, you can try working him loose over them. Most horses take to this readily; if we leave the trotting poles out, and our stallion Nivalis is loose in the *manège,* he will often deliberately trot over the poles and back again!

Training aids

As I said in Chapter 8, there *is* a place for training aids, in work on the lunge (and also, as we shall see, in loose work).

Green horses, or those with conformational and/or psychological prob-

Nivalis loose jumping. It is best to introduce this type of work without the weight of a rider *(L. Skipper)*

lems, may need help with finding the correct way of working. We cannot teach the horse how to be a horse (see Chapter 10), but we *can* help him to work efficiently, in a manner that will be of most benefit to his developing muscles. The rider who sits correctly, and uses the aids to help the horse rather than just command him, can actually influence him to use his back muscles properly and engage his hind legs. The horse being lunged without a rider does not have this influence to guide him, so unless he is the athletic kind who rounds and engages naturally, he may need more help from the ground. Conversely, he does not have the added weight of the rider to cope with, so the effects of any training aid (correctly used, of course) are more readily apparent, and may be more easily gauged.

The trainer can determine which horses will benefit from training aids on the lunge by watching the horse move loose in the field, as well as by observing how he carries himself on the lunge. Some trainers will use training aids in lungeing as a matter of course, but I believe it is better to treat each horse as a separate case and decide according to his individual conformation and way of going. If it ain't broke, don't fix it!

Side reins can properly be described as training aids. They can be very useful in lunge work, both to regulate the amount of bend and to encourage the horse to lower his head. However, they must not be adjusted so that they tie the horse's head down; he must still have freedom of his head and

Arabian mare Fanci, owned by Shana Young, is lunged in correctly-fitted side reins by Dr Thomas Ritter *(Diane Webber)*

neck. Their great disadvantage is that, when adjusted so that they are effective for trot work, they must then be readjusted for work in walk and canter, otherwise the horse's head movements in those gaits would result in him being caught in the mouth at each stride. Even so, correctly used, by someone who understands how to adjust them, they can be very beneficial in suggesting to the horse how he should carry his head and neck.

Apart from side reins, the two basic training aids which are widely used (in Europe, but not in the English-speaking countries) in lunge work, were named after their inventors, the French cavalry officers Chambon and de Gogue. Both devices work on principles aimed at encouraging the horse to lower his head and neck, without the use of any backward force. Of the two, the Chambon is the simpler (see Fig. 9.2). Its use in continental Europe is so extensive that many people there regard it as an essential piece of lungeing equipment.

Both the Chambon and the de Gogue resemble a type of running martingale. They can be used in conjunction with a cavesson or, if the horse is to be worked loose, with just a bit, preferably a soft mullen-mouth snaffle (we use a Nathe bit).

The Chambon only comes into action if the horse raises his head above

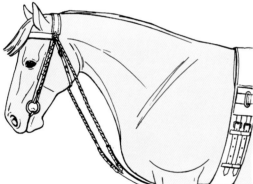

LEFT **Fig. 9.2** The Chambon

BELOW **Fig. 9.3** The Chambon in action

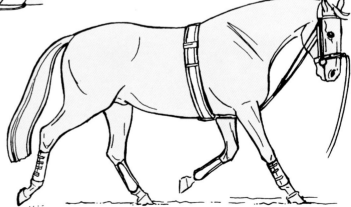

a certain level, which depends on how the device is adjusted (see Fig. 9.3). There is no backward pull, such as one might find with draw reins or running reins. The felt poll pad exerts a mild pressure on the poll: this is very gentle and, if the Chambon is correctly adjusted, not at all restrictive. The horse is still free to move his head and neck in any direction other than above the defined limit. Balance and stride are unaffected, as the horse can still use his head and neck, and there is no forcible stretching of the nuchal ligament.

The Chambon thus encourages the horse to lower his head and neck – the key word here being 'encourages', not 'compels'. Provided the horse is sent forward by the trainer, and that forward momentum is maintained, the effect will be to encourage the flexion of the lumbo-sacral joint and the joints of the hind legs, with subsequent raising of the back.

The action of the de Gogue is similar in principle to that of the Chambon, but somewhat more sophisticated. Like the Chambon, the de Gogue resembles a running martingale (see Fig. 9.4), but it has a potentially more powerful effect than the Chambon. Like the latter, it should be adjusted in such a way that the horse still has almost complete freedom of his head and neck. The action on the poll is more direct, although again it should only be gentle, and as with the Chambon there is no suggestion of backward pulling.

The de Gogue can also be used in ridden work,[1] and is not, therefore, simply a variation on the Chambon, although its use in lungeing and loose work is very similar. In lungeing it can be used with more precision than the Chambon, which is why we tend to use it, and is a little more versatile.

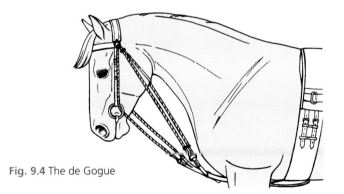

Fig. 9.4 The de Gogue

---

1 Use of the de Gogue under saddle is beyond the scope of this book and is, in any case, a specialized skill.

The de Gogue encourages Toska to stretch forward and down. Care must be taken to keep the horse's hind legs active *(L. Skipper)*

I cannot emphasize enough that if a horse throws his head up, or carries it too high, you should in all cases make every effort to find out *why* he does this. This applies even more to ridden work. The only time we ever use a Chambon or a de Gogue is when we have eliminated physical pain or disability (from whatever cause).

Whether you use a Chambon or a de Gogue, initially both are best used in loose work to allow the horse to accustom himself to unfamiliar tack. They should be fitted rather loosely to begin with, although care should be taken to ensure that they are not so loose that a horse who suddenly becomes rather enthusiastic about lowering his head and neck cannot accidentally put a forefoot through the straps. Generally this can be avoided by making sure the horse is moving forward briskly; this will help to counteract any tendency to 'hoover' the ground with his nose, which is not really what we want!

Ridden work is undoubtedly the best way to train a horse for any discipline. However, where there is a need for remedial, preparatory or therapeutic work *before* serious training can begin (or between spells of ridden work), I believe the benefits of working from the ground are potentially enormous and well worth pursuing, no matter what your ultimate aim may be.

CHAPTER TEN

The rider

W E ARE OFTEN REMINDED that horses were not designed specifically to carry riders, and this is true enough. It is also frequently implied that correct riding is something of a damage limitation exercise, and again there is some truth in this: there is an enormous amount of potential for damage to the ridden horse through bad riding and poor saddle fitting. However, riding can also be a therapeutic exercise for the horse and this is often overlooked. So how can we help the horse through ridden work?

Before we can understand how to answer such a question, we have to know what tools we have at our disposal. In particular, this means considering the aids used to communicate with the horse from the saddle.

The aids

Let us think about that term, 'aids'. In the late twentieth and early twenty-first centuries the trend has been to think of the aids in the sense of something we do to *control* the horse, or a series of signals by means of which we let him know what we want. But what does the word 'aid' actually mean? In its equestrian sense it means exactly what it does in everyday life: help, assistance, support. The original English term was 'helps', derived from the French *aider,* meaning literally to help, to aid, to assist. This suggests that the aids are there not just to tell the horse what we want, but to *help* him to fulfil our requests.

Most modern textbooks on training and riding tend to assume that horses can only be trained by means of what are known as conditioned responses. I covered this subject in some depth in my book, *Inside Your Horse's Mind,* where I explain how horses learn and why there is so much confusion over just what it is we are trying to teach them under saddle. Briefly, a conditioned response is what we get when we teach a horse to move away from the leg: if he complies, we reward him (or we should!); if he does not, we keep trying until he does. Eventually he will come to associate the reward with moving away from the leg; in time this response will become automatic and he will move away even without the reward. In other words, he has become 'conditioned'.

In theory, using such an approach, we can train horses to do almost anything of which they are physically or mentally capable and in practice this appears to be so. But is it necessarily the most effective one to use?

The 'conditioned response' school of thought tends to assume that the horse has to be taught everything we want him to do under saddle, from moving away from the leg to performing a half-pass, or whatever. However, we have only to watch horses at liberty, especially in play, to realize that this cannot be right. They can run, jump, move sideways, backwards, pirouette, trot in circles, perform *piaffe, passage,* or just about anything else we might

Nivalis, excited by the presence of other horses, executes a natural, if tense, version of the passage. His hindquarters are not engaged, and his back is hollow, but in a less exciting situation he can produce a beautifully rounded passage *(L. Skipper)*

ask them to do. They already know how to be horses! Every movement we could possibly ask them to perform, they already know how to do. They do not have to be taught what to do, any more than a foal has to be taught how to stand up and run about.

Obviously, some horses are more athletic than others. Although they already know how to perform various movements or how to jump, they just might not be very good at it. All we can really teach them is a better way to make use of their natural abilities. We do this by teaching them to accept our aids, by helping them to cope with our weight on their backs and to find their balance, and by developing their muscles by means of progressive gymnastic training. This is the sole purpose of school movements; if we talk of 'teaching' the horse such movements as ends in themselves, then we have missed the point.

So, we can certainly teach the horse to change gait, jump, or to perform movements by rote by, for example, tapping him on the shoulder (or using any other signal we may choose) when we want to canter, and rewarding a correct response and ignoring an incorrect one. The problem is that this does nothing to help the horse to understand *how* we want him to perform the change of gait, take a jump, execute a half-pass, etc.

This is where our approach to the use of the aids is crucial. Are exercises under saddle something we impose on the horse, or are they something he will offer willingly once we have shown him what we want, and made it easy for him to comply?

Helping the horse

The greatest masters of equitation realized, long ago, that there are numerous ways in which we can help the horse to perform under saddle. Have you ever watched truly great riders and wondered how on earth they manage to get the horse to perform the most intricate manoeuvres while remaining so still in the saddle and appearing to do nothing at all? The answer is that they communicate with the horse by means of the subtlest, most minute signals – a touch of the leg here, a tiny shift in weight or increase in muscle tone there – and because these signals evoke a natural response in the horse, he can interpret them exactly as the rider intends (see Fig. 10.1).[1]

---

1 I described the nature of these natural responses in Chapters 11, 12 and 13 of my earlier book, *Inside Your Horse's Mind*.

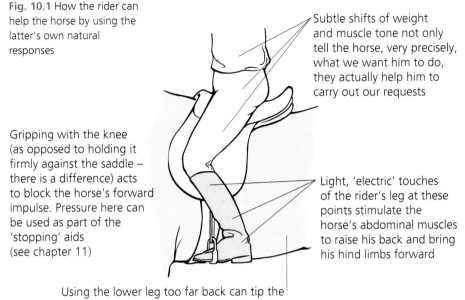

Fig. 10.1 How the rider can help the horse by using the latter's own natural responses

Subtle shifts of weight and muscle tone not only tell the horse, very precisely, what we want him to do, they actually help him to carry out our requests

Gripping with the knee (as opposed to holding it firmly against the saddle – there is a difference) acts to block the horse's forward impulse. Pressure here can be used as part of the 'stopping' aids (see chapter 11)

Light, 'electric' touches of the rider's leg at these points stimulate the horse's abdominal muscles to raise his back and bring his hind limbs forward

Using the lower leg too far back can tip the horse on to his forehand by making him raise his loins rather than the centre of his back

In Chapters 4 and 5 I mentioned the internal and external oblique abdominal muscles. Stimulation of these muscles by the rider's leg makes them contract, flexing the hip joint and bringing the hind limb forward.[2] This is an example of a natural response. South African trainer Karin Blignault, who has studied occupational therapy and neuro-developmental therapy, enlarges on these natural responses. She uses concepts devised for use in remedial work which encourages normal movement in spastic children. These concepts are: Facilitation and Inhibition of Movement. Facilitation, she explains, is

> the term used to describe the manner in which we encourage the horse to produce the correct movement – in other words, the aids. We explain to the horse, with our body, what to do with his body. Thus it is a body language which explains, very specifically to the horse, which muscles to contract. We use the aids in a very specific way to influence the horse's natural balance and righting reactions and therefore facilitate the movement we want.[3]

2 See also Sara Wyche, *Understanding the Horse's Back*, Crowood Press , 1998, p.51, and Üdo Burger, *The Way to Perfect Horsemanship*, (1st pub. in Germany as *Vollendete Reitkunst*, 1959) tr. Nicole Bartle J. A. Allen 1986 (reissued 1998) pp. 240 –241.

3 Karin Blignault, *Successful Schooling*, J. A. Allen, 1997, p.10.

In the same way, she explains, the aids can be used to inhibit, or prevent, unwanted movement such as when we want to halt the horse, or slow him down. (See Blignault's excellent book, *Successful Schooling,* Chapters 1 and 4, for a fuller understanding of these concepts.).

This idea of 'facilitating', or helping, the horse is at the heart of the ethos of classical riding, already mentioned in Chapter 1. Anyone who is familiar with the idea of classical riding only through passing references in magazines, might be forgiven for thinking that it is simply a rather refined and esoteric form of dressage, with no relevance to the ordinary rider. They could not be more wrong. The classical principles of equitation were worked out over many centuries by masters of the art of riding, and have

The classical principles of equitation were worked out over many centuries by masters of the art of riding. An eighteenth-century engraving of M. de Kraut *(Charles Parrocel, c.1733)*

stood the test of time. They emphasize working in harmony with the horse's conformation, physiology and psychology. This means nothing more or less than the training and riding of horses in accordance with their nature and working towards mutual understanding – rather than resorting to force – to help to restore the horse's natural balance and enhance his gaits under saddle. All this is as relevant as anything could be to the everyday rider, no matter what their chosen discipline, or even if all they want to do is enjoy riding their horse. As Dr Deb Bennett says, 'All domestic horses belong to one species and have one skeletal design operated by one set of physiological reflexes. Therefore, there are really only two ways to ride – with the horse or against him'.[4]

This kind of training and riding is not, of course, exclusive to riders and trainers who call themselves 'classical' (and not all of those who label themselves 'classical' do in fact follow classical ideals). Regardless of how they perceive themselves, though, I think it would be true to say that those who do follow those ideals are most likely to understand – and to make use of – the aids as a means of helping the horse rather than simply commanding him. On the other hand, among those who hold fast to the idea of the aids as commands, and to the concept of all training being a matter of conditioning and shaping the horse's behaviour, there are some who even deny that the natural responses referred to above actually exist.

However, countless horsemen and women – myself among them – have found that such natural responses do exist, and that they are of paramount importance in ridden work. Yes, training horses involves conditioning: praise and reward, for instance, motivate the horse to repeat something he has done well, and this is of course a form of conditioning. But to suggest that stimulus-and-response training is all there is to it, is to overlook an essential part of the horse's nature – and the one we can best make use of to help him through any difficulties.

The point I am making here is that if we use only the 'conditioned response' approach, and ignore the importance of the natural responses in helping the horse, then it often happens that only the most naturally talented horses may respond in such a way as to make high levels of performance possible. So we have the excuse that 'the horse isn't good enough', when in fact it may simply be that the quality of the riding and training is what is preventing the horse from performing well!

It would be wrong, though, to think that we can get on a totally green horse and expect him to respond as a trained horse would. First of all, there are simply too many new sensations (such as the unaccustomed weight on

4 Dr Deb Bennett, 'True Collection', *Equus*, 198, April 1994 p.58

his back) that the horse has to cope with, for him to be able to respond immediately to the rider's aids. Secondly, the horse's muscles may be insufficiently developed. Much also depends on the skill of the rider, especially on how much control they have over their own body, so that they do not make any unintentional movements to confuse the horse.

Having said that, there are some green horses who do respond immediately. For example, our Arabian stallion Nivalis, and the Warmblood gelding Toska, when first ridden, proved extremely sensitive and responsive to the seat and to the leg. They 'mirror' the rider; in other words if, for example, the rider simply turns their body, they will respond by turning in the same direction as the rider.

The effective rider

In fact, all horses, not just the very sensitive ones, can be made responsive in this way. Once the rider learns how to use their body effectively in communicating with the horse, it is astonishing how many problems can disappear overnight, and how much easier the horse finds it to comply with our requests.

However, this requires some effort on the part of the rider. Anyone who tells you that you should be so relaxed on a horse that you go all floppy (advice I have actually heard given to novice riders!) does not know what they are talking about. The great twentieth-century piano teacher Nadia Boulanger used to say, 'Loose is not beautiful. Loose is loose'.[5] A floppy rider is a dead weight; paramedics who have to move people who are unconscious, dead drunk, or simply dead, will tell you how difficult it is, compared to the ease with which they can move someone who can at least take responsibility for some of their weight. To ride effectively you need muscle tone: not, as many people imagine, in your arms and lower legs, but in your back (especially the lower back), abdomen and thighs. By stabilising the centre of your body, this muscle tone will help to hold you in position on the horse without the need to grip with your lower legs (which makes it impossible to use them subtly). It will also give you greater control over the extremities – the arms, hands and lower legs – so that you can begin to use these with delicacy and finesse.

I have a theory about why there were so many good riders in the seventeenth and eighteenth centuries: the people who practised riding as an art, rather than just as an everyday necessity, were gentlemen, and in those days

5 Playing the piano requires an effort, too!

every gentleman learned the art of fencing and swordplay. This 'centred' them and toned up their 'riding muscles', making them exceptionally effective in the saddle (see Figs. 10.2–10.6).

I hope the above has made it clear that the way in which a rider sits on a horse, and how they apply the aids, is of overwhelming importance, whether you are riding on the flat or over jumps – indeed, no matter *what* your chosen discipline might be.

Unfortunately this aspect of riding, so vitally important, is woefully neglected in the majority of our riding schools (with some honourable exceptions). Many of our teachers, if they are themselves effective riders, have no clear idea of exactly what they do in the saddle, because it comes so naturally to them. So they describe what they *think* they are doing, and pass this on to their pupils. Have you ever been told to use your seat to influence the horse? And if you have, did anyone explain really clearly *exactly* what you should be doing? If they did, you were exceptionally lucky. Most riding-school pupils are not so fortunate.

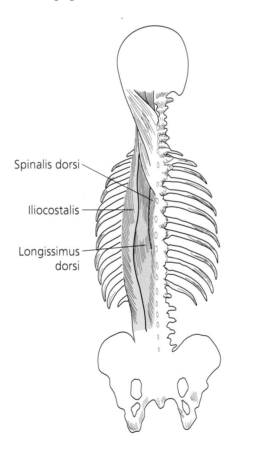

Spinalis dorsi

Iliocostalis

Longissimus dorsi

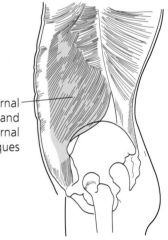

External and internal obliques

LEFT **Fig. 10.2** The riding muscles: the erector spinae muscles of the lower back. This group of muscles acts to support, extend, flex and rotate the spine

ABOVE **Fig. 10.3** The riding muscles: the oblique abdominals support and rotate the spine, and assist in lateral flexion

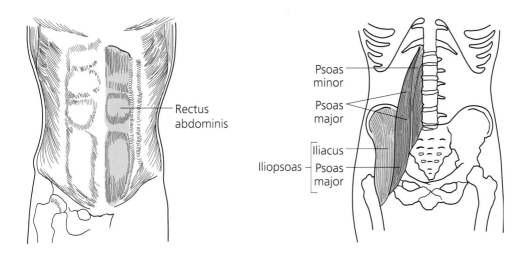

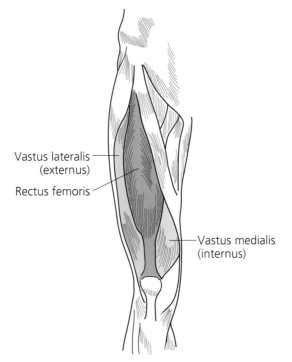

ABOVE **Fig. 10.4** The riding muscles: the rectus abdominis muscles. Muscle tone here helps to hold the rider in place; a momentary contraction and relaxation of these muscles acts as a very powerful aid (see Chapters 11 and 12)

ABOVE RIGHT **Fig. 10.5** The riding muscles: the iliopsoas muscles aid hip flexion and help to support and mobilize the spine

RIGHT **Fig. 10.6** The riding muscles: the quadriceps muscles of the thigh extend the knee and flex the hip joint. Well-toned 'quads' give the rider great stability in the saddle

While there are many excellent books on riding, comparatively few of them actually teach the rider *effectively* how to achieve the elusive 'seat' (see Fig. 10.7). Fortunately, the last few decades of the twentieth century produced some outstanding teachers who have been able to do just that, and whose ideas have been put forward in books and videos. Some of these teachers have made worldwide names for themselves, and their teaching

Balanced seat
This rider can take responsibility for their own weight, which is distributed down the thighs as well as through the seatbones and crotch

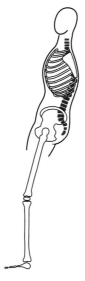

Chair seat
Whether the knees are straight or bent, this rider is out of balance, with the weight being concentrated on the back of the seatbones – very uncomfortable for the horse!

Fork seat
Insecure and ineffective, this will put the horse on his forehand and will impede free forward movement

ABOVE **Fig. 10.7** The balanced, chair and fork seats

has been a revelation for many riders struggling to achieve what they had previously felt to be impossible.

Among the most successful are Sylvia Loch, Sally Swift, and Mary Wanless. Although each adopts a different approach, for the most part they are saying basically the same kind of things. Sally Swift makes great use of images and sensations to convey her ideas. Sylvia Loch has a very sympathetic, inspirational approach which often draws on analogies outside riding to make her point and to illuminate her ideas. Mary Wanless also uses analogies, but hers is a much more technical, analytical approach than that of the other two. For that reason many people find it rather daunting, although it is well worth the effort necessary to grasp some of the more complex ideas she puts forward.

The classical seat: riding from your centre

Basically, all three of these teachers are describing what is often called the 'classical seat', which, because it is a balanced seat (see Fig. 10.8), is the only truly effective way to ride on the flat. Although this may seem to have little relevance to jumping, in fact the position adopted by riders in showjump-

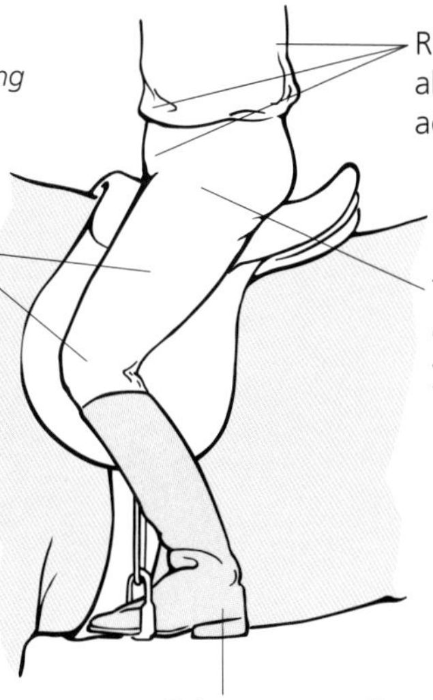

If we were to take the horse out from under this rider, they would land on their feet. Think of standing up around a horse, rather than sitting as if you were in a chair.

Rider's back and abdominal muscles act to stabilize the seat

The thigh and knee should remain snugly against the saddle. Taking the knee away from the saddle (except briefly, as part of a specific rider exercise) as riders are sometimes taught, destablizes the rider's position and makes subtle use of the lower leg impossible

The hip joint needs to be open – think of pushing your belly towards your hands, but without hollowing your back

Riders are usually told to lower their heels, but pushing the heels down makes the lower leg come forward. It is perfectly aceptable for the sole of the boot to be horizontal, as here.

Fig. 10.8 The balanced seat

ing is simply the basic classical seat adapted for the forward position: instead of remaining upright, the rider 'folds down' at the hip joints (the body should not be thrown forward, with the backside sticking up in the air, as is so often seen; this is not a balanced seat).[6]

In *The Classical Seat* Sylvia Loch describes it thus:

> The expression 'three point seat' is one of imagery. It indicates a broad base of support represented by the entire pelvic floor rather than being isolated to the back of the seatbones only, sometimes known as a 'two point seat'…Contact throughout this entire area leads to far greater support for the pelvis, the abdomen and ultimately the rider's spine …[7]

Mary Wanless goes even further and defines the rider's seat as encompassing not only the seat itself but the inner thighs right down to the knees. In this way the area of contact with the horse is maximized, and the rider's weight distributed over as large an area as possible.

All three of the above teachers lay great emphasis on the concept of the horse 'mirroring' what his rider does. Sylvia Loch and Mary Wanless both

6 For an excellent description of how the forward seat should really work, see Mary Wanless, *Ride With Your Mind* Masterclass, Methuen, 1991, pp.187-218

7 Sylvia Loch, *The Classical Seat*, Unwin Hyman, 1988, p.30

M. Philippe Karl of the Cadre Noir shows an exemplary jumping position as he tackles this cross-country fence with Selle Français stallion Stupefiant de Retz *(A. Laurioux; reproduced from* Long Reining *by Philippe Karl, with kind permission of M. Karl)*

stress the importance of recognizing, and correcting, the rider's own asymmetries, which may compound, or even create, similar asymmetries in the horse. How often the horse is blamed for being crooked, when in fact it may be the rider who is making him so!

As one who has had to fight a hard battle to achieve – and maintain – a decent position in the saddle, I know only too well how elusive that perfect poise and balance can be, even when you know what you should be doing and how you ought to be sitting. I can therefore wholeheartedly sympathize with riders who feel that their efforts to improve their horses are doomed from the start by their own lack of effectiveness in the saddle. However, they need not despair. I am no great horsewoman, and never will be. For one thing, in spite of a childhood spent in adoration of the horse in all his shapes and forms, I did not take up riding seriously until well into adult life, when I had already suffered various injuries which greatly impaired any small athletic ability I might ever have had. For another, my shape (short and dumpy) works against me. Finally, apart from brief spells when I had the help of an excellent teacher, I have had to work mostly on my own, and so am virtually self-taught. Yet I still managed to learn how to influence my horses effectively, through subtle aids and the use of my position. If I can do it, anyone can!

As I have already suggested, riders need to assess the standard of their own riding very critically. I do not mean this in a destructive way but, unless we are aware of our faults and weaknesses, we cannot even begin to improve. Watch some videos of very good riders such as Arthur Kottas, Reiner Klimke (or his son Michael) or Carl Hester. If you can get hold of a copy of Kalman de Jurenak's *Classical Schooling* video, you can see how much difference good riding can make to the horse, as one horse is shown being ridden first of all by a relatively inexperienced rider, and then by a master, Hans-Heinrich Meyer zu Strohen. Try to imagine what makes these riders as effective as they are, and when you ride, carry with you an image of how they look, think how it might feel to look like that, and try to reproduce that feeling in yourself.

In doing this, do not make yourself stiff and tense. In her excellent video, *The Classical Seat II,* Sylvia Loch exhorts riders to 'project the horse forward from an open, upright body position', saying 'The rider must project from the abdomen'. (See under Recommended Reading.) Think of riding from your centre, using the muscle tone in your thighs, abdomen and

The classical seat: M. Philippe Karl on Selle Français stallion Raid II *(A. Laurioux; reproduced from* Long Reining *by Philippe Karl, with kind permission of M. Karl)*

lower back. If you lack tone in those areas, you may find that martial arts training helps (it will also help to centre your thoughts and emotions),[8] in the same way as the practice of swordplay would have done in the seventeenth and eighteenth centuries. Once your muscles are properly toned, you will be surprised by how relaxed you can feel, without going loose and floppy or losing that centred feeling.

Riding in an indoor school with mirrors helps you to take a critical look at yourself, or if you are out hacking and happen to pass any shops with large windows close to the road, you can glance at your reflection as you go past. Do not do what I once did, though: one day I was hacking out on a placid old horse we used to have and I was so busy admiring our combined reflections in a shop window that I almost ran the horse into the back of a parked car!

It would be even better if you could get someone to photograph or video you riding. Once you know what you are looking for, this can be a real eye-opener! If you see all kinds of quirks, deficiencies and horrible habits in your riding, do not despair; everybody has them (yes, even the best riders). It is just that some of us have a few more than others, and need that bit of extra help to iron them out. If you find that almost involves learning to ride all over again, then think of it positively, as a chance to be a 'born-again' rider.

In Chapter 1 I suggested that it would be best, if possible, to find a classically trained teacher. Even better would be such a teacher who also had their own, classically trained schoolmaster horse. By 'schoolmaster' I do not mean the kind of horse who will perform 'movements' or jump fences mechanically and by rote[9], no matter what the rider does. Such cleverly trained horses can make success possible even at high levels of competition, in spite of poor and even ugly riding, but they teach the rider nothing. I mean the kind of horse who is well-schooled enough to give the rider a correct 'feel' for what is right, but who will only make the correct response when the rider's position and use of the aids are right (or almost right!).[10]

Once you have felt what is correct – whether it is a good transition, the feel of a horse working properly on the bit, or any other moment in riding – you can then store this feeling away for future reference, so that when

---

8 Riders may also benefit from lessons with an Alexander Technique teacher or a Pilates tutor (see Appendix II). Joni Bentley's *Riding Success Without Stress* (J. A. Allen) gives an excellent view of how the Alexander Technique can help riders; the Pilates Method is also very good.

9 They look and feel mechanical, too.

10 Such a schoolmaster may be difficult to find, but if you can locate one, make the most of the opportunity.

you come to try to reproduce the transition, school movement or whatever, you will know when you have succeeded. The more often you experience such a feeling, the easier it will be for you to recognize what you are doing (or not doing!) to bring it about.

There is much, then, that we need to improve in ourselves before we can think of improving our horses. If we are humble enough to recognize this, we are already halfway there. As Sylvia Loch says, 'Once we start to ride from the centre, all sorts of miracles can happen.'[11]

11 Video, *The Classical Seat II*.

CHAPTER ELEVEN

Improving the horse I
Understanding the movement

ORSES ARE CREATURES of movement. Their whole lifestyle is geared to almost constant movement, albeit mostly at a fairly leisurely walk. When grazing, they spend very little time in one place. They will crop a very small area of grass and then move on, maybe less than a metre, perhaps several metres, and begin grazing again. In this way, feral and free-ranging horses can cover great distances in a day; even Dobbin in his field will have travelled quite a number of kilometres in the space of just a few hours.

Forward movement

The horse's forelimbs act mainly as shock absorbers and to support the forehand. Most of the 'drive' for forward movement comes from the hind limbs, with the horse's long back muscles acting as the 'transmission'. Free, forward movement depends on the ability of these muscles to contract and relax again freely, which is one reason why horses who normally move with grace and freedom at liberty can sometimes move badly under saddle; the fault in such cases frequently lies with poor saddle fitting and/or unbalanced riding.

Some textbooks state that, even when galloping, most horses will not bring their hind feet further forward than a line dropped down from the umbilicus. If this were the case, then they would have a very restricted hind leg stride as the umbilicus is generally situated almost directly in line with the point of hip. In fact it is not true, as simple observation, let alone the evidence of countless photographs, films and videos will testify. Nevertheless, this idea is often repeated by people who ought to know better, giving a distorted picture of what is possible for horses in movement.

Attentive readers will no doubt have noticed by now that, apart from a very brief mention in Chapter 8, I have so far ignored something that some people might regard as being important: this is the centre of gravity. We do not need to know where it is in order to tell whether the horse is moving correctly or not; we can assess that perfectly well by eye, or by the feel he gives us under saddle. So I will say no more on the subject, which tends to cause a great deal of confusion; we can manage perfectly well without it.

Basic types of movement

The basic type of movement is dictated by the skeletal structure. Other factors, such as muscle tone, hoof balance and shoeing, the way the horse is ridden or handled, the type of ground, etc., may affect that movement, but they cannot alter it beyond the limits imposed by the way in which the bones of various joints impinge on each other. Because of this, the range of motion of which a horse is capable is already established by the time he is four months old. Within those limits, however, we can – as we saw in Chapter 4 – increase the range of motion by means of suppling exercises.

Although the amount of increase possible is limited by the respective lengths of the scapula and humerus in the forehand, the pelvis and femur in the hindquarters, and the angles they make with each other, it is still possible to extend the range of motion to a very noticeable extent. This is because a small movement in the shoulder or stifle area is considerably magnified by the time it is transmitted to the lower limb (see Fig. 11.1). So although we cannot expect a horse with an upright shoulder and horizontal humerus to develop an extended trot similar to that of a purpose-bred dressage horse, we can still increase the mobility of the joints to the extent that the horse produces longer, more flowing strides.

First of all, though, we need to know what kind of movement we are dealing with. We saw in Chapter 4 how the length and angle of the scapula and humerus affect scope and length of stride. They also affect the *type* of movement, as Table 6 shows.

We must not forget, however, that it is the *hind legs* which provide the impulsion. Here again, angles give us the necessary clues. Length of stride, power, and engagement of the hindquarters depend on the angles of the

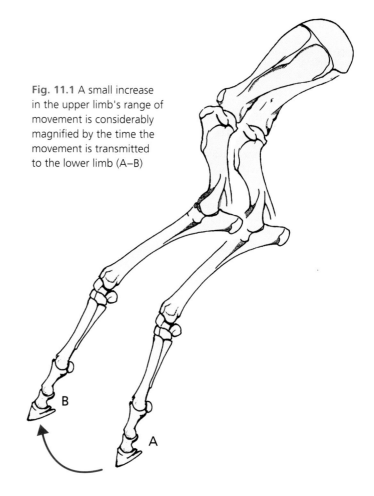

Fig. 11.1 A small increase in the upper limb's range of movement is considerably magnified by the time the movement is transmitted to the lower limb (A–B)

pelvis, hip joint, stifle and hock. If the horse is to move well, the angles made by the pelvis (ilium) and the femur with the ground, and of the ilium with the femur, should not differ too greatly from the corresponding angles made by the scapula and humerus.

There should be sufficient angulation in the hocks to allow good flexion (but not too much, or the result is a camped-out and/or sickle hock formation). A long line from hip to hock, with a well let down hock and short cannon, gives a long, powerful stride; a shorter line from hip to hock, coupled with higher set hocks and long cannons gives a higher, shorter stride. A relatively straight hock gives low movement with a swinging stride; the hind leg conformation that gives good average angles of all the hind leg joints (see Fig. 3.26) brings with it more flexion of the hock and stifle.

No one type of movement is intrinsically 'better' than another; it all depends on the job the horse has to do and the most functional and efficient movement for that job. As the different breeds have for the most part

Table 6 How skeletal structure of the forelimb affects the type of movement

Scapula	Humerus	Cannon	Type of movement	Remarks
Upright (near 60 degrees)	Long (at least 50% of the length of the scapula) and steep (angle between scapula and humerus wider than 90 degrees)	Fairly long, with high knees	High; can fold high and tight at the knee	Gaits may lack forward reach and elasticity, and the limbs may be inefficient at absorbing concussion; could give a rough ride under saddle
Upright	Short (less than 50% of length of scapula) and steep	Long or short	Short and choppy	As above
Moderately sloping (50–55 degrees)	Long and moderately steep (angle between scapula and humerus at least 90 degrees)	Medium to short	Medium, with sufficient scope for general ridden work	Gaits generally are free and elastic
Moderately sloping	Short and moderately steep	As above	As above, although somewhat lacking in scope	Movement may be rather stiff
Low (slope of around 45 degrees)	Long, moderately steep	As above	Fairly low, slightly round action. Some scope, but may not be able to fold sufficiently for high jumping	Gaits usually very comfortable
Low	Long, horizontal (angle between scapula and humerus less than 90 degrees)	As above	Low action, often of the type known as 'daisy-cutting'. May find it difficult to raise the forearm to the horizontal	As above, but may be lacking in 'spring' and elevation
Low	Short and horizontal	As above	Low action, may also be short and rather flat	Greater stride frequency may make for an uncomfortable ride

been selectively bred for specific types of work, their conformation reflects that work and with it the type of movement. Low, sweeping movement with little flexion of the limbs, such as that found in many Thoroughbreds, favours speed rather than collection, but is perfectly suited to a racehorse or to hunters travelling over fast country.

On the other hand, many of our modern breeds, especially the Warm bloods, would have originally been used as cavalry horses, who would need to be able to move efficiently over varied and often rough terrain. This would dictate a medium type of movement, neither too low and ground-hugging, nor extravagantly high and uneconomical. Arabians, who were originally bred exclusively as war-horses, generally have this type of movement. They are often described as having a 'daisy-cutting' style of action, but this is incorrect for the Arabian, as is a 'bicycling' movement of the hind legs[1] often seen in show horses. Travelling over uneven and often rocky ground, an Arabian war-horse with daisy-cutting action would be prone to stumble; in any gait, a war-horse would need to be able to lift his feet well in order to get over the ground safely.

This also applies to horses used for working stock over rough terrain, such as the Iberian breeds and their derivatives. These have a somewhat higher, rounder action than most Warmbloods and Arabians; this is often referred to as 'baroque' action. One often reads statements to the effect that dishing is a characteristic of these breeds, and it is true that a great many Andalusians (and perhaps fewer Lusitanos[2]) do dish noticeably. Dishing was an unwanted side effect of breeding for a certain 'look'. The flashy effect of high, wide action, especially in horses intended for parades, meant that this action was specifically bred for; the fact that it is wasteful of energy mattered little when the horse was only going to be ridden for an hour or so. However, it is unsuited to the working stock horse who may have to be ridden for many hours over rough or slippery terrain. Indeed, some Spanish stockmen refuse to work with horses who have a pronounced dishing action, because of the risk of the horse becoming unbalanced on hard ground.

The prevalence of dishing in Spanish horses may also, in part, be due to the preference many Spaniards have for horses who are too broad in the breast; as we saw in Chapter 4, dishing may be a result of the horse's efforts to compensate for this excessive broadness.

Extremely high action, such as we see in the American Saddlebred and Hackney, while fine in the show ring, uses up far too much energy, as well as increasing the risk of concussion damage on hard ground. In fact, although these breeds do have naturally high action, it is usually artificially enhanced by the use of weighted shoes.

The above is a rather crude division of horse movement into three basic types: low, medium and high. Susan E. Harris[3] divides movement into six different types, and I have used her examples as a basis for the types summarized in Table 7.

---

1 That is, where there is plenty of hock action but little forward movement. This is usually caused by stiffness in the back muscles, and is often the result of the way these show horses are trained to stand and trot, with the head and neck in the air and the back hollow.

2 Portuguese breeders are trying to breed out this faulty action.

3 See *Horse Gaits, Balance and Movement*, Howell Book House, USA, 1993. Recommended for a fuller understanding of the subject.

Table 7 Types of movement (adapted from *Horse Gaits, Balance and Movement* by Susan E. Harris, Howell Book House, USA 1993)

Type of movement	Description	Found in	Useful in these disciplines
Short and low movement	Short, low strides with little flexion of knees or hocks. Horses with this type of movement may be agile and handy	Horses of many different breeds and types	General purpose riding; dressage and showjumping at Riding Club level
Long and low movement	Ground-covering action with little suspension or flexion of knees and hocks; often referred to as 'daisy-cutting' or 'grass-clipping'. Good extension and forward balance; less suited to collected gaits or movements requiring great suspension	Some Thoroughbreds, Thoroughbred crosses and hunters; show ponies	Hunting (depending on the type of country being hunted); eventing; endurance
Medium movement	Elastic, ground-covering movement showing both elevation and flexion of knees and hocks; however this is not as marked as that found in baroque movement. Capable of both collection and extension	Warmbloods, especially those bred for dressage; many Arabians; some Morgans; some Thoroughbreds	Competitive dressage; show-jumping; eventing; endurance; general purpose riding
Round movement	Combines forward reach with considerable flexion of knees and hocks, without the extreme flexion of high action	Some Morgans, some Welsh Cobs, and many ride-and-drive types	General purpose riding; showing; dressage and showjumping at Riding Club level
Baroque movement	This type of movement was typically found in horses used in High School manège riding of the seventeenth and eighteenth centuries. Flexion of knee and hock joints is marked, although less so than in horses having high action. Movement is round and elevated, with great suspension and elasticity	Andalusians, Lusitanos, Lipizzaners and various breeds derived from the Iberians	High School dressage; Spanish *doma vaquera* riding; showjumping; general purpose riding
High movement	High head carriage; great flexion of knees and hocks; forearm often raised beyond the horizontal, tightly folded at the knees. Movement up and down exceeds forward movement	American Saddlebreds, Hackneys, and some other horses with Saddlebred or Hackney blood	Show classes for Park horses; these classes are extremely popular in the USA, but are less common elsewhere

Note This table should be used as a guide only, within every breed you will find horses with different types of movement, and horses with a specific type of movement will not necessarily be restricted to the kinds of discipline suggested in the table. Many factors, besides conformation and movement, combine to make a horse suitable for a specific discipline; not least of these are temperament and an individual's past history and current state of health, both mental and physical.

Short and low movement:
Arabian x Belgian Warm-
blood gelding Kruger
(*L. Skipper*)

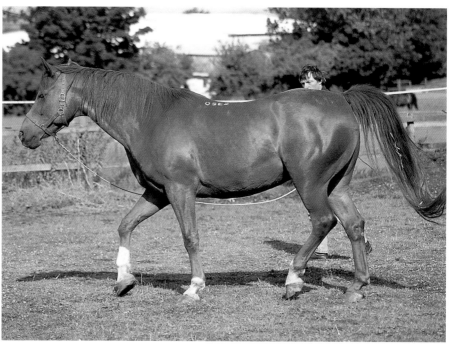

BELOW Long and low
movement: Cleveland Bay x
Thoroughbred mare Kiri and
her daughter Imzadi, by
Arabian stallion Nivalis
(*L. Skipper*)

ABOVE Medium movement: Arabian gelding Jaleel Ibn Dawn Star *(Photo Sweet)*

Round movement: Stormydown Black Diamond, Section D Welsh Cob, Welsh Pony & Cob Society Silver Medal winner and Supreme Champion in-hand. Bred by Mr & Mrs John Cooke *(John Cooke)*

165

Baroque movement:
Andalusian stallion Kan VIII
(Yeguada Iberica)

High movement: American
Saddlebred *(Bob Langrish)*

The quality of movement

Although the *type* of movement may be dictated by the horse's conformation, the *quality* of the movement may often be improved beyond all recognition by correct training. This is because that quality is to a large extent dictated by the state of the horse's muscles, and while these may leave a lot to be desired in some cases, this may only be a reflection of the horse's current level of training or of wellbeing.

The information given in this chapter, together with your conformation and movement profiles, will help you to understand the type of movement your horse has. However, conformation is not everything. As always, look at the whole horse!

A horse's state of mind can also affect his movement. As Sara Wyche points out, a horse who feels intimidated (whether by other horses, humans, or specific situations), may restrict his freedom of movement as a result of perceived repressive influences, whereas a bold, confident horse may move in such a way that underlying unsoundness may be masked.[4] Past injuries, even when long since healed, can also affect a horse's way of going; the horse may have got into a habit of moving in a certain way in order to protect an injured limb or muscle. Although pain may no longer be present, the habit often persists, so, when assessing a horse's movement, remember to take account of any recent injuries (or any old ones, if details are known).

Improving the gaits

Having established what kind of movement the horse has, how do we go on to improve it?

One way in which you will *not* improve the gaits is by trotting endlessly in circles. Unfortunately, many riders confuse this with schooling, which gives the school exercises a bad name. Yet this is hardly surprising; watch a lesson (especially a group lesson) in any number of riding schools in the English-speaking countries, and what will you tend to see? Horses and riders trotting endlessly in circles!

No, the key to improvement of the gaits lies in transitions, in pole work, and in the various mounted and dismounted suppling exercises, mentioned in Chapters 4, 5 and 12.

---

4 See Sara Wyche, *Understanding the Horse's Legs,* Crowood Press, 2000, p.57

The gait which has proved most useful for training purposes is the trot. This is because it is a symmetrical gait (i.e. the legs move in diagonal pairs); for similar reasons, it is also the easiest gait to improve. However, before we can start to improve the trot or any other gait, we must ensure the horse is moving with *impulsion*.

Many people confuse impulsion with speed, but it has little to do with the latter. Instead it is a feeling of contained power, projecting the horse forward rhythmically and giving his movements 'lift' and forward impetus. Impulsion is generated by the horse first of all flexing the hip, stifle and hock joints and then thrusting against the ground as he extends these joints again (see Fig. 11.2). This is why the ability to flex the joints of the hind legs is so important.

This contained power is essential for athletic performance; without it, the horse will not only be less manoeuvrable, he will be more likely to injure himself. This means that in the case of lethargic horses, we will have to stoke up this impulsion by asking for more 'go' in their movements. In other cases, we will often have to slow the horse down.

At faster gaits than the walk, a four-legged animal is never really stable. We often talk about horses being balanced while in motion, but this is not

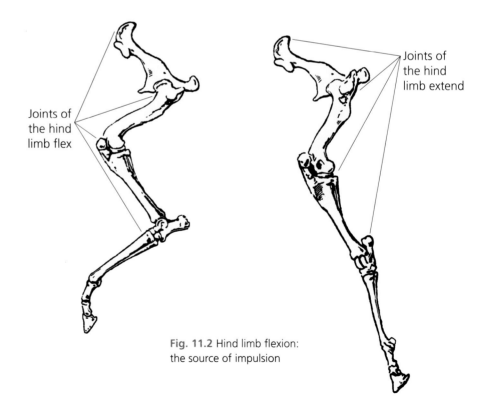

Joints of the hind limb flex

Joints of the hind limb extend

Fig. 11.2 Hind limb flexion: the source of impulsion

strictly correct, because the word 'balance' suggests something that is static. In forward motion, horses (and humans) are actually in a continual state of losing their balance and then regaining it. This is called *dynamic equilibrium* and it means that it is the forward motion itself which enables the horse (or human) to regain the balance lost as the body falls forward under the influence of gravity. As the body moves forward, its weight is taken up by the supporting limb or limbs and projected forward, this process being repeated each time a supporting limb is placed on the ground.

Dynamic equilibrium means that at higher speeds any loss of balance can be easily corrected because the feet touch the ground in quick succession. So, even though in the trot, canter and gallop the horse has two, one or no feet in contact with the ground, the forward momentum ensures that he does not fall over (a good analogy here is with a bicycle: at faster speeds

Kruger in canter: at one point in the stride, there is only one foot touching the ground. Note how far the horse's hind legs reach under his body. *(L. Skipper)*

balancing on two wheels becomes easy, whereas at slower speeds the bike may start to wobble or even fall over). At slower speeds the intervals between footfalls are much longer, so the horse either needs more feet on the ground in each stride in order to maintain stability, or – and this is one of the main aims of training – a greater degree of control over his muscular actions, in order to maintain that dynamic equilibrium at slower speeds.

This is why horses tend to rush; it is easier, as the alternative means harder work for them. Think of a ballet dancer on her pointes. She makes it look effortless, but the degree of muscular control she has acquired in order to keep her balance is the result of years of training.

It can be tricky deciding how much a gait needs slowing down or speeding up. The one thing we do *not* want to do, especially with green horses, is to stifle the desire to go forward, by holding them back. You need to find the horse's natural rhythm and tempo, which is best done on the lunge, so you can observe how he moves unencumbered by a rider.

So how *do* we slow the horse down? This might seem like a silly question until you really think about it. How do *you* slow your horse down? Many people simply pull on the reins, and this might have the desired effect

Toska: to maintain stability in the walk, the horse must keep at least two (and usually three) feet on the ground, and must move them in the correct order (usually left fore, right hind, right fore, left hind)
(L. Skipper)

in some cases (although in others it might have the opposite result – remember what I said in Chapter 7 about the action of the bit, especially a snaffle). However, pulling on the mouth does nothing to affect what the horse does with his hind feet; horses slowed down or halted in this fashion usually do so by braking with the front legs. They are probably already on the forehand, so they simply become even more so. No, the rider has to learn how to slow the horse with their own body.

If you have the firm, independent seat described in Chapter 10, you will find it relatively easy to slow or halt the horse. For such riders, a momentary bracing of the muscles of the back and abdomen will be sufficient to slow the horse in walk, sitting trot and canter; in rising trot, keeping your thighs and abdomen firm and rising from the knees rather than the stirrups, you simply slow the timing of your rise, and the horse (who would really much rather follow you than have you follow him all the time) will slow down in response. Sound too easy? I promise you it will happen, but only if you have sufficient control over your own body actions. This requires muscle tone, as described in Chapter 10.

On the lunge, you can combine a vibration on the lunge line with a change in body position so that you are slightly ahead of the horse. To this body language, add voice aids. We have found that most horses respond readily to words such as 'steady' uttered in a low, long drawn out, calming tone. Horses also respond to rhythm, which is one reason why dressage to music has been so outstandingly successful. In trot, imitate the ticking sound of a metronome by repeating 'trit-trot, trit-trot' in the rhythm and speed at which you want the horse to work. Provided they are relaxed, and you have their attention, most horses will slow down in response to this.

As I said earlier, with more lethargic horses you may need to 'stoke up' the impulsion (but if your horse is always lethargic, do have him checked for any physical conditions which might be creating the lethargy; also make sure he is getting sufficient energy from his diet). On the lunge you can use your body language to urge him forward, by getting slightly behind him and trailing the lunge whip after him, at the same time clicking your tongue (a very effective way of urging a horse forward). Whether you are bringing on a young horse or improving an older one, you need to get him used to the idea that he must move forward, or be ready to move forward, at all times – even in halt! Under saddle, do not repeatedly squeeze or thump his sides with your legs; that will only make him dead to the leg because he learns to ignore your signals in order to protect himself from discomfort. Instead, use your legs in quick, light touches just behind the girth (see Fig.10.1); these will act like small electrical impulses to stimulate the muscles which move the horse's legs forward, and he will be walking more briskly before he has time to even think about it. For the really 'ploddy' horse, French trainer Dominique Barbier makes a very useful suggestion: imagine you and the horse are in a barn, the roof is going to collapse, and you have only five seconds to get out. If your imagination is convincing enough, your horse will pick up on your emotions and it is amazing what a galvanising effect this can have on even a sluggish horse!

Once you have found the right rhythm and tempo for your horse, you can start to use transitions, pole work and school figures to improve the gaits.

Table 8 Gait problems: remedial action

Note Some gait abnormalities, such as dishing or paddling, cannot be remedied, as they are caused by the horse's skeletal structure. However, good basic training can help to ensure that the horse carries himself in a manner which will minimize any problems caused by such faulty gaits.

Irregularities of gait are often signs of back, limb or foot problems. They may also be the result of past injuries, so before attempting any remedial work, please have the horse thoroughly examined by the vet and the farrier to establish possible causes. Suitable remedial action can then be decided as required.

Problem	Remedial action	Further reference
Excessively high action with insufficient forward movement	Stretching exercises to increase range of fore and hind limb movement. Lungeing with two lines, interspersing work on circles with work on straight lines, encouraging the horse to move forward actively. Riding in a straight line, especially out on a hack; cantering and galloping in a controlled manner. Riding over poles placed on the ground in a fan shape, to encourage lengthened strides.	Chapters 4, 5, 9 and 12
Excessively low, daisy-cutting action with insufficient flexion of limbs and/or engagement of the hindquarters	Work on circles will help with engagement, while lungeing or riding over raised poles or cavalletti will encourage the horse to take higher steps.	Chapters 9 and 12
Short femur (short, rapid hind leg strides)	As above. Encourage the horse to adopt a slow, regular rhythm in trot, while sending him actively forward. Work on circles, especially spiralling in and out.	Chapters 4, 5, 9 and 12
Short, choppy gaits	Stretching exercises will help to increase the range of motion of fore and hind limbs. Under saddle: in trot, send the horse forward energetically but keep the trot slow by timing your rise. Lungeing and riding over trotting poles, gradually increasing the distance between the poles, will encourage the horse to lengthen his stride. Work over raised poles and/or cavalletti will help him to establish a more regular rhythm, and encourage him to pick his feet up. Riding up hills and over a variety of different terrains will also help.	Chapters 4, 5, 9 and 12
Stumbling (i.e. not picking feet up)	Ensure the horse's feet are correctly trimmed and that shoes fit properly. Have the horse checked for back or limb problems. If the horse is sound, lungeing and riding over raised poles or cavalletti will encourage him to pick his feet up. Try riding over a variety of different surfaces in succession (e.g. sand, pebbles, gravel, small stones); this will help him to be more aware of where he is putting his feet. Riding over different terrains will also encourage better awareness, on the horse's part, of what he is doing with his feet.	Chapters 3, 4, 5, 9 and 12

CHAPTER TWELVE

Improving the horse II
Training strategies

N O ONE BOOK CAN TEACH the rider everything they need to know about the kind of exercises which will improve the gaits and increase the horse's suppleness and lightness of the forehand. That can only be achieved by the right kind of experience, by thinking about, and understanding, what you have learnt, preferably working with someone on the ground to keep a watchful eye on horse and rider, and by further reading. Fortunately there are a number of good books and videos which will expand on, and clarify, what you read here. These are listed under Recommended Reading, but there is one in particular which, although its title implies that it is aimed at dressage riders, I have no hesitation in recommending to riders of all disciplines; remember what I said in Chapter 1 about dressage being nothing more than the basic education of the horse. The book in question is Sylvia Loch's *Dressage in Lightness* (J. A. Allen, 2000). It sets out, with simplicity and yet with great clarity, the principles of training, the role of the rider, and how the horse responds. It gives the reader a logical, progressive training programme which is flexible enough to suit different kinds of horse, explains the purpose of each exercise, describes precisely how the rider should give the aids, and – in one of the book's most valuable features – gives some insight into how the horse might respond to what the rider does in the saddle, by means of a 'commentary' from the horse on each of the exercises. This book (which I suggest is best read in conjunction with the same author's *The Classical Seat*) provides a solid base from which to build your knowledge.

Another two books which I thoroughly recommend are Karin Blignault's

Successful Schooling, J. A. Allen, 1997, and Erik F. Herbermann's *Dressage Formula,* now in its third edition (J. A. Allen, 1999). Do not be put off by the title; this is a brilliant book for anyone who wants to enhance their understanding of the principles of training horses. Even the more knowledgeable rider would do well to absorb what these books have to offer; none of us is so good that we cannot benefit from another's insights.

I suggest, therefore, that you think of this chapter as an introduction to the exercises recommended later in the chapter, rather than as a complete guide.

You do not need a purpose-made manège in order to carry out the exercises in this chapter, but a level, marked out schooling area certainly helps. Some of the exercises can be carried out while out on a hack, but be careful in choosing when and where to do this; a busy road is definitely not the place for schooling!

Schooling need not be boring. If you approach it in the right frame of mind, instead of thinking of it as a dull routine, it can become a stimulating challenge for both horse and rider.

Starting work

The traditional way of getting horses fit enough to start serious work is by means of roadwork, but many people (like myself) live in areas where the roads are becoming suicidally dangerous to venture out on, with even small country roads being used as racetracks by drivers who never seem to expect animals on the road in the country. If you are in this situation, do not despair. Half an hour's lungeing is as good as an hour's hacking (if your horse is green, or unfit, do build up to this gradually); additionally, if you have large enough fields to ride in, you can often cover as much ground as you would on a hack.

Praise and reward

In all the exercises which follow, these are two of the most important components. Praise and reward your horse (with a stroke on the neck – not a hearty slap; a scratch on the withers; verbally, in a tone of voice that tells him you are pleased, as in 'Good boy!', or a mint, or whatever you know gives him pleasure[1]) whenever, and as soon as, he gets something right,

---

1 Which, of course, you *will* know, if you have constructed your personality profile of him.

even if it is only a step in the right direction. Release the contact; stop giving the aid. Take the pressure off! And never, *ever,* punish him for getting something wrong.[2] A horse cannot work properly if his mind is crippled by the fear of making a mistake. Reward every effort in the right direction; ignore mistakes. Do not always correct him; if the horse offers canter, say, when you ask for trot, pretend it was what you wanted to do anyway, and make the most of it. The chances are that it was the aids which were not clear enough! Think positive, *be* positive, and so will your horse!

Warming up

As I said in Chapter 4, it is essential to warm up muscles before they are asked to do any work. How you warm up depends on the individual horse, but a good idea would be to loosen him up and relax him first, before you actually sit on his back. You can do this by just walking him around quietly in hand for a few minutes. This gives him a chance to look around, take stock of his surroundings, and get into the rhythm of walking. If he has already been introduced to shoulder-in (see page 191), then once he has started to relax you can just ask him for a few steps of shoulder-in on a small circle around you. This will help to loosen and round his back in preparation for being ridden.

If you want to start from the saddle, simply walk the horse around on a loose rein for five to ten minutes, again letting him have a good look at his surroundings. Then you can, if you wish, do a few circuits of the schooling area in trot on a loose rein. With some horses it is best to do this in canter, again on a loose rein. Horses generally prefer the canter to the trot when moving about loose in the field at anything other than a walk, and for this reason many of them relax more readily into canter than in trot; it all depends on the individual horse. The idea is to have the horse going forward freely and without tension, reaching out and seeking a contact with the bit. Once he has relaxed and is moving freely, you can pick up the reins and start work, but throughout a schooling session, you should intersperse serious work with a few minutes' relaxing walk on a loose rein. Always end a session like this, to help the horse to unwind.

---

2 Punishment for bad behaviour is something entirely different, but be sure it is bad behaviour, and not just the result of pain or fear. See *Inside Your Horse's Mind* for more about this.

Relaxation

Horses cannot give of their best if they are tense and worried. However, relaxation in this context does not mean 'totally relaxed': it simply means that only those muscles required for posture control or movement should be under tension, and then only for as long as it takes to perform their function.

Tense, spooky horses; horses who go above the bit

Tension and a tendency to shy often go together: where this is the case, eliminating the tension will very often do away with the shying. Correct tack fit in particular is a must; if the horse is uncomfortable or in pain from ill-fitting tack (especially the saddle), tension will be the inevitable result, unless he has an abnormally high pain threshold for a horse. As always, the rider must check their position and riding technique: check, check and check again.

On the ground

Walking round in hand as described above does wonders for many tense, spooky horses.

In the saddle

For obvious safety reasons, carry out this exercise in an enclosed area, especially if your horse is really spooky. Once you are sitting correctly and in balance, ask the horse to walk forward on a fairly loose rein. Watch his ears to see where they are pointing; if they are pricked forward, he is not paying attention to you. If this is the case, you need to regain his attention. I find that a slight (and I mean slight!) tap with a schooling whip on the shoulder usually does the trick, or, failing that, a light vibration with the leg just behind the girth. Whatever you do, do not increase tension by tapping too hard. We are asking him to listen to us, not punishing him. We are effectively saying, 'Excuse me, this is a partnership, and your partner is talking to you. Please pay attention!'

Lengthen the rein; it may help some horses if you widen and lower your hands until they are resting on the neck on each side of the withers, as this invites the horse to stretch forward and down. Do not throw the reins away; you still maintain a light contact and, if the horse is accepting the bit, he should reach forward to seek that contact. If he does not do that, or if he tries to pull the reins out of your hand, do not worry; simply ask him to walk on more briskly. Eventually he will get the message!

The very act of lowering the horse's head helps to relieve tension, as he cannot do this freely and remain tense in his neck and back. Once the physical tension starts to disappear, so will the mental tension, and in most cases you will find that as soon as he lowers his head and neck, he will start to relax and pay more attention to you. Instead of pricking forward and sideways, looking for potential causes for alarm, his ears will be turned sideways and slightly back, focusing on *you*.

Feed the reins out to their full length – right down to the buckle! Give away the contact completely for a few circles. Once the horse is relaxed and walking forward freely, provided he is using his hindquarters properly, you should feel his back start to lift and fill out underneath you (you may need to ask for a little more impulsion before this happens). Then you can start to shorten the reins and take up a polite contact again, asking the horse to 'come up'. If you have widened your hands, bring them closer together once the horse has raised his head again; remember what I said in Chapter 7 about the position of the hands.

Now see if you can find the correct rein length, i.e. one which will allow the horse to reach forward to take the bit politely, while allowing you to retain a fine control of the reins without having to pull back at any time (which can happen if the reins are too long). How long the reins should be, and how much contact the horse takes, are matters between you and the horse. What you should be aiming for is a light, elastic and yet positive feel down the reins, with the horse accepting the bit quietly. The horse reaches out, his neck arching forward and up from the withers; he seeks for the bit, and takes it forward. This is *not* the same as leaning on the bit or taking a pull. It is a sensation that is very difficult to describe, and even more difficult to grasp until you have actually felt it. Then all becomes clear and you find yourself thinking, 'So *that's* it!'

If the horse starts to tense again when you pick up the reins, repeat the exercise until he remains relaxed throughout (remember to maintain the impulsion). Next try some transitions (see below). Walk forward for six paces, then halt. Walk forward another six paces, then halt again. Repeat this until the horse can take the transitions without becoming tense again. Then you can go on to try the same thing in trot.

Even if you spend an entire session like this, it will not be wasted. Start every session in this way, and gradually you will find that it takes less and less time for your horse to start relaxing. Then you can start to work!

Bear in mind that you will achieve nothing worthwhile until your horse *does* learn to relax.

The walk

Many riders are afraid to do much work in walk, because they have been given dire warnings about how easy it is to spoil the gait. Well, so it is, if you work the horse in a kind of false collection which destroys the forward impulsion. It is also true that the trot, having more impulsion than the walk, is better for most gymnastic exercises. However, work in walk can be – and should be – a valuable component in schooling. The walk exercises more muscles than either the trot or the canter, which is one reason why it is so valuable for warming up. It is also the best gait in which to introduce new exercises such as shoulder-in. You need to ensure that the walk is active and forward-going; from this you can go on to ride all manner of circles, demi-voltes (half-circles, returning to the track – see Fig.12.1), loops, serpentines, figures-of-eight, etc. which will all help to supple the horse.

Work on a circle

Although in Chapter 11 I warned against 'endless trotting in circles', systematically ridden circles are an essential component of schooling. This is because the horse travelling on a circle has to flex one side of his body while stretching the other. The inside hind leg must flex more and come further under the body, while the outside hind leg has further to travel. The circle is thus an invaluable suppling tool.

When riding a circle, too many riders try to pull the horse around with the reins. The hands are there only to guide and support! The rider's inside leg at or fractionally behind the girth acts as a pillar for the horse to bend around, while the outside leg is held slightly further back, to prevent the horse's hindquarters from swinging out. The rider's shoulders are parallel with the horse's (but do not twist to the inside, or the horse will 'jackknife'). The outside rein, held against the horse's neck, acts only to support the rider's outside leg. Think of how you position your body when walking a circle on the ground and if you put yourself into that position on top of the horse, he will 'mirror' your actions.

What kind of exercises can you do on a circle? The possibilities are endless. Since work on circles encourages the horse to engage from behind, as he starts to engage more, you can ask for smaller circles, which will improve engagement still more.

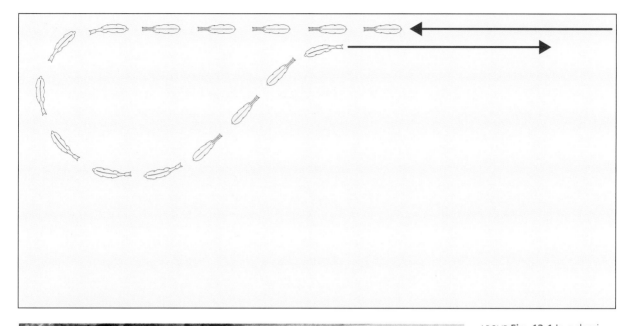

ABOVE **Fig. 12.1** In a demi-volte, the rider turns off the track, makes a half-circle, then returns to the track on a diagonal line and continues in the opposite direction from the original one (figure not shown to scale)

Riding on a circle helps to engage the hind legs: here Nivalis's inside hind leg steps under his body as he starts the turn into the circle (*L. Skipper*)

Spiralling in and out on a circle is an excellent exercise. In trot, begin with a 20 metre circle and spiral in until the horse is making the smallest circle of which he is capable. Then spiral back out again. Ride a figure-of-eight and do the same thing at the other end of the schooling area.

You can ride figures-of-eight using large circles, or, when the horse can comfortably trot in smaller circles, you can do a series of figures-of-eight using 10 metre circles (see Fig. 12.2). Once the horse can manage a really small circle (approximately six metres in diameter), you can do one of these in each corner of the schooling area, in the middle of the long side, or anywhere else! Your imagination is the limit, but do take care not to ask your horse for a smaller circle than he can comfortably manage, or you will risk injury. The size of circle you can ask for depends on the individual horse and his level of training. Our Arabian stallion Nivalis could trot a circle of the same diameter as his own length even before his training started, but very few horses are as naturally supple as that (and even many advanced dressage horses could not trot a circle that small). So be guided by how you feel the horse is responding – if he feels as if he is struggling, he probably is. In that case, go back to larger circles until he can manage the smaller ones.

Do not get so carried away by working on circles that you neglect to spend a good part of the time riding in straight lines. After every circle exercise, ride forward in a straight line. If the work on the circles has been correct, you should find the horse's muscles becoming more evenly developed, and he will find it easier to travel straight.

Fig. 12.2 You can make a series of small figures-of-eight anywhere in the school (figures not shown to scale)

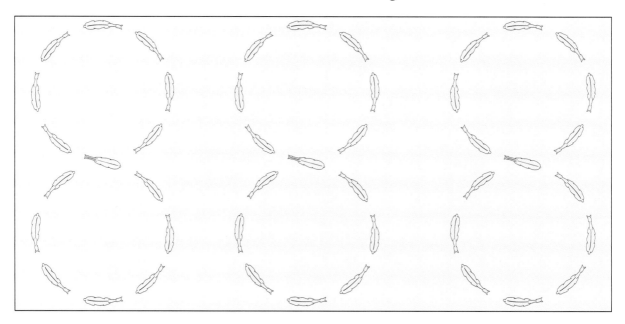

Trotting poles and cavalletti

Trotting poles consist simply of wooden (or, increasingly, plastic) poles, about 3–3.5 m (10–12 ft) in length. They can be used flat on the ground, or raised on blocks, cavalletti or other solid supports.

The benefits of pole work are:

- The spacing of the poles helps to develop a regular stride and rhythm.

- As the horse's neural pathways adapt to this regularity, his natural gaits will be much improved.

- It improves the horse's balance and co-ordination.

- The horse must lift his feet, which leads to increased activity from behind.

- Since the distance between the poles can be adjusted, the horse can also be encouraged to take longer steps, thus improving his length of stride.

- As the horse has to think about where he is putting his feet, it helps to improve his concentration.

Cavalletti (see Fig. 12.3). are widely used in continental Europe but far less frequently in the English-speaking countries. They may consist of poles simply resting on cross-pieces, or the poles may be fixed to the cross-pieces or supports. The fact that some horses have been injured through incorrect use of cavalletti has made some trainers, especially in the United Kingdom, understandably reluctant to use them, or to recommend their use. However, any risk involved in their use is no greater than that of asking a horse to jump a fence, even a low one, and I believe the potential benefits far outweigh any possible risk.

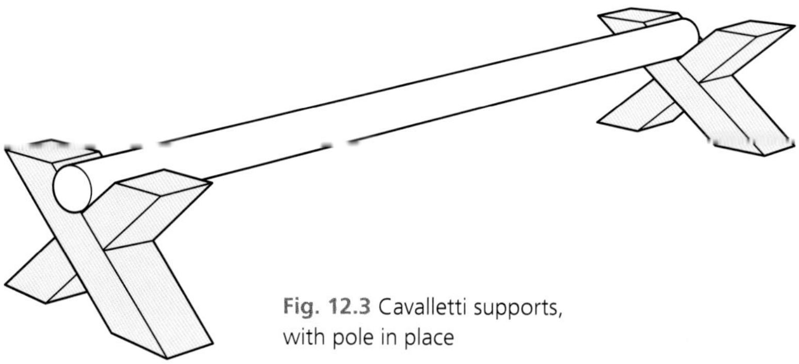

Fig. 12.3 Cavalletti supports, with pole in place

The benefits of cavalletti work are:

■ It is extremely valuable for exercising and strengthening the horse's muscles.

■ Because the horse has to lift his feet higher than he would normally do, he must also flex the joints of his limbs, stifle and the lumbo-sacral joint.

■ This also exercises all the related muscles, and promotes engagement of the hindquarters and hind limbs.

■ The fact that the horse has to take higher steps will help to give his gaits more elevation, especially in the trot.

■ Cavalletti work is excellent for loosening up the horse's muscles, especially those of the back.

■ It helps to build stamina, by improving the action of the cardio-vascular system.

If proper cavalletti are not available, poles can be rested on any firm supports as long as they are stable. The standard working height is 15–20 cm (6–8 in) but the advantage of proper cavalletti supports is that their construction means you can vary the height.

As with any other aspect of training, pole work is only of value if used correctly. Improperly used – whether by incorrect placing of poles or by overwork – they can be harmful, damaging the very muscles they are supposed to be strengthening. Any such work must therefore be preceded by careful planning.

Every precaution must be taken to ensure safety. In particular, you must be careful to place the poles at the correct distance for individual horses, as stepping repeatedly between poles placed either too close together or too far apart can result in strain injuries. In walk, start off with poles placed approximately 90 cm–1 m apart (3 ft–3ft 4 in); in trot they will need to be 1.2–1.7 m (4 ft–5 ft 3 in) apart. This is an approximate guide only. Every horse's stride is individual, and the length will depend on the size of the horse as well as the type of movement. The idea is for the horse to step halfway between two poles; you will need to adjust the distance between the poles after you have seen how your horse's stride length fits in. Once he is working confidently over the poles, you can then vary the distance to encourage him to lengthen or shorten his stride, but be careful not to make the distance too great or too little for him to manage without strain or injury; vary it by only a little (5–8 cm [2–3¼ in]) at a time. Only close observation can tell you what is correct. As with lunge work, whether or not to use boots or bandages should be decided on an individual basis.

Lead the horse around for five to ten minutes before mounting and starting work; this will help to relax him and let him see the poles. Take him up to them and let him sniff them if he is unaccustomed to them. 'Old hands' may be quite blasé about this kind of thing!

Exercises

Remember that all the exercises described in this chapter should be carried out on both reins.

Most of the following pole exercises can be carried out on the lunge, over raised poles or poles laid flat on the ground, although Exercises 3 and 4 should be carried out under saddle, and in Exercises 4 and 5 there would be no advantage in raising the poles. See how inventive you can be in making up your own patterns, but make them logical: think about what you are trying to achieve and, as always, have a care for safety and the horse's well-being.

EXERCISE 1

If your horse consistently strikes off in canter on the wrong lead, a pole on the ground, placed diagonally across the corner of the arena or schooling area, will usually encourage him to strike off on the correct leg, because horses will normally change legs when cantering over the pole. As he grows accustomed to the new sensation, he will eventually start to make a correct strike-off.

EXERCISE 2

Place four to six poles parallel with each other in a line. Walk over the poles in a straight line. Repeat this on the other rein, then vary it by going over the poles first to the right of the centre, then to the left. Repeat in trot. This will help to improve accuracy.

The same exercise carried out over poles with alternate ends raised will help to improve the action of the hocks and shoulders.

EXERCISE 3

Set a line of four to six poles close to a long side of the arena, or along a hedge or fence. Walk over the poles in a straight line, then ride a demi-volte, returning over the poles in a straight line. Repeat on the other side, riding back over the poles. Repeat the exercise in trot.

Riding over poles raised at alternate ends will help to improve the action of hocks and shoulders *(Horse & Rider)*

EXERCISE 4

Set out a line of four to six poles approximately 3 m (9ft 3 in) apart down the centre of the arena or working space and walk the horse in a series of serpentine loops round the ends of the poles.

EXERCISE 5

Set out two poles end to end, with a space of approximately 1.5 m (4 ft 11 in) between the ends, in the centre of the arena or working area. Ride a circle round each pole, first in walk, then in trot. After this ride round the poles in a figure-of-eight. This will help to make your circles regular.

EXERCISE 6

To encourage the horse to lengthen his stride, place three to six poles in a fan shape at each end of the arena or working area. Arrange the distances so that your horse's normal trot stride falls somewhere near the centre of the fan (see Fig.12.4). Ride down the long side (or equivalent if working in a field), then trot over the poles at point A on the diagram. Do the same at the other end. Trot over the poles again, this time at point B. Repeat at the other end. You can gradually move out on the poles to increase the distance

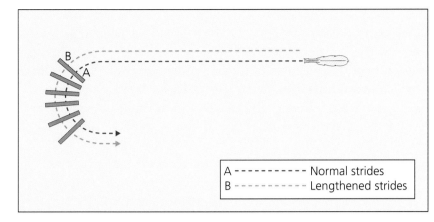

Fig. 12.4 Riding over a fan of poles as in this exercise will encourage the horse to lengthen his strides

A - - - - - - - Normal strides
B - - - - - - - Lengthened strides

still further but, as always, be careful not to ask your horse to lengthen more than he is able to without straining himself. It would be helpful here to have someone on the ground watching where your horse places his feet.

'Deep' work

In Chapters 5 and 9 I mentioned the benefits of working the horse with his head and neck lowered, the topline rounded and the hindquarters engaged. When carried out under saddle, this kind of work is often referred to as 'deep' work, and it has long formed a part of the basic education of horses in all the traditional centres of equestrian excellence. However, in the last decade or so of the twentieth century a fashion grew up in certain dressage circles for working the horse with extreme flexion of the neck, and with his nose pulled in until it almost touched his chest. This is akin to the kind of overflexion we get with horses worked in draw reins, and it has nothing to do with the kind of therapeutic work I described in Chapter 5.

In true deep work there must never be a suggestion of pulling the horse's head in, nor must the horse be allowed to lean on the bit, or fall on his nose. For the work to be of any use, the topline must be rounded. If the horse simply stretches his neck out and pokes his nose, his back will be hollowed and he will be on his forehand. Green horses will be unable to engage properly under saddle to begin with, so for such horses the work is best gradually introduced on the lunge, while they are free from the weight of a rider. Later, when the back and abdominal muscles have already been strengthened by work on the lunge, and the horse can start to engage under saddle, an element of deep work can be introduced.

The horse should not be asked to work in this way under saddle until he has already loosened up and started to engage. From an active trot on a large circle, ask the horse to lower his head and neck by lowering (and, if necessary, widening) the hands, as described on page 176. As with that exercise, the horse should take the bit forward and down without pulling or snatching. If the horse has enough impulsion, and he is engaging his hind legs, you should be able to feel his back come up and 'fill out' underneath you. Ease your seat forward slightly without tipping forward – just 'fold' forward a fraction from the hip joints and take more weight down your thighs.

As with work on the lunge, do not overdo this kind of work. Five to ten minutes on each rein should be sufficient; any more than that and you could risk straining the horse's muscles and ligaments.

Because it is so easy for the rider to allow the horse to work on the forehand in this work, it is best to have a knowledgeable eye on the ground to make sure the work is being carried out correctly. Properly carried out, deep work is an invaluable tool, but caution is needed![3]

3 See Sylvia Loch, *Dressage in Lightness,* Appendix: 'Long and Low, Deep and Round'.

Here you can see that Nivalis's whole topline has rounded up *(L. Skipper)*

Transitions

These are some of the key components of training horses and among the most neglected as far as the average rider is concerned.

Think about what happens if you are running and suddenly slow down or stop. Fractionally before you want to walk or halt, you brace the muscles of your back and abdomen. This enables you to pass from one gait to another, or stop altogether, smoothly and without jerkiness or stumbling. From the walk or halt thus achieved, you can – because you have retained your poise and balance – immediately move off again, at whichever gait you choose.

On the other hand, if you run in a sloppy manner, with flaccid muscles and your upper body inclined forward, you will find it almost impossible to halt or return to walk quickly and smoothly. You will find yourself taking a few little 'pottery' running steps before you can make the transition, at the end of which you will either fall into the new gait or come to an ungainly, shuddering stop.

Exactly the same applies to horses. A horse who is collected and balanced will be able to make transitions or come to a halt smoothly, and be instantly ready to move off again. One who is more or less on his forehand will flop out of one gait into another and instead of stopping quickly, smoothly and squarely, will drag himself on for several strides until he finally grinds to a halt. Does this apply to your horse? If it does, do not worry; it can be remedied. Collection is not just something that happens only after the horse has reached a certain level of training. Even relatively untrained horses are capable of a certain degree of collection; how much, depends on the individual horse and his conformation. This existing ability is something we continue to build on throughout the horse's training, and perfecting the transitions is one of the ways in which we do this. By this I mean either transitions from one gait to another, or within a gait, i.e. lengthening and shortening of the stride. Watch any really good rider schooling, and you will see that in some cases they will ask for several transitions in the space of a single minute. However, the benefit lies not just in the number, but in the *quality* of the transitions. Get these right, and everything else will fall into place.

Correct transitions will:

- get the horse working with greater impulsion;

- lead to sharper responses;

- help to establish engagement, because the horse must bring his hindquarters more underneath him in order to make a transition easily;

- improve the horse's balance;

- make collection easier for the horse;

- have a suppling effect on the horse.

Finally, because of all the above factors, the gaits themselves will start to improve.

When riding transitions, you will need to give the horse as much help as you can, especially if he has been accustomed to falling in and out of changes of gait. This means concentrating on your own position. It is not enough to ride transitions just with the leg and hand; you must use your body.

Suppose you want to move from trot to walk. Decide in advance where you want to make the transition. Just before you reach that point, prepare the horse with a half-halt (of which I will say more in a moment). Then, when you arrive at your pre-determined spot, close your legs softly against the horse's sides, fractionally further back than usual. At the same time, firm up your back, abdomen (think of pushing your stomach towards your hands but *without* hollowing your back), and thighs, taking slightly more weight on the crotch and, in the process, lightening the seatbones. Finally, you softly close your fingers on the reins. In this way you slow the forward momentum by partially blocking it with your body, which no longer 'goes with' the movement of the horse. The lightening of your seat (which is still in full contact with the saddle) enables the horse to lift his back and 'step through' into the new gait. The instant he does this, give with your hands and release your body just enough to allow the movement to come through, but do not collapse or grow floppy, or the horse – mirroring you – will also flop onto his forehand. He will probably also raise his head and hollow his back, as this is less hard work for him than collecting himself would be!

If you get all this right, the horse should move smoothly from the faster gait to the slower one. You may need to practise this a lot before it starts to improve, but as soon as you and the horse start to make correct transitions, you will be astonished by the difference this makes. Your horse will feel – and look – much more 'uphill' in his transitions, and the quality of the resulting gaits will be far better as a result.

Transitions to halt are made in exactly the same way, except that the 'stopping action' of your body and thighs is rather stronger. Closing the knee more firmly, and at the same time increasing the weight in both stirrups, will increase the stopping action even further. The lower leg asks the horse to move into the halt, while the hand remains lightly closed on the rein a fraction longer. There must still be a release once the horse has halted; it is just delayed a little. The horse will quickly come to understand that he does not move off again until you give the signal to do so. If he has a tendency to move off unasked, practise standing still a little longer than you would normally, until he gets the idea. As always, reward any correct action, no matter how small it may be!

Upward transitions are not very different, except that instead of the stopping movement we have a 'go' signal – a slight bracing forward of the rider's abdomen and back, accompanied by a light, electric touch of the lower leg to stimulate the horse's belly muscles and ask for the forward movement of the hind legs. The fingers, having closed slightly on the rein to warn the horse that you are about to ask him to do something, now release to allow the forward movement. If the transition is correct, you should feel a lifting sensation as the horse moves up smoothly into the new gait.

Whether riding upward or downward transitions, always remember to ride *forward* into the new gait.

The most basic transition is the walk to halt. Make sure you can do this correctly before you go on to practise the walk–trot/trot–walk, and trot–canter/canter–trot transitions. As the horse's training advances, more difficult transitions such as walk–canter/canter–walk, and eventually halt–canter/canter–halt, will improve his way of going still further, but these should not be attempted until the basics are correct!

You can practise transitions anywhere: in the school, in a field, even out on a hack, where you can plan to do a transition at, say, the next telegraph pole, the next tree, the next gate, or whatever takes your fancy.

Plan your transitions, and prepare yourself and the horse. When you ask for a transition at a marker, try to do so as your body comes level with the marker. This will give you something to aim for and help to improve accuracy. Remember, though, that the *quality* of the transition is all-important; when you get it right you will be able to ask for a transition wherever you want.

Half-halts

What is a half-halt? Classical trainer and FEI judge Charles de Kunffy says that the half-halt should be thought of as a 'mini transition', and I think this is a very good description. The half-halt – a momentary bracing of the muscles of the abdomen and lower back, and a fractional closing of the fingers on the reins – helps to warn the horse that he is about to be asked for something, but even more, it helps him to rebalance and gather (if you like, 'collect') himself, and prepare for the action that is to come.

Exercises

Always start off with the most basic exercises. To begin with, try this one.

EXERCISE 1

Walk forward for six paces, then halt. Walk forward again six paces, then halt again. Repeat this as often as you like, until you feel the horse starting to 'come through' from behind, and he will halt without hollowing his back and/or raising his head.

EXERCISE 2

On a large circle, establish an active working trot. Ask for a transition to walk, walk for six strides, then ask for trot again. Trot half a circle, and ask for a transition to walk again. Walk for five strides, then go back to trot. Repeat this exercise, reducing the number of walk strides each time, until finally you do only one stride of walk before going back to trot.

EXERCISE 3

Once the horse is confirmed in shoulder-in (see page 191), you can combine it with transitions. Using the long side of the arena (or, in a field, a fence or hedge), ride a small circle at one end. As you come out of the circle, ask for several strides of shoulder-in. From shoulder-in, ask for a transition to trot or canter.

Lateral work

Many people think of lateral work as something that is only needed for dressage competitions, or as something that is too difficult for the average horse and rider. In fact lateral work should be an essential part of the training of any horse. Basic lateral work is not difficult as long as we understand what we are trying to achieve and as long as we do not ask too much of the horse too soon.

Note I have not included leg yielding in this section, even though it is usually the first (and often the only) experience many riders will have had of lateral work. I have omitted it because, although it is useful for introducing horse and rider to the idea of moving sideways as well as forwards, it does little to actually improve the horse, since it does nothing to encourage him to flex his hocks and step under himself. There are other exercises, such as the shoulder-in, which are far more beneficial in that respect.

Shoulder-in

This is the king of exercises, developed by the great de la Guérinière from earlier, similar, exercises.

The great beauty of the shoulder-in is that, unlike some of the other lateral exercises such as the half-pass, the horse can be introduced to it at a relatively early stage in his training. Once he can bend properly on a circle, you can start to use the shoulder-in.

When the shoulder-in is executed correctly, the inside foreleg crosses over the outside foreleg, and the inside hind leg crosses in front of the outside hind leg. The exercise can be ridden on four tracks (as it is at the Spanish Riding School and by many classical trainers) or on three tracks (as it is in modern dressage competition). Both are technically correct but for our purposes the three-track shoulder-in, being less demanding, will be of more use.

In the classical four-track shoulder-in the horse's forehand is brought in so that the forelegs follow tracks separate from those of the hind legs. In the three-track shoulder-in the inside foreleg follows a separate track from the hind legs but the outside foreleg follows the same track as the inside hind leg (see Fig. 12.5).

Regardless of whether the horse is travelling on three or four tracks, he must move more forwards than sideways. If the exercise is carried out with very little bend in the body it is known as a **shoulder-fore** (see Fig. 12.6), which is especially good for introducing the horse to the shoulder-in proper (see photograph on p. 192).

The benefits of shoulder-in are:

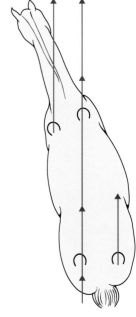

Fig. 12.5 The king of exercises: the shoulder-in.

- It prepares the horse to take more weight on the hind legs, because with each step he must carry his inside hind leg under his body and cross it over the outside hind leg, which he can only do by flexing the joints of the inside hind limb.

- Because the hind legs take more weight, the shoulders are freed, allowing the forelegs greater freedom of movement.

- Since the horse must cross both the fore and hind legs over one another, he acquires greater agility in all legs, and both shoulders are suppled.

- This increased suppleness helps to straighten the horse.

Fig. 12.6 The shoulder-fore, where the horse's body is not as bent as in the shoulder-in proper, is a good introduction to the exercise *(from* Academic Equitation, *by General Decarpentry)*

RIGHT Nivalis's first-ever shoulder-in exercise. This is really more of a shoulder-fore, as there is insufficient bend in his body. However, this is a creditable first attempt by a novice horse *(L. Skipper)*

The aids for riding a shoulder-in are virtually the same as those for riding a circle. Just as the horse starts to turn off the track to begin the circle, make a half-halt and encourage the horse to move sideways with a gentle nudge of your inside leg, fractionally behind the girth.

Before riding the shoulder-in, try walking through the exercise yourself on the ground, moving sideways as well as forwards, just as you are asking the horse to do. Then, when you actually come to ride the exercise, try to reproduce the sensations you felt when you walked through it on the ground. In other words, you put yourself into the shoulder-in position on top of the horse. If you can do this effectively, your horse will simply mirror your actions.

Start the exercise by riding a small circle – the smallest your horse can manage comfortably without stiffening – at one end of the arena or training area. Then, as you return to the outside track, imagine you are about to

ride another circle, but instead of coming off the track again, continue up the long side (or along the fence or hedge), keeping the bend of the horse as if he were still on the circle. Only ask for a couple of strides to begin with, then ride another circle and continue straight up the long side.

Some horses find this exercise difficult, some find it easy. Ask for only a little at a time; one or two good steps of shoulder-in are worth a dozen poor or inadequate ones. As soon as your horse responds, make a big fuss of him.

Once he is comfortable with the shoulder-in, you can go on to invent all kinds of patterns (see, for example, Fig. 12.7).

Initially, introduce the shoulder-in at a walk. Although the exercise is eventually more beneficial in trot, where there is more impulsion, the walk gives both horse and rider more time to sort themselves out. Progress to shoulder-in at a trot once the horse is comfortable with the exercise (and yes, you can ride it in rising trot).

American classical trainer Paul Belasik demonstrates a true three-track shoulder-in *(from* Dressage for the 21st Century, *by Paul Belasik, J. A. Allen 2002) (Karl Leck)*

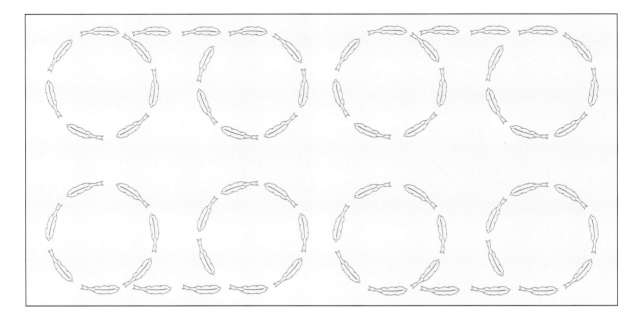

Fig. 12.7 Shoulder-in: ride a small circle, and as you return to the track, continue up the track in shoulder-in for a few steps, then ride another small circle. This exercise can be repeated anywhere in the schooling area (figures not shown to scale)

Note This is one exercise where, certainly to begin with, you really need a knowledgeable pair of eyes on the ground, to tell you whether the shoulder-in is correct.

Turn on the haunches

Another extremely useful exercise once the horse is capable of some degree of engagement, is the turn on the haunches, carried out in walk. This exercise helps to counteract stiffness because increased flexion to the inside means a corresponding stretching of the outside of the horse's body. It also helps the horse to take more weight on his hind legs.

In the turn on the haunches (often referred to as a 'quarter turn'), the horse pivots around his inside hind foot which does not, however, stay 'rooted' to the ground but takes a small step, either returning to the same spot or slightly in front of it, each time it leaves the ground. The outside hind foot, and the two forefeet, move around the inside hind leg, the hind foot with small steps, and the two forefeet with larger steps, which carry the horse's forehand round in a 90 degree turn. Ideally this should take no more than two or three steps.

To begin with, ride the turn on the haunches from a small circle. As you return to the track, ride straight forward for a few steps, keeping the horse slightly flexed to the inside. As you reach the point where you want to turn, make a half-halt, at the same time moving your inside seatbone forward a fraction; this shifts your weight slightly in the direction of the turn. This invites the horse to move in that direction, as he will want to step under your weight in order to retain his balance (remember the concept of influencing the horse's natural balance and righting reactions, mentioned on page 146). The inside hand opens slightly to indicate the turn, while the outside hand maintains a polite yet positive contact. The outside hand may move towards the withers but should never cross over them; the rein lies against the horse's neck, encouraging him to move round in the new direction. Do not be tempted to pull the horse around with the reins, as this will do nothing to help him to engage his hind legs. It is the outside leg which asks the horse to move into the turn; the knee and thigh, together with the lower leg acting slightly behind the girth, gently nudge the horse round. The inside leg acts as the supporting pillar around which the horse turns.

This exercise is only beneficial if executed properly. Forward momentum must be maintained, even though the horse is stepping sideways more than forwards. Once the horse can make the turn correctly, you can work it into your schooling patterns (see Figs. 12.8 and 12.9).

Work hard on improving the transitions, the lateral work and the pole exercises, and you will be surprised by how quickly you will see an improvement, not only in the horse's ability to collect himself, but in his overall gaits.

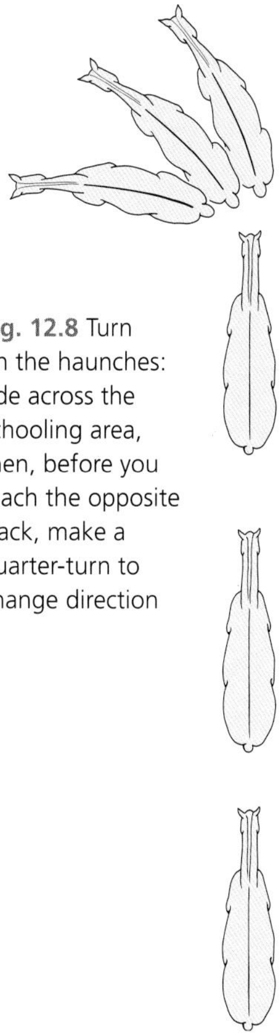

Fig. 12.8 Turn on the haunches: ride across the schooling area, then, before you reach the opposite track, make a quarter-turn to change direction

Fig. 12.9 Turn on the haunches: you can use these turns to change direction in a series of serpentine loops

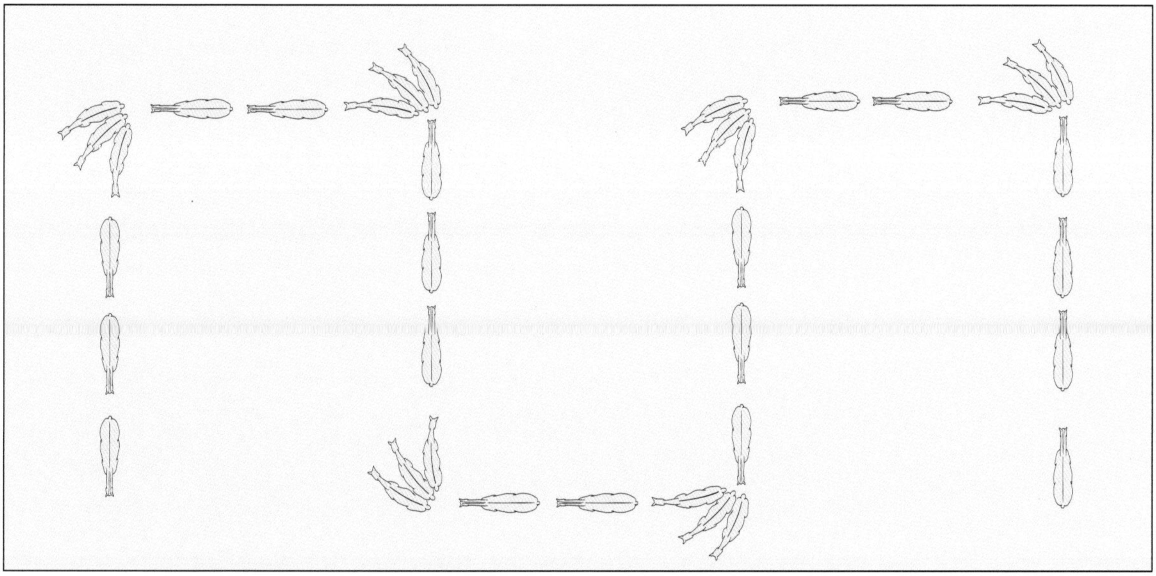

CHAPTER THIRTEEN

Glowing with health

THE OLD SAYING, 'beauty is only skin deep' is only partly true. With horses, a superficial gloss can certainly be achieved by dint of much grooming and application of products designed to add shine to the coat and hair, as well as by clever presentation (in show horses, often enhanced – if that is the right word – by specially designed equine make-up). However, none of these techniques and products can achieve that appearance of radiant good health, both physical and mental, which can make the less obviously glamorous horse appear truly beautiful.

We have seen how correct training will build up muscles and help the horse to carry himself in a way that not only enables him to work more easily, but makes him appear more elegant and shapely. To be fully effective, this training must be backed up by good nutrition and health care, mental welfare being one of the most important aspects of the latter. This means looking critically at the way in which your horse is kept; for instance, does he have enough time out in the field to relax and play with other horses, as well as fulfilling his need to graze and move around? Does he have the companionship of at least one other horse with whom he gets on well? Failing that, does he have the company of an animal of another species, such as a goat or a sheep, and can you give him enough quality time with you (other than while he is working)?[1]

Following on from this, what about your training methods? Are they appropriate for this particular horse? Too many people fail to look on their

---

1 What constitutes 'enough' of any of these things depends very much on the individual horse. For a fuller account of the kind of things that matter to horses, see my earlier book *Inside Your Horse's Mind,* and *Equine Welfare* by Dr Marthe Kiley-Worthington, J. A. Allen, 1998.

horse as an *individual* and try to apply training methods and techniques rigidly, without making allowances for that individuality and its quirks and variations (see Chapter 14, Know Thy Horse).

Tension and stress

Stress is an ill-defined word which is often misused. It means literally mental, physical or emotional strain or tension. Organisms need some degree of stress in order to function properly. Indeed, the whole process of conditioning horses for athletic activities involves some stress, as the resulting changes to the tissues involve an element of damage and subsequent repair. However, when the amount of stress becomes too great for the organism to cope with, it starts to break down. In horses, the most obvious evidence of this is when the horse goes lame, or develops muscle spasms. But mental stress can be just as destructive to horses as physical lameness or injury. If the horse does not understand what is being asked of him, or if he is asked to perform in a way for which he is unprepared, he may still do his best to comply, but if this situation goes on for too long he may develop behavioural problems. The same applies to horses who are harshly ridden, or whose trainers and riders do not allow them sufficient time to relax either at the start of, or during, training sessions. The resulting tension can not only make the training much more difficult than it needs to be, it may actually cause physical as well as mental damage. A tight, tense horse cannot function properly. Fortunately, if tension is the enemy, we can help to prevent it before it occurs, or alleviate it as soon as it appears.

Where tightness in the muscles is a problem, you will need to consider whether it stems from physical discomfort or from inappropriate management. Here, the profiles you built up earlier will help you to decide where the problem lies and what action is necessary. The stretching exercises and warm-up routines described in Chapters 4, 5 and 12 will help to alleviate this unwanted tension.[2]

Massage

Massage is a great therapeutic medium. Some of the methods used are extremely ancient, while others are very modern. All, however, make use of the same kind of basic techniques.

---

2 Tension in *some* muscles is necessary, as explained in Chapters 5, 8 and 12. A horse completely free from muscular tension would be flat out on the ground!

Stroking, which is the basic relaxation technique, uses very light pressure applied with the tips of the fingers or the palms of the hands. The direction of the stroke should be the same as the lie of the coat hair, and preferably along the length of the muscles. The masseur uses their body weight to apply pressure, pushing the hands away from them and then removing the pressure as the hands move back to begin the next stroke.

Effleurage is a gliding movement with the hand in full contact, making use of the fingers and the palm. With this technique there is slightly more pressure than with the simple stroke. Each effleurage stroke should be carried out with an even pressure, in a slow rhythm (1–2 strokes per second). It can be used as a general stimulant, or to soothe the horse and enhance circulation.

Some other basic massage techniques are: **kneading**, also used to help circulation; **muscle squeezing**, for relaxing tense muscles; **skin rolling**, to help maintain elasticity of the skin; and **pounding** (not as fearsome as it sounds, when applied properly).

In order to carry these out safely you should have some basic knowledge and understanding of the principles, otherwise you may hurt the horse and damage underlying tissues. However, the average, intelligent horse owner is quite capable of learning sufficient about basic massage techniques to be able to use them safely and wisely to benefit their horse.[3] If they are carried out properly, most horses appear to enjoy such massage sessions.

In fact, one of the most effective massage techniques used to be commonplace in almost every stable, although it seems to have fallen out of use in recent years. This is the old practice of 'wisping'. This is a vigorous form of massage using a pad or 'wisp', formerly of hay or straw, which assists in toning up muscles, stimulates the blood supply to the skin, and helps bring a shine to the coat. The wisp is dampened slightly and brought down with a bang in the direction of the lie of the horse's coat. The main areas to benefit are the sides of the neck, the quarters and thighs (avoid bony projections and the loins). Most horses appear to enjoy being wisped, if it is done properly. The old advice, to make a wisp by twisting a rope out of hay or straw, is no longer practical, as modern cutting and harvesting techniques mean that most hay and straw is chopped too short for making wisps. However, the ready-made wisping pads you can buy, usually of suede stuffed with wool, are equally effective and, properly cared for, will withstand years of vigorous use. At the time of writing I have one that has been in continuous use for over eleven years, and it is still in good condition!

3 An excellent place to start is with Mary Bromiley's *Massage for Horses* (Threshold Picture Guide No. 38), Kenilworth Press, 1996

One aspect of massage therapy which is often overlooked is that which stimulates the reflexes which govern the horse's use of his 'ring of muscles', i.e. the belly lifts described on page 90. This type of therapy is similar to the way in which a rider's legs stimulate these reflexes, but with the advantage that the horse does not also have to cope with the weight of a rider.

Grooming

Even ordinary grooming can be considered a form of massage. If you have ever watched films or TV programmes about feral or free-ranging horses (or been fortunate enough to observe them in their natural setting), you may have been struck by how shiny and well-kept their coats appear. Yet most of these horses have never been touched by human hands; their grooms are other horses belonging to the same group.

Have you ever really observed two horses grooming each other? They are surprisingly vigorous, using their teeth and lips to remove accumulated dirt, dead skin and loose hair. They use their mobile muzzles with an

ABOVE This strapping pad, belonging to the author, has been in constant use for more than eleven years (*L. Skipper*)

Many horses find grooming both relaxing and stimulating. Nivalis shows by his lowered head and neck that he is enjoying this grooming session! This is also a good way to encourage the horse to stretch his topline (*L. Skipper*)

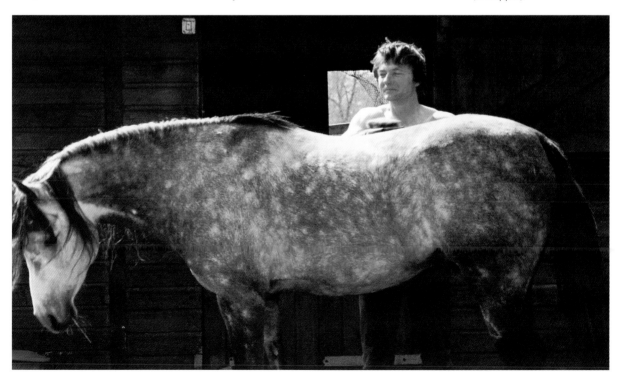

Kiri (RIGHT) and her daughter Imzadi (BELOW) keep their coats clean and shining by mutual grooming when turned out together
(L. Skipper)

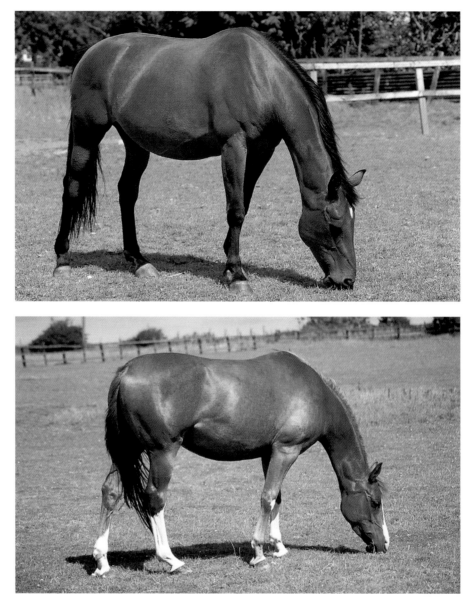

energetic, side-to-side action to massage the skin and underlying muscle, stimulating the circulation and improving muscle tone as they do so.

Sometimes these sessions are quite brief, lasting only a few minutes, but sometimes two horses who are very close emotionally will prolong their mutual grooming sessions to ten or fifteen minutes or, in the case of two of our own horses, as much as twenty minutes at a time. This is because mutual grooming is one of the most important social activities for horses, as it is for many other species: apes, monkeys and cats (both wild and domestic) for example.

Mutual grooming is an extremely important aspect of equine social life. Here, Zareeba grooms with his girlfriend Roxzella, removing dead skin, loose dirt and hairs, and stimulating the skin (*L. Skipper*)

As well as serving the obvious purpose of keeping the coat clean, mutual grooming, because of the very great degree of intimacy involved, helps to establish and strengthen bonds of attachment. The latter are extremely important in equine society, as they help to strengthen the cohesion of the group, whose survival largely depends on its stability.

So, if we approach grooming in the right way, we can use it as a very effective means of creating a bond with our horses, as well as contributing to their physical wellbeing. If you and your horse have established mutual trust, you can make this a two-way process, and allow your horse to reciprocate by grooming *you*. Many people already do this, but if you have not tried it before, be warned: horses can be surprisingly rough and, although a well-mannered horse is unlikely to hurt you deliberately, you could end up with a few bruises! You might even be bitten, or at least nipped, if the horse concerned has never learned appropriate behaviour, or has a tendency to bite or nip anyway, so be careful in your choice of a grooming partner. If (like me) you do not mind being roughed up a little by an equine friend (or having your clothes mistreated), then you may find the experience of mutual grooming with your horse a very satisfying one – but proceed with caution!

If your horse can be trusted not to nip, you can indulge in mutual grooming with him: the author with Zareeba (*Brian Skipper*)

Many horses dislike being groomed with a brush, but will tolerate, and even enjoy, being groomed by human fingers.[4] Perhaps because they find it similar to being groomed by an equine companion, the action of the fingers appears to stimulate and relax them at the same time. Grooming like this can be an excellent opportunity to check the state of the horse's musculature. You will need to learn how to tell the difference between tension and muscle tone, between slackness and relaxation, and what degree of muscle tone is normal for a particular horse. This is something which only comes with experience and practice; see if you can try this with as many different horses as possible (but be careful when dealing with horses you do not know, and always ask the owner's permission, explaining to them what you want to do and why).

Variations on a theme

There are numerous very effective variations on basic massage techniques referred to above. **Ttouch**, designed to reduce stress and encourage the horse to relax, was developed by Linda Tellington-Jones. It improves the horse's awareness of his own body, and by doing so increases his athletic ability. Ttouch involves touching the horse in a series of circular movements, using varying degrees of pressure and hand positions. The basic Ttouch movement is a circular one called the Clouded Leopard (all the movements have fanciful names, which make them easier to remember). The toucher places the left hand lightly on the horse, and holding the fingers of the right hand in a lightly curved position, uses the latter to push the horse's skin around in a circle and a quarter, followed by a release. The thumb is used to steady the fingers. This is the foundation for the many different forms of Ttouch. This technique has proved highly effective, and can be carried out by anyone willing to study it.[5]

Shiatsu (literally, 'finger pressure' in Japanese) is similar in many ways to acupuncture, except that instead of needles it uses the pressure of the hands and fingers. Shiatsu seeks to rebalance the body's energy by touching specific parts of the body. According to the principles behind the technique, these parts are connected by channels, or meridians, corresponding to the bodily functions, such as the heart, bladder, kidneys etc.

Like Ttouch, shiatsu is a two-handed technique. One hand supports,

4 In the Near and Middle East, this is the traditional form of grooming.

5 A good introduction to this method may be found in Linda Tellington-Jones's book, *Getting in Touch with Horses,* Kenilworth Press 1995 (paperback edition 1998).

while the other works along the meridian, applying a vertical pressure which alternately sinks in, releases, then sinks in again. Either finger-tip pressure or palm pressure may be used. Although it is not clear how this process works, horses respond very positively to it.[6] People using the technique report that their horses have become more relaxed and easier to handle.

Some excellent books on massage and related subjects (including stretching exercises) are listed under Recommended Reading.

After working my horses, especially in summer, I like to give them a stimulating, refreshing body wash. I sometimes use a proprietary wash, such as Vet Lin by Absorbine, the same company's RefreshMint, or Effol's Horse Refreshment. Sometimes I make up my own wash by adding seven to ten drops of lavender oil to a small quantity of boiling water, then adding cold water until the wash is lukewarm. Most horses enjoy this and find the scent soothing and relaxing. Do not use undiluted essential oils directly on the horse's skin, as they may cause irritation. Always use them well diluted with water.

Interior wellbeing

While grooming and massage will certainly improve the state of a horse's skin and coat, a shining coat is as much a reflection of the horse's *interior* state as it is of its exterior condition. The coats of bays and chestnuts will often show dappling as a result of this overall wellbeing, or the coat may take on a much richer colour than normal. Look at the photograph of Cleveland Bay X Thoroughbred mare Kiri (page 204). This was taken when she was in foal, and her glowing good health is apparent in the richness and shine of her coat, which in summer is normally a light bay, almost paling to dun.

Good nutrition, of course, plays a major part in creating this healthy state. All responsible horse owners are familiar with the Golden Rules of feeding:

- Feed little and often

- Feed according to work

Assessing your horse's precise requirements can be difficult, as there are so many variables to take into account, such as individual body type (see the

---

6 See *Shiatsu Therapy for Horses* by Pamela Hannay, J. A. Allen, 2002. See also Appendix II for details of the Shiatsu Society.

Cleveland Bay X TB mare Kiri, here shown when she was in foal, and positively glowing with health *(L. Skipper)*

section on Condition later in this chapter), the kind of forage, grazing etc. available, the type and duration of your horse's normal exercise, and many other factors. For this reason a detailed discussion of equine nutrition is beyond the scope of this book. If you want to make an accurate assessment of your horse's individual requirements, you should consult an equine nutritionist. All the major feed companies employ these, and most have a Helpline for you to contact for advice. The advice given may (understandably) tend to be biased in favour of the company's own products, but in general you can expect good, sound advice.

In particular they can advise you whether your horse's diet requires supplementation. Some pastures, for instance, are deficient in certain essential minerals and trace elements. In some cases these deficiencies may create actual health problems, or in other cases the effects may be purely cosmetic. For example, certain deficiencies may lead to loss of skin pigmentation around the eyes; my Arabian gelding Zareeba is prone to this. The pigmentation does return, depending on the type of forage he is being fed, but sometimes supplementation is required; I have found seaweed extract to be very effective in the case of this horse. However, do not be tempted to

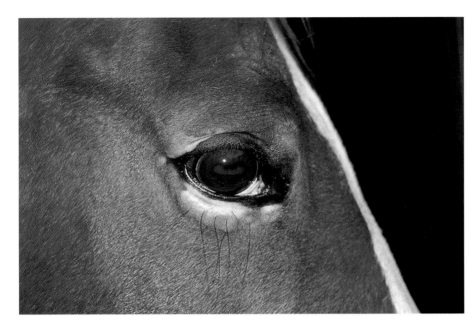

Zareeba periodically suffers some loss of skin pigment around the eyes; the pigmentation eventually returns (L. Skipper)

stuff your horse full of supplements indiscriminately; this can cause more harm than good. This is especially true if you are feeding supplements which contain large quantities of certain trace elements and minerals; too much zinc in the diet, for example, will 'lock up' any copper present in the feed or forage, and may result in a copper deficiency. Always consult your vet, together with a nutritionist, if you think your horse may benefit from diet supplementation.

The same caution applies to herbs. Many people assume that because herbs are 'natural', they must therefore be harmless, and that it is safe to feed them in large quantities. Nothing could be further from the truth! Many herbs which are beneficial in small or moderate quantities can be toxic or even fatal in large enough doses, so always use a proprietary brand of herbal supplement, and follow the instructions regarding feeding.

A well-balanced diet should provide everything your horse needs for his coat to have that shine which comes from inner wellbeing. However, if you want to enhance it still further (and always bearing in mind the warnings given above), you can add oils such as vegetable oil, cod liver oil, or soya bean oil to the diet. However, these should not form more than about 0.5 per cent of the overall diet, as they are rich in energy. Other good coat conditioners are seaweed extract and fenugreek seeds (again, use proprietary brands and feed according to instructions).

Good nutrition, then, can improve the horse's overall looks to a remarkable degree – remember the transformation of Elmo, described in Chapter 1. However, also remember that this transformation was due in part to judicious exercise on the lunge to build up Elmo's muscles. Avoid the temptation to build up a false topline by overfeeding; the result will be a fat horse with limited athletic ability.

Condition

How do we decide what is an acceptable weight for a horse? As with humans, much depends on the individual horse. Advice given to humans often assumes an ideal weight that will be applicable to all humans of the same height and sex. Yet this is not so; at my supposed ideal weight I look severely undernourished, whereas at *his* ideal weight my husband would be too fat for his body type. The latter is the clue: body type varies, and this is increasingly been taken into account in publications giving advice on health matters. Even here, though, people do not fall into neat categories; many people may fall between two different body types, and so their 'ideal weight' will differ from both.

The same applies to horses. We might say, for instance, that a horse of 152 cm (15 hh) should weigh X kilograms, but what kind of horse are we talking about? Do we mean a sturdy native cross, or are we referring to an ethereal Thoroughbred? Even within a breed, type can vary enormously while staying within the acceptable parameters for that breed. Our four pure-bred Arabians, for example, vary considerably in type, from the dainty (Nivalis) to the chunky (Zareeba). With a difference in height of only 2.6 cm (1 in), Nivalis's 'ideal weight' will differ considerably from Zareeba's!

As long as we recognize that differing types will have varying 'ideal weights', we can still determine what is more or less correct for our horses. We do this by using a combination of weight measurement and what is usually referred to as 'condition scoring'.

The most accurate method of weighing horses is to use a weighbridge. However, access to these is not always readily available, so we can make do with a less accurate but still perfectly acceptable substitute: a weigh-tape. These are generally available from the larger tack shops and mail-order specialists, and their use is extremely simple; reliable makes come with instructions.

Using a condition-scoring system is not quite so straightforward, because this is a somewhat subjective measurement. Some books and magazine articles give a simple diagram showing the shape of a horse's back and hindquarters at varying levels of the condition-scoring system being used. The problem with these is that they are usually rather over-simplified, and the diagrams themselves can be misleading. For instance, in most of these diagrams a horse classed as 'normal' would, if encountered in real life, be severely undermuscled along the back and over the hindquarters! The classical Greeks and Romans knew what they were doing when they chose what they called 'double-spined' horses (this referred to the musculature on either side of the spine); riding horses (as opposed to racehorses) need plenty of musculature and padding in those areas.

However, we can still use a condition-scoring system to assess our horses reasonably accurately. Table 9 gives such a system.

Table 9 Condition score for horses [7]

Score	Condition	Description
1	Poor	Very emaciated. Bone structure very prominent, especially spinous processes, ribs, hips, pelvis etc. No apparent fatty tissues.
2	Very thin	Emaciated. Neck structures, withers and shoulder prominent. Some fat covering over base of spinous processes, but the latter are still prominent, as are the ribs, hips, pelvis etc. Transverse processes of lumbar vertebrae can still be felt.
3	Thin	Neck thin. Spinous processes and ribs can still be easily seen; some fat cover on ribs. Transverse processes of lumbar region can no longer be felt. Fat covering about halfway up spinous processes; pelvis still clearly defined.
4	Moderately thin	Spine still visible, but individual vertebrae cannot be seen. Withers, shoulder and neck lean but not too thin. Ribs can just be seen.
5	Moderate	Back and loin area relatively level. Ribs cannot be seen, but may be easily felt. Withers rounded over spinous processes; neck and shoulders join body smoothly. Fat around tailhead, starting to feel spongy.
6	Moderate to fleshy	Neck, shoulder and withers more filled-out. Some fat along sides of withers, behind shoulders, and along the neck. Fat over ribs and tailhead feels spongy. Slight crease along spine.
7	Fleshy	Increased fat along neck, withers and behind shoulders. Space between ribs filling up with fat, although individual ribs can still be felt. Noticeable crease down back; fat around tailhead soft.
8	Fat	Neck noticeably thickened and 'cresty'. Crease down back now prominent; ribs cannot be easily felt. Fat deposits along withers, behind shoulder, and inner buttocks.
9	Extremely fat	Neck, withers, shoulder, inner buttocks and tailhead bulging with fat. Patchy fat over ribs; crease down back now very prominent.

7 Adapted from Hayes, *Veterinary Notes For Horse Owners (Revised edition)*, Stanley Paul, 1987, p.585, and Henneke, DR. Potter, GD. Krieder, JL. 'A condition score relationship to body fat content in mares during gestation and lactation.' In: *Proceedings of the 7th Equine Nutrition and Physiology Symposium*, Warrenton, VA. 1981, p 105.

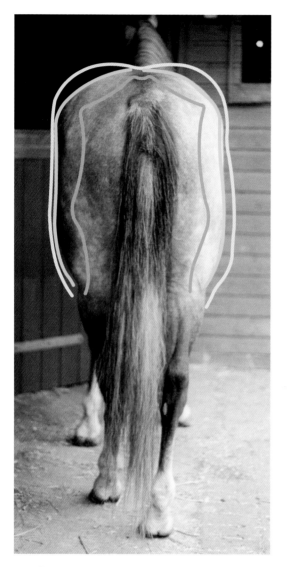

Condition score – contrasting extremes with a moderate condition outline showing good muscle development in the hindquarters.

very fat ··········· moderate ——— very poor ▬▬▬

Using a condition score can help you to maintain your horse's weight at the right level

Most horses will probably fall into categories 4, 5 or 6, with some overlap in certain cases, and this is fine. However, if your horse comes into category 3 or 7, you should take action to build your horse up or slim him down; if he comes into any of categories 1, 2, 8 or 9, there is a serious health problem which needs to be addressed very quickly!

Be aware that some horses may appear to have a fat belly, when in fact they are simply lacking in abdominal muscle tone, which makes the belly sag. This usually goes with a lack of topline development. If your horse has this problem, check his diet (and his teeth, to make sure he can chew his food properly), and start to build up his muscle tone by means of the conditioning processes described throughout this book.

The holistic approach

I have deliberately not used the term 'holistic' so far because for some people it conjures up a picture of rather airy-fairy New-Age-type alternative therapies. This is a great pity, because many so-called 'alternative' therapies do in fact appear to be highly effective and should be regarded as 'complementary' rather than 'alternative'. As for the term 'holistic', this is nothing more or less than a way of looking at the complete organism and how its various parts interact. Anyone seeking a greater understanding of this could not do better than to contact a holistic vet (see Appendix II).

If we pay attention to every aspect of our horse's care and training – in other words, if we are 'holistic' in our approach – then I see no reason why he should not become truly beautiful, both inside and out.

CHAPTER FOURTEEN

Know thy horse

I F YOU FOLLOWED THE advice given in Chapter 2, and created a personality and behaviour profile for your horse, you should by now have a pretty good idea of how he responds in a wide variety of situations. Even if you have not yet created such a profile, if you have had your horse for some time you may already have a good deal of insight into his character. If not, then now is the time to start developing that insight. This is important, because one of the greatest barriers to developing horses' potential is a failure to recognize that they are all – no matter how similar their breeding or upbringing – *individuals*.

One idea popular at the moment is that certain personality traits are determined by genetic inheritance. People who believe this fall into the trap of thinking of traits of temperament or personality as *things,* rather than concepts which help us to understand why individuals think and behave as they do. To describe someone (whether human or equine) as having, say, a bold temperament is not like saying they have red (or chestnut) hair; a *bold* temperament is not an observable, measurable trait, it is a description.

An animal (and this includes humans) may have certain general tendencies or qualities which are inborn, but an animal's temperament, as well as its overall personality, is shaped by a very complex interaction of internal and external influences. *Personality* (including temperament) is therefore the sum of those qualities with which the animal was born, together with its lifetime experiences. The innate qualities can be affected, shaped, developed or suppressed by those experiences; this is why, from the moment they are born, the ways in which horses are handled can have such a profound effect on their later development.

No matter how much alike they may appear, every horse is a unique individual: Trakehners H G Flambe and H G Fresco *(Holme Park Stud)*

We cannot know, for example, how many of the world's greatest horses would have achieved what they did had they been raised and trained in different circumstances. I do not mean to imply that such horses were not exceptional in themselves, but beyond doubt their abilities were nurtured and allowed expression by the conditions of their upbringing, training and the manner in which they were ridden.

Some of the greatest horses have been difficult and/or complex characters, needing great tact and expertise to bring out the best in them. Would the wayward and headstrong Murphy Himself be remembered as one of the greatest three-day-event horses, if he had not first of all fallen into the hands of Ginny Elliott, and then gone from Ginny to Ian Stark? What

How foals are handled right from the start affects their entire psychological development: Arabian mare Tiff (Mikenah), shown here as a four-day-old foal with breeder Sara Debnam *(Lynn Debnam)*

BELOW This foal is confident yet well-mannered with humans: Nivalis's daughter Foxton Velvet with her human friend Lorraine *(L. Skipper)*

about those splendid dressage stars, Ahlerich and Rembrandt, neither of them easy characters – would either of them have been able to fulfil their potential without Reiner Klimke or Nicole Uphoff-Becker? And what about Halla, the showjumping star of the 1956 Olympics? Halla was considered crazy, and virtually unrideable, but Hans-Gunter Winkler thought other-

The wayward and brilliant Murphy Himself, with Ian Stark *(Elizabeth Furth)*

BELOW Not the easiest of horses: the great Rembrandt with Nicole Uphoff at the 1992 Olympic Games *(Elizabeth Furth)*

wise, and he and Halla went on to clinch the team gold medal for Germany, as well as winning the individual gold medal. I could give countless other examples, in every sphere of equestrian activity.

The key to the success of such partnerships lies not only in the natural talent of all those concerned, but in the fact that all the riders mentioned above tailored their management and training methods to the individual characters of their horses. Yet a great deal of the literature concerning the behaviour, management and training of horses tends to give the impression that all horses will behave in the same manner, with little if any variation. The advice given by all too many trainers and instructors, as well as the training given to those wishing to obtain recognized equestrian qualifications, too often appears to assume that the same methods must be used, regardless of the horse's individual character traits.

Failure is generally held to be the result of the horse's inadequacies, rather than of methods unsuited to that particular horse. The assumption also seems to be that horses should learn specific things within a specific time frame, when in fact the best trainers will always make allowances for different rates of learning in different horses.

The classical principles of training do not change from horse to horse, but when it comes to the actual method used, this must vary according to the individual horse. As long as you are not asking the horse to do something he is physically or mentally unprepared for, you can make up your own routines to suit your horse. For example, some horses benefit from being schooled every day, when a couple of times a week might be adequate for others. Some might even need a couple of sessions a day, broken up into shorter periods. Some need a good spell of riding in, when others might only need a few minutes of warming up first. With some horses, certain exercises have to come before others, and so on. One horse may need to be loosened up in canter before you start trot work, where another might find canter easier after doing some work in trot, and so forth.

Thinking of horses as individuals gives us greater flexibility in how we handle them. Instead of using set procedures to deal with problems, we can instead 'read' the individual and use our knowledge of their character to decide what approach to take.

Taking time to observe your horse and learn about all his little quirks of character can help tremendously when we come to deal with situations where a horse behaves in a manner that is out of character. If you have not had your horse all his life (as many – perhaps most – people will not have done), it helps enormously if you can find out as much as possible of his past history. I know this is not always easy, and in many cases may be impossible; even so, try to find out whatever you can, because knowing about a horse's past experiences can make all the difference when working out how to deal with problems.

When we come up against difficulties in training – as we inevitably will – one thing to remember is that horses seldom set out to be difficult for the sake of it. They are mentally geared towards co-operation rather than conflict. In wild or free-ranging situations, they co-operate as a group, because that is the only way to ensure their survival, whereas conflict tends to destroy the integrity of a group.

This strongly ingrained inclination towards co-operation means that horses seldom set out to be bloody-minded for the sake of it (although some seem to do so!). We on the other hand often provoke conflict by our refusal to see the horse's point of view.

You must establish respect, but this has nothing to do with domination, or showing anyone 'who's boss'. It has instead to do with mutual understanding and establishing a partnership, in which one party holds the controlling interest, but the other still has a voice. This means being firm but fair; never arbitrary, yet consistent without rigidity; flexible without being lax, and taking the trouble to listen to your horse.

You and the horse form a group, so it is in his interest to co-operate with you. If he does not, it may be because he cannot. Perhaps he does not understand what you want; perhaps he is confused or emotionally upset. Maybe he is physically incapable of doing as you ask. It may be that he has not yet recognized you as the other member of his group. In this case you may need to use the kind of technique made famous by Monty Roberts, known as 'join-up'.[1] It is the trainer's responsibility to take stock of possible causes, and decide on the correct course of action.

If you feel you have really come up against an intractable character, you may need to seek advice from a trainer who specializes in reforming truly difficult horses (see Appendix II)

Give your horse the benefit of the doubt before you assume he is 'trying it on'; deception does not come easily to horses. That is not to say that they are incapable of deception;[2] individuals can certainly fool us on occasion.[3] In general, though, it probably does not occur to most of them even to try. It can certainly be very difficult, sometimes, to know whether a horse

---

1 The best way to learn how to do this is by attending demonstrations and seminars. See Appendix II. See also Kelly Marks's excellent little book, *Creating A Bond With Your Horse*, J. A. Allen, 2000.

2 Some behavioural scientists maintain that only humans and certain primates are capable of deception, but this is based on a number of prior assumptions which, as we learn more about animal behaviour, are increasingly being challenged.

3 See Chapter 9 of *Inside Your Horse's Mind*.

cannot do something that we ask of him, or whether he just does not *want* to do it. There are times when we must be firm, when we must insist that the horse takes notice of us even though he might not feel like doing so. But the art lies in knowing *when* to do this, and in knowing just how much we can insist on before we provoke resistance, and a wearisome battle of wills. This is something that, again, can only be learned by really getting to know your horse and what makes him tick, as well as by being flexible in your outlook. So when we are faced with problems, we have to look at all possibilities, and that includes the horse's own character and temperament.

Ultimately, how you approach training and handling is up to you. The more knowledge you have gained about your particular horse's personality, the greater your range of options in dealing with any problems, and the easier it will be for you to draw up a flexible training plan which takes account of changing needs and priorities.

Intelligent training can help horses learn how to learn. The more mental stimulus you give your horse, the more his capacity for learning and understanding will increase. As with all aspects of training, you must not push him too hard; you must learn to recognize what his limits are at *any particular time*. The thing to remember is that if you approach training in the right frame of mind, you can make a bright horse even brighter, and a seemingly dull horse blossom into a much more mentally alert individual.[4]

4 For a detailed examination of how horses learn, see *Inside Your Horse's Mind*, Chapters 11 and 16.

Imaginative training can make horses more intelligent: Nivalis with Brian (*L. Skipper*)

Note using straw bales for this kind of training is not generally recommended, as they are too unstable, and the horse could catch a foot in the baling twine

Above all, remember that horses, like humans, may have their off-days; they may get headaches, feel tired or just generally out of sorts. Younger horses may be teething (a process that can go on until they are five, or even six years old), which may make them reluctant to accept a bit, or go forward. Even of there are no outward signs of lameness, the horse may be feeling discomfort from an aching limb, a stiff neck or a sore back. Pain, fear and emotional distress may affect a horse's personality in many ways and we need to know what an individual horse's normal responses are in order to tell when he is indeed feeling below par.

Some days you will seem to make rapid progress and others you will feel as if you have taken a few steps back. So what? It happens. Do not get flustered, frustrated or despondent. Sort out any problems that *can* be sorted out, concentrate on the good things, and before you know it, nine times out of ten the problems will have disappeared. If they have not, and whatever you have tried has not worked, then try something else (always taking care not to compromise the correct principles of training).

In the last chapter I mentioned the holistic approach, which so many people are now exploring. In relation to what we do with horses, that means getting to know our horses as well as we possibly can – all their little quirks of character, their likes and dislikes, what is normal for them as far as health is concerned, what their usual behaviour is in as many situations as possible, how they respond to other horses, how they respond to humans – and most importantly, of course, to ourselves. In doing this it is

Like other horses (and humans), Nivalis has several sides to his character. He can be extremely sweet-natured (as here, with his friend Joanne)…

...or bad-tempered, as he is when Max the dog annoys him by trying to lick his nose (*L. Skipper*)

tempting to try to pigeon hole them, for example by saying that this horse is bold, that one timid, this one laid-back, that one flighty, this one even-tempered, that one bad-tempered etc. etc. Horses, like humans, can at times be any or even all of those things. One aspect may predominate at most times, but it is dangerous to assume that that is all there is to the horse. Know your horse; know the individual. Tailor the management and training to suit that individual, not the other way round. It may take up more time, but in the process, you will not only learn more about your horse, but also about yourself. And if that helps you to forge a better partnership with your horse, then surely the effort will be worthwhile.

Conclusion

Now we have come this far, what next? You may have been reassured by what you have read; your horse may have no major faults (or not enough to create real problems) and may be well suited to the kind of activities you want to pursue.

On the other hand, you may be somewhat discouraged to learn that your horse has more faults than you suspected and in some cases these may be severe enough to make a radical reassessment of your goals necessary.

If you have your heart set on competing in a specific discipline and it is apparent that the horse you have is going to need a lot of help in order to achieve your goal, you may need to decide whether this is really the horse for you. If, for example, you want to start competing now and it is going to take you several years, a lot of hard work and, possibly, outside assistance which may be expensive to obtain, before you can even think about competitions, then you may decide that your best course of action is to part with the horse you have, and look for one more suited to your immediate needs.

On the other hand, it may be that you simply do not feel you have the time, the necessary experience, patience, or facilities to undertake what may be a laborious course of training. Again, the decision to part company may well be a very sensible one; it is a decision that no-one else can make for you, and certainly no-one but you can decide whether it is the right one to make.

However, I would ask anyone in this situation to consider very carefully. The decision to enter into a partnership with another sentient being (and if you doubt that horses are sentient beings, please read my book, *Inside Your Horse's Mind*) is not one to be taken lightly. Having made that decision, parting company should not be taken lightly either. In some cases it may well be the best for all concerned, especially if there is a clash of temperaments, or if a rider is over-horsed; in such cases safety, and the wellbeing of both parties, have to be paramount considerations.

Certainly, we should not discard a horse simply because he has certain traits or features which may be inconvenient for us. That would be to treat him as an object, rather than a living creature with thoughts, needs and feelings of his own. Some horses seem resigned to being passed from one owner to the other as soon as they have outlived their usefulness in one particular 'home'. Some adapt to this better than others, and will continue to perform well in spite of the trauma of being uprooted every so many years. Nevertheless, I do believe that the best partnerships are those which are founded on lasting bonds of mutual respect and affection. Horses need such bonds in order to thrive; they are one of the most basic features of equine social life. My personal feeling is that we should only consider parting with a horse with whom we have already established such a bond, for truly compelling reasons. However, as I said above, such a decision is for the individual to make. All I would ask is that, whatever you decide, you make it only after long and careful consideration.

Perhaps you may need to re-evaluate your goals. Whatever these may be, how important is it to you to achieve them? I have had to re-evaluate mine several times, not through any fault of my horses, but because of personal injury or debility. Is competing that important to you? If so, why? Is it simply that you enjoy the atmosphere, the camaraderie (or, sometimes, the rivalry!), the challenge, or the simple fact of taking part? Or is winning your main goal? Asking yourself these questions will help you to decide what to do next.

Suppose the horse you have has shortcomings which mean that, even with careful training, you are unlikely to achieve the level of success you had hoped for. Is that the end of the world? Do you part with that horse in the hope that if you buy a 'better' horse, this will bring success? (I hope that what you have read in these pages will have given you the answer to this question.) Or do you try instead to see what you *can* achieve with your horse?

If you decide on the latter course, you may find (indeed, I hope you will) that you become so fascinated with the *process* of training, and watching your horse's capabilities expand and grow, that you will tend to forget about specific goals. Instead you may find yourself exploring new possibilities that are revealed as the work progresses.

For most of us, in the western world at least, riding horses is no longer a matter of daily necessity, or of life and death, as it used to be for so many people. We ride instead for pleasure, for *fun*. Yet all too often we tend to forget this in our desire for measurable achievements. When I started riding again after a long break, forced on me by the effects of old injuries, I was initially so anxious about picking up our abandoned training programme that my anxiety and resulting tension transmitted themselves to my responsive little horse. However, all that tension disappeared once I forgot about goals, and started to relax and enjoy myself. This, I thought, is what it is really all about: a harmonious partnership with a much-loved companion. From the way he responded, I think Zareeba agreed with me!

To be able to work with a creature so powerful, and yet so trainable and co-operative as the horse, is a wonderful experience. This process of training – watching them learn, grow stronger and more beautiful, and exulting in their athletic prowess – to me, is not a chore, but a great privilege. I hope you will find it so, too.

Appendix I
Kruger: a brief analysis

Registered name: Count Kruger
Registered with the Arab Horse Society as part-bred Arab (50%)
Warmblood X Arabian
Sire: Eugano VII Dam: Solkie

We originally acquired Kruger as a companion for his half-brother, Zareeba (with whom he had spent the first year of his life), and as a second horse for Brian to ride. He was a funny-looking foal and yearling; he was very pretty, but there was no hint of the substance he would later develop. His breeders had hoped that by putting their small Arabian mare to a big Warmblood they would get a good-sized jumping horse, but it seemed as if Kruger was going to stick at not much over 157 cm (15.2 hh). This did not bother us, as size is of little importance to us, and 157 cm is ample height for the average-sized rider.

Kruger (Arabian x Belgian
Warmblood gelding)
(L. Skipper)

However, we were surprised when Kruger, long past the age when most horses have stopped growing, put on a sudden spurt of growth, until at the age of eleven he stood a fraction under 163 cm (16 hh).

He is a nicely made, powerfully built and well-proportioned horse, who tends to put on weight easily. His forelegs are placed a little further back than I would really like to see, which makes his forehand slightly heavier than it would otherwise be. His topline is well muscled, with a nice long line from point of hip to point of buttock. The scapula is a good length, and slopes at around 55 degrees to the ground, which is a little on the upright side, but still fine for a general riding horse. The hoof/pastern axis in fore and hind limbs is good. Kruger's forelegs are straight, with short cannons and a long, well-muscled forearm.

The angle made by Kruger's humerus with his scapula is about 95 degrees, and the angle made by the humerus with the radius and ulna is around 130 degrees. This is excellent for a riding horse, although the slight uprightness of the scapula detracts from this a little. This does mean that the humerus is not as upright as the angle with the scapula would suggest. We can predict from this that Kruger will not have quite as much scope or length of stride as he might otherwise have done. This is in fact the case, although the length of the humerus (around 50 per cent of the scapula) compensates for this to some extent. He has well-developed hindquarters and a nice long femur, which makes his hind leg action much better than that of his forelegs. There is just enough angle in his hocks.

Kruger's forelimbs are straight as seen from the front (although this is not apparent from the photographs (see pages 26, 29 and 32), as he was not standing quite square), but since his breast is rather wide, he toes-in slightly to compensate. Because of this he also dishes slightly, although not enough to interfere or restrict his forelimb movement still further.

Kruger is actually capable of much better movement than we see in the photograph in Chapter 11 (see page 164), which shows him in trot. Although his forelimb movement is fairly short and low, it is far from being as low or restricted as that photograph suggests. He has a fair turn of speed, and can keep up with all but the fastest of our other horses. However, his shorter stride means he has to work much harder, and take many more strides, in order to travel the same distance!

Kruger's head and neck are nicely set on, and he finds the neck-telescoping gesture easy. It is his temperament, more than his conformation, which tends to put him on the forehand. Although very good natured and easy to manage, Kruger is all in favour of making life as easy as possible for himself. He can flex his croup and his hocks, and engage his hindquarters nicely, but he prefers to travel on the forehand, as this is less hard work for him. His habit of slapping his front feet down in trot, instead of springing lightly from one diagonal to the other, resulted in several splints when he was a young horse. Happily these never caused lameness, and the unsightly knobs have disappeared as the bone has remodelled itself. Indeed, apart from injuries resulting from external forces such as kicks, Kruger has suffered from no lameness apart from that caused by a foot abscess when he was younger, and a very brief attack of mud fever.

A horse of great charm and character, Kruger has quite a complex personality. His desire to go forward was regrettably stifled early in his ridden career by some misguided dressage training which employed the notion, deplored in Chapter 13 of *Inside Your Horse's Mind,* of driving the horse into a fixed contact. Kruger resisted this hard; it resulted in him gripping the bit and using the rider's hands as a prop. It has taken us a great deal of patience and effort to remedy the psychological effects of all this. He now takes a nice polite contact but will still try to seek support from the bit if he can, even though his degree of muscle development means he has no need to do so.

If properly motivated, he is a horse who will give 100 per cent to his rider, but he is easily bored, and will 'switch off' very quickly if not in the mood for serious work. Working him over poles to encourage him to lift his feet can be difficult, as he would sometimes rather blunder straight through the poles than go to the trouble of picking his feet up (I should add that there is no physical condition making it difficult or painful for him to do so).

When younger he did quite well in dressage competitions (being placed on his first outing) and in ridden showing classes, but soon demonstrated his boredom with these, and although he can jump reasonably well, showjumping is really not his scene. What Kruger really enjoys more than anything else is going out for long hacks, and it is when being ridden out that he has produced some of his best work, showing sustained impulsion, lovely elevated gaits and a lightened forehand. If we were more geared to competition he would probably have done well in competitive trail rides, but would have needed very careful schooling and riding to ensure he did not slop about on his forehand and put excess strain on his forelegs. For that reason I doubt whether he would have been successful at higher levels.

However that may be, we value Kruger not for what he might have been, but for what he is: a great horse to have fun with, a delightful friend and companion whose positive characteristics far outweigh his quirks and limitations, and – because he continually challenges our perceptions and our abilities – an invaluable teacher from whom we continue to learn.

Appendix II
Useful organizations

The Classical Riding Club

The Classical Riding Club was started in January 1995 by Sylvia Loch, as a means of bringing together like-minded people who were interested in a more philosophical approach to riding. This approach puts the happiness and pride of the horse above all else, even above winning and being seen to be successful.

The Classical Riding Club has a worldwide membership, composed of people from every walk of life and with widely differing equestrian backgrounds and levels of ability. The CRC welcomes everyone with a genuine interest in the classical ethos, but above all its aim is to bring this ethos to the everyday rider, to enhance our understanding of the horse.

The benefits are: a quarterly newsletter which contains instructional articles, book reviews, members' letters and articles by members; as well as these the newsletter carries details of demonstrations, seminars, open days, teach-ins, lectures etc. Membership of the CRC also gives members access to a general equestrian helpline, as well as expert advice *via* the network of regional liaison members. There is also a list, available at a nominal charge, of trainers/instructors who have signed a declaration to say they promise to teach under the classical principles and ethos as laid down in the Club's Charter.

The Classical Riding Club also runs a series of training tests, intended to complement the standard competitive dressage tests. These training tests emphasize harmony and empathy between horse and rider; the idea is to encourage riders to improve their equitation and to become aware of aspects which need attention. For this reason they are of value to all riders, not just those interested in dressage. Details are available from the Classical Riding Club office (address given below).

The Classical Riding Club is a very friendly, informal organization, whose members have proved more than willing to share ideas and information. If you wish to join, please write to: The Classical Riding Club, Eden Hall, Kelso, Roxburghshire, TD5 7QD, UK. Fax: +44 1890 830667, or send an e-mail to Lesley Skipper (UK Internet liaison member) on crcuk@ashtree33.freeserve.co.uk

The Intelligent Horsemanship Association

This is an organization dedicated to bringing together the best horsemanship ideas from around the world in an effort to promote understanding and fair treatment of horses at every opportunity.

It was founded by Kelly Marks, the popular equine expert featured on BBC1's prime time programme *Barking Mad*. Kelly is a pupil of Monty Roberts and the first teacher of his methods worldwide. She was inspired by the thought of all the horses and people that could be helped by the use of his simple and yet revolutionary techniques.

Intelligent Horsemanship Association membership: open to everyone; annual fee £20. For this you will receive the *Listening Post* newsletter which will keep you in touch with all the latest news and events from Monty and Kelly, also from other experts including Mary Wanless and Mark Rashid.

To join, call Angela Hobbs, Association Secretary on +44 (0) 1672 541155 during office hours. You can email on listening.post@kirion.net or fax +44 (0)1672 541185. Kelly Marks can be contacted at: Lethornes, Lambourn, Hungerford, Berkshire RG17 8QS. Tel: +44 (0)1488 71300 fax: +44 (0)1488 73783.

Readers in other countries who are interested in learning about Monty Roberts's techniques could try contacting the **Monty Roberts International Learning Centre**, P.O. Box 246, 901 E. HWY 246, Solvang, CA 93464, USA. Tel: +1 805-688-3483, fax: +1 805-693-8223 email: mrilc@montyroberts.com

Parelli Natural Horsemanship

Another teacher of 'natural horsemanship' who has had remarkable success in dealing with 'problem' horses is Pat Parelli, mentioned in Chapter 7. For more information about Parelli Horsemanship, contact

Parelli Natural Horse·Man·Ship, PO Box 3729, Pagosa Springs, Colorado 81147, USA.
Tel: +1 800-642-3335 or +1 970-731-9400, fax: +1 888-731-9722 or +1 970-731-9722.

Equine performance and rehabilitation

Dr. Gail Williams has a first class honours degree in equine studies and a doctorate in equine biomechanics from the University of Bristol's Veterinary School. She is a regular contributor to *Your Horse* magazine and is the author (with Martin Deacon FWCF) of *No Foot, No Horse – Foot balance the key to soundness and performance,* recommended in this book. Dr Williams offers advice and investigation of poor performance, performance development advice, and performance support programmes for the conformationally weak horse. Contact: **Dr Gail Williams, Equine Performance and Rehabilitation Centre**, 1 The Green, Wilmcote, Stratford upon Avon, Warks, CV37 9XJ, UK. Tel. and fax: +44 (0)1789 269425, email: gail@eparc2.powernet.co.uk

Farriers and corrective foot treatment

Advice may be obtained from:

The Farriers' Registration Council, which regulates farriery in Great Britain. Address: Sefton House, Adam Court, Newark Road, Peterborough, PE1 5PP. Tel: +44 (0)1733 319911, fax +44 (0)1733 319910.

The American Farriers' Association, 4059 Iron Works Pkwy, Ste. 1, Lexington, KY 40511, USA. Tel: +1 859 233 7411, fax: +1 859 231 7862.

World Wide Farrier Directory website: http://www.farriers.com

McTimoney chiropractors

For more than forty years McTimoney animal chiropractors have been helping horses and other animals with a non invasive technique which involves no drugs or anaesthetics and which most animals accept quite readily. Animal chiropractic aligns and balances the animal's musculoskeletal system. It helps to restore and maintain health, soundness and performance. It works holistically to eliminate the cause and not simply treat the symptoms.

Contact: **McTimoney Chiropractic Association**, 21 High Street, Eynsham, Oxford, OX18 1HE, UK. Tel: +44 (0)1865 880974, fax: +44 (0)1865 880975.

The Alexander Technique

The Alexander Technique is a practical method developed by F.M. Alexander (1869–1955) for improving the way we 'use' ourselves in the activities of everyday life. The Technique can be learnt by anyone and can help in as many ways as there are individuals. It does not seek to 'treat' specific ailments but, through learning how to change habits that do harm, the therapeutic benefits of applying it are considerable. Contact: **The Society of Teachers of the Alexander Technique**, 129 Camden Mews, London, NW1 9AH. Tel: +44 (0)20 7284 3338, fax: +44 (0)20 7482 5435. This organisation has a worldwide directory of Alexander teachers.

Pilates

Developed in the 1920s by the legendary physical trainer Joseph H. Pilates, the Pilates Method (a fusion of western and eastern philosophies), is a series of approximately 500 exercises which teach you about breathing with movement, body mechanics, balance, co-ordination, positioning of the body, spatial awareness, strength and flexibility.

Pilates and yoga share similar goals, with both systems believing in individual progress in a non-competitive arena, with emphasis on stretching as well as strengthening muscles. However, the Pilates system works the body as a whole, co-ordinating the upper and lower musculature with the body's centre. This dramatically improves strength, flexibility, posture and co-ordination. Contact: **The PILATESfoundation® UK Limited**, 80 Camden Road, London E17 7NF . Tel: +44 (0)7071 781 859, fax: +44 (0)20 8281 5087, email: admin@pilatesfoundation.com

Global Independent Pilates Reference Source

You can use this database listing over 700 Pilates studios and 650 Pilates instructors in 37 countries to search for a Pilates instructor or studio close to you. Search by instructor or studio, country, state/county, studio name or surname. Website: http://www.pilates.co.uk

Shiatsu

If you are interested in Shiatsu, you can find out more from The Shiatsu Society. For details of training in Shiatsu or to obtain a list of Registered

Practitioners by area, please contact: The Shiatsu Society, Eastlands Court, St Peter's Road, Rugby, CV21 3QP, UK. Tel: +44 (0)1788 555051, fax: +44 (0)1788 555052. email: admin@shiatsu.org , website: www.shiatsu.org

Holistic veterinary surgeons

You may be able to find a holistic veterinary surgeon through the following contacts:

Royal College of Veterinary Surgeons (RCVS), Belgravia House, 62–64 Horseferry Road, London SW1P 2AF. Tel: +44 (0)20 7222 2001, fax: +44 (0)20 7222 2004, website: http://www.rcvs.org.uk

American Holistic Veterinary Medical Association Directory
Tel: +1 410 569 0795, website: http://www.altvetmed.com
AltVetMed is a website produced by J. A. Bergeron, VMD, and S. G. Wynn, DVM, of the American Holistic Veterinary Medical Association. This site includes a variety of information on complementary and alternative veterinary medicine including herbal, holistic, homeopathic and nutritional therapies. There are articles on specific topics such as dental care, flea control and vaccination, useful bibliographies of books and periodicals, and a directory of members of the American Holistic Veterinary Association.

Recommended reading

In the course of my research, I consulted hundreds of technical books and scientific papers, many of which are only obtainable through specialist libraries. Because of this, and as this is not an academic book but a guide for the everyday rider, I felt that a full-scale bibliography would be inappropriate and that a Recommended Reading guide would be of more practical use. Most of the titles listed below should still be in print, but if any of them are no longer in print, they may still be obtainable through the numerous second-hand book services available via the Internet. Try Amazon (www.amazon.co.uk in the UK, or www.amazon.com in the USA), Barnes & Noble in the USA (www.barnesandnoble.com) or W. H. Smith Online (www.bookshop.co.uk). These all provide an excellent service.

Breeds, specific and general

Edwards, Elwyn Hartley *The Ultimate Horse Book* Dorling Kindersley 1991
—— *The Encyclopedia of the Horse* Dorling Kindersley 1994
Llamas, Juan *This is the Spanish Horse* (tr. by Jane Rabagliati) J. A. Allen 1996
Loch, Sylvia *The Royal Horse of Europe* J. A. Allen 1986
Skipper, Lesley *The Arabian Show Horse* J. A. Allen 1997

Classical riding

Loch, Sylvia *The Classical Rider: Being at One With Your Horse* J. A. Allen 1997
—— *The Classical Seat* Hyman Unwin 1988

Conformation and movement

Bennett, Dr Deb K. *Principles of Conformation Analysis, Vol I* Fleet Street Publishing 1988
—— *Principles of Conformation Analysis, Vol II* Fleet Street Publishing 1989
—— *Principles of Conformation Analysis, Vol III* Fleet Street Publishing 1991
(These three little booklets are difficult to obtain, but well worth the effort, because they are by far the best guide to conformation I have ever read; I made extensive use of them in preparing this book.)
Harris, Susan E. *Horse Gaits, Balance and Movement* Howell Book House, USA 1993
Loving, Nancy S. *Conformation and Performance* Breakthrough, USA 1997
McBane, Susan *Conformation for the Purpose* Swan Hill 2000
Oliver, Robert, and Langrish, Bob *A Photographic Guide to Conformation* J. A. Allen 1991
Smythe, R.H. and Goody, Peter C. (rev. Peter Gray) *Horse Structure and Movement* J. A. Allen 1993
Wagoner, Don (ed.) *Equine Photos & Drawings for Conformation & Anatomy* Equine Research Inc., Tyler, Texas, USA 1999

Equine anatomy and physiology

Goody, Peter C. *Horse Anatomy* (paperback ed.) J. A. Allen 1983
Williams, Gail and Deacon, Martin *No Foot, No Horse* Kenilworth Press 1999
Wyche, Sara *Understanding the Horse's Back* Crowood Press 1998
—— *Understanding the Horse's Legs* Crowood Press 2000

Horse psychology and management

Kiley-Worthington, Dr Marthe *The Behaviour of Horses in Relation to Management and Training* J. A. Allen 1987
—— Equine Welfare J. A. Allen 1997
Marks, Kelly *Creating A Bond With Your Horse* J. A. Allen 2000
Rees, Lucy *The Horse's Mind* (1st pub. 1984; paperback ed. 1993) Stanley Paul 1993
Roberts, Monty *The Man Who Listens to Horses* Hutchinson 1996
Skipper, Lesley *Inside Your Horse's Mind: A Study of Equine Intelligence and Human Prejudice* J. A. Allen 1999

Physiotherapy and massage

Bromiley, Mary *Equine Injury, Therapy and Rehabilitation* (2nd ed.) Blackwell 1993
—— *Massage for Horses* Kenilworth Press 1996

—— *Natural Methods for Equine Health* Blackwell 1994

Denoix, Jean-Marie and Pailloux, Jean-Pierre *Physical Therapy and Massage for the Horse* (tr. Jonathan Lewis) Manson Publishing 1996

Giniaux, Dominique *What the Horses Have Told Me* (tr. by Jean Claude Racinet. Originally published by Editions Lamer, Paris, 1992) Xenophon Press 1996

Hannay, Pamela *Shiatsu Therapy for Horses* J. A. Allen 2002

Hourdebaight, Jean-Pierre *Equine Massage* Ringpress 1997

Tellington-Jones, Linda *Getting in Touch with Horses* (paperback ed.) Kenilworth Press 1998

Wyche, Sara *The Horse Owner's Guide to Holistic Medicine* Crowood Press 1996

Training and riding

Albrecht, Brigadier-General Kurt *Principles of Dressage* J. A. Allen 1987

Blignault, Karin *Successful Schooling* J. A. Allen 1997

Burger, Üdo *The Way to Perfect Horsemanship* (Allens Classic Series edition) J. A. Allen 1986 (reissued 1998)

Decarpentry, General *Academic Equitation* (tr. Nicole Bartle) (Allens Classic Series edition) J.A. Allen 1987 (reissued 2001)

d'Endrödy, Lt. Col. A. L. *Give Your Horse a Chance* (first published 1959) (Allens Classic Series edition) J. A. Allen 1999

Dietze, Susanne von *Balance in Movement* (tr. Heike Bean) J. A. Allen 1999

Edwards, Elwyn Hartley *The Complete Book of Bits and Bitting* David & Charles 2000

Henderson, Carolyn *Training Aids* Compass Equestrian 1999

Klimke, Reiner *Cavalletti* (rev. ed.) J. A. Allen 2000

Loch, Sylvia *Dressage in Lightness* J. A. Allen 2000

Mairinger, Franz *Horses are Made to be Horses* Rigby, Sydney, Australia 1983

Mashanaglass, Marquis McSwiney of *Training from the Ground* J. A. Allen 1987

Moffett, Heather *Enlightened Equitation* David & Charles 1999

Oliveira, Nuno *Reflections on Equestrian Art* (tr. by Phyllis Field) J. A. Allen 1976

Podhajsky, Colonel Alois *The Complete Training of Horse and Rider* (tr. by Colonel V. D. S. Williams and Mme Eva Podhajsky) Harrap 1967

Sivewright, Molly *Thinking Riding, Book 1* J. A. Allen 1984

—— *Thinking Riding, Book 2* J. A. Allen 1985

Stanier, Sylvia *The Art of Long Reining* (rev. ed). J. A. Allen 1993

—— *The Art of Lungeing* (rev. ed). J. A. Allen 1995

Swift, Sally *Centered Riding* St Martin's/Marek (USA) 1985

Wanless, Mary *Ride With Your Mind* Methuen 1987

—— *Ride With Your Mind Masterclass* Methuen 1991

Video tapes

Bennett, Dr Deb *Dr Bennett's Secrets of Conformation*
Bromiley, Mary *Hands On with Mary Bromiley*
Hannay, Pamela *Shiatsu for Horse and Rider*
Klimke, Reiner *Cavalletti*
Kottas-Heldenberg, Arthur *The Art of Classical Dressage* (8 tapes)
Loch, Sylvia *The Classical Seat* (3 tapes)

(The above are all available from Weatherbys Allen Ltd,
tel: +44 (0)1933 440077, fax: +44 (0)1933 270300,
email: turfnews@weatherbys-group.com,
website: weatherbys-group.com/turf)

Index